h
10/01/08

TRADITIONS IN SOCIAL THEORY

Series Editors: Ian Craib and Rob Stones

This series offers a selection of concise introductions to particular traditions in sociological thought. It aims to deepen the reader's knowledge of particular theoretical approaches and at the same time to enhance their wider understanding of sociological theorising. Each book will offer: a history of the chosen approach and the debates that have driven it forward; a discussion of the current state of the debates within the approach (or debates with other approaches); and an argument for the distinctive contribution of the approach and its likely future value.

Published

PHILOSOPHY OF SOCIAL SCIENCE: THE PHILOSOPHICAL
FOUNDATIONS OF SOCIAL THOUGHT
Ted Benton and Ian Craib

CRITICAL THEORY
Alan How

STRUCTURATION THEORY
Rob Stones

MARXISM AND SOCIAL THEORY
Jonathan Joseph

Forthcoming

FEMINIST SOCIAL THEORY
Sam Ashenden

STRUCTURALISM, POST-STRUCTURALISM AND POST-MODERNISM
David Howarth

MICRO SOCIAL THEORY
Brain Roberts

DURKHEIM AND THE DURKHEIMIANS
Willie Watts Miller and Susan Stedman Jones

Further titles in preparation

Marxism and Social Theory

Jonathan Joseph

First published in 2006 by
PALGRAVE MACMILLAN
Houndmills, Basingstoke, Hampshire RG21 6XS and
175 Fifth Avenue, New York, N.Y. 10010
Companies and representatives throughout the world.

PALGRAVE MACMILLAN is the global academic imprint of the Palgrave Macmillan division of St. Martin's Press, LLC and of Palgrave Macmillan Ltd. Macmillan® is a registered trademark in the United States, United Kingdom and other countries. Palgrave is a registered trademark in the European Union and other countries.

ISBN-13: 978–1–4039–1563–4 hardback
ISBN-10: 1–4039–1563–6   hardback
ISBN-13: 978–1–4039–1564–1 paperback
ISBN-10: 1–4039–1564–4   paperback

This book is printed on paper suitable for recycling and made from fully managed and sustained forest sources.

A catalogue record for this book is available from the British Library.

A catalog record for this book is available from the Library of Congress.

10 9 8 7 6 5 4 3 2 1
15 14 13 12 11 10 09 08 07 06

Printed in China

Contents

Acknowledgements

Many thanks to Catherine Gray, Sheree Keep and the staff at Palgrave, and to Rob Stones who read the manuscript and gave me some useful advice. I would also like to thank Doug Stokes who has offered many useful suggestions and Hiroki Ogasawara and colleagues at the faculty of cross-cultural studies at Kobe University for their generosity during my stay as a visiting scholar. Thanks also to Maureen, Simon and Sarah. I particularly want to mention Ian Craib who suggested this book as part of the Traditions in Social Theory series he was editing. We shared many ideas and theories and he made many helpful comments on early chapters. He continued doing this despite suffering from a terminal illness and his early death is a very sad loss. Finally, many thanks to my wife Ai Saeki for all her support.

1

Introduction

The Challenge of Marxist Theory

Marxism is perhaps the most influential, yet most criticised and most misunderstood of all social theories. Indeed, even the question of its status as a social theory is open to debate since few Marxists would define themselves as social theorists first and foremost. The sheer scope of Marxism causes most problems to the interested reader. For Marxism spans philosophy, sociology, economics, politics, history, cultural studies and many other fields. Yet Marx himself, and many of his followers, refuse to consider such 'academic' categorisations, stressing instead that Marxism is more than just a theory, it is a way of understanding the world and acting upon it. Marx frequently criticised philosophers and political economists for being trapped in their own systems of thought and failing to see the broader picture of the way the world is. If any ideas are put forward, then this should be with the purpose of practically engaging with the world to improve the conditions of social life. In this respect, Marxism is unparalleled in its ambition. Seeking to gain a comprehensive understanding of the *totality* of social life – indeed insisting that individual components of the social world can only be comprehended within a totalising framework – Marxism claims to link this understanding to practical action aimed at remedying this situation. No other set of ideas links such a range of theories to human practice in such a comprehensive way. It is a testimony to the power of Marxist thinking that this tradition is still developing and being engaged with so long after Marx first started to write.

This book has two aims. First, it is intended to introduce the reader to a range of schools and debates within Marxist social theory. Then it aims to summarise those debates and to critically assess Marxist theory in order to consider potential strengths and weaknesses. This is done by looking at two contemporary theories that have offered a critique of orthodox Marxism – the post-Marxism of Laclau and Mouffe and the critical realism of Bhaskar and others. First, a number of different schools of Marxism are examined, then some areas of application are discussed, then debates over Marxism's role and the validity of its claims is addressed.

In a sense, such an approach is in keeping with Marxism's own advice. Of course it is necessary to present Marxist ideas to the reader. But it is also

1

necessary to subject these ideas to critical scrutiny. One of the fundamental principles of Marxist theory is to approach the social world in a critical way and to suggest how it might be changed for the better. But the social world is a complex terrain comprised of both material and discursive or ideational elements. Ideas are an important part of the social world and Marxism itself constitutes a set of ideas. Thus Marxism must confront itself and subject its own ideas, claims and status to critical scrutiny. If elements of Marxist social theory are found wanting, then these too must be subject to transformative action. Although this book tries to hold back on most of its criticisms when introducing different Marxist theories, the final two chapters are more consciously critical. In the conclusion, a number of suggestions are made as to where Marxist ideas are problematic and where they should be challenged.

However, although this book ultimately adopts a critical stance, it is necessary to state that this is a Marxist book – or at least it attempts to stay within the Marxist framework. It rejects the post-Marxist idea that we have to pass through Marxism in order to resolve social theoretical issues. It may well be considered unfashionable, but the argument here is that Marxism continues to provide the best possible framework for understanding the social world. It is also the only social theory that succeeds in combining a theoretical account of the social world with a practical attempt to change it. In today's postmodern climate, Marxism also stands out in advocating a social scientific approach that believes that we can make intelligible claims about the social world. The key issue for this book, therefore, is not whether or not to adopt a Marxist framework, but what sort of Marxist framework to have. It therefore sets out the different schools of Marxism – classical, structuralist, critical and so on – in order to determine the most appropriate ways to understand the social world. These different schools vary quite considerably and indeed this may pose the question as to whether these can all be considered to be variants of the same species. For a Marxist might be broadly defined as a follower of the ideas of Karl Marx. But then among these followers are followers of other followers – Leninists, Trotskyists, Luxemburgists, Gramscians, Althusserians, Habermasians and many others. Then again, if there are problems with the ways these different Marxists have interpreted Marxism, the answer is not simply to go back to Marx and find some pure form of his ideas. Marxism should always remain true to its critical spirit and should continue to criticise its own claims. It should move on from its claims about the world to see if the world itself is changing and if those theories that attempt to explain this world are themselves in need of change. Marxism is at its best when it is doing social theory. It usually runs into difficulties when it tries to incorporate this into some grander philosophical scheme of things. Or else it runs into difficulty when clinging dogmatically to some old ideas when they are no longer able to explain the way that things are. Marx's own theories were developed during an earlier stage of capitalist development. The world has changed since Lenin theorised imperialism. Marxists usually describe themselves as historical materialists. That means we have to see Marxist ideas as being historical products themselves. As time passes, so theories need to be adapted or developed. Rather than simply trying to impose a Marxist conceptual framework onto the social world, the Marxist who is true to the critical spirit of Marx will examine the complex interplay between the social world itself and the concepts we use to try and explain it. This is the difficult task faced by Marxists today. But it is to Marxism's great credit that it is still capable of responding to the challenge.

The Structure of the Book

Chapter 1 of this book explores the work of Karl Marx and Freidrich Engels, the founders of Marxism and the originators of most of the ideas discussed in this book. It starts with their early work and the emergence of Marxism out of classical German philosophy (particularly the work of Hegel) and their attempt to understand the issue of human estrangement or alienation. This emphasis eventually leads Marx to a study of the importance of the economy and the way in which alienation results from the private ownership of property and the nature of the production process. The Marxist theory of ideology starts with the notion that the ruling ideas in society are the ideas of the ruling class. But it develops to account for the way that capitalist relations of production and exchange produce a misleading or fetishised form of consciousness that treats human relations as relations between things while bringing to life the commodified form of social objects.

Marx's economic theory introduces such things as the labour theory of value and the way that exploitation within the capitalist system is founded upon the extraction of surplus value from the worker. The working class is defined by the non-ownership of the means of production. In working for a wage, they produce more value for the capitalist than they receive back in wages. However, these conditions of common exploitation produce among the workers a growing class consciousness. The relationship of the working class to the production process gives them the potential to transform the system through collective action.

This leads to a discussion of political action and forms of class struggle. It also opens up the question of how to confront the power of the state. This in turn raises the issue of the role of the state and how it fits into the social system. Traditionally, Marxist theory has understood the role of the state in terms of the base-superstructure model whereby the economic base gives rise to a legal and political superstructure. Subsequent chapters challenge this model.

Chapter 3 considers classical Marxism and explores how the immediate heirs of Marx and Engels provided a very rigid and mechanical interpretation of their ideas. Their philosophical and historical views try to explain social change but end up making complacent claims about its inevitability. This in turn generates a more 'revisionist' approach whereby the leaders of Marxist parties could get on with the day-to-day business of practical politics even if this included supporting the First World War. Such a capitulation led to a strong challenge from Lenin and Luxemburg and new debates over forms of political party and revolutionary activity. It also led to new theories of world politics and the notion of imperialism. Lenin's view was that imperialism reflected new pressures to expand markets and that this opened up an era of wars and revolutions. Economic rivalries would break out among the big powers, while other parts of the world were being hastily developed by overseas capital. This created new conditions in those countries that might allow a revolutionary situation to develop. This process was theorised by Trotsky as uneven and combined development.

The revolution in Russia was described by Gramsci as a revolution against Marxist ideas. He believed that by taking matters into their own hands the Bolsheviks had acted against the idea that history has to follow a certain course of development before social revolution can take place. Gramsci is an advocate of praxis or human action. Chapter 4 looks at how praxis Marxists like Gramsci, Lukács and Sartre oppose the mechanical approach of orthodox Marxism and instead emphasise human subjectivity, class consciousness and class struggle. There is also a renewed emphasis on the concept of alienation (or in Lukács's idea of reification, the transformation of relations between people into relations between things). Lukács and Sartre pay a lot of attention to overcoming this and to the development of consciousness. Gramsci offers more in the way of concrete theory by developing the concept of hegemony to explain how class rulership has to be constructed and how it is necessary to win the consent of the masses. The revolutionary party must engage in a hegemonic struggle to gain influence in civil society and build a power basis to stake a claim for state power

The approach of Althusser and Poulantzas draws heavily upon Gramsci. However, their structuralist Marxism rejects the praxis approach and switches attention from social agents to social structure. At the same time Althusser wishes to challenge the way Marxist theory sees social structure through the model of economic base determining political–cultural superstructure. He offers an alternative that gives relative autonomy to the political, cultural and ideological and he focuses on the unevenness of social development which is described as being overdetermined. Althusser contributes greatly to the Marxist theory of ideology while Poulantzas does important work on the existence of class fractions. However, both are criticised for downplaying the role of human agency as well as their 'theoreticist' or 'scientistic' approach to Marxist social theory.

The final school of Marxism that is covered here in Chapter 6 is that of critical theory. Like the structuralists they criticise some of Marxism's assumptions about the role of the economy and the inevitability of socialist transformation.

Adorno, Horkheimer and Marcuse examine the changed conditions of advanced capitalism where developments in technology allow for the material satisfaction of the working class while the culture industry provides for their cultural needs. The workers are kept in a state of blissful ignorance, no longer capable of playing a radical role. Instead Marcuse turns to the new social movements for inspiration. However, Adorno and Horkheimer are more pessimistic, believing that society has become totally integrated and dominates over individuals. Their negative view of the rationality of modern society is perhaps a product of the 1930s and the twin triumphs of fascism and Stalinism as well as the commercialisation of the United States and is challenged by the later critical theory of Habermas. But Habermas's optimism is founded upon the potential of human communication and mutual understanding and thus moves a long way from the traditional focus of Marxism.

Having examined the different schools of Marxism, Chapter 7 is an examination of some areas that have presented particular challenges to Marxist analysis. Marxism has made a tremendous contribution to a wide range of social theories from anthropology through to film studies, so this chapter selects four areas that have seen considerable contemporary discussion. The issue of feminism has been selected because it receives little coverage in the main theories discussed in this book and yet it is one of the most problematic issues in Marxist theory. Given that Marxism lays so much stress on class relations, how should feminism's concern with gender divisions be understood? Is gender exploitation an issue that can simply be reduced to women's place in the capitalist system, or is there a separate basis for the oppression of women? This raises the issue of whether socialism can do away with gender divisions as a site of oppression. A similar question emerges in relation to national divisions – another issue selected because of its controversial nature. How should national movements be understood in relation to socialist movements? Can nationalism be used for progressive purposes? This section challenges the complacency of many Marxists who tend to regard the national question as a secondary issue when compared to the struggle for socialism.

Debates over the national question entail debates about the Marxist theory of history. Since theories of historical development are so fundamental to Marxist theory, this section confronts the issue of whether history should primarily be understood in terms of class struggle or economic development. The latter is raised by G.A. Cohen's functionalist account of how social development is driven by the productive forces. This is compared with approaches like Richard Brenner's that instead emphasise the role of class struggle as the main historical factor (in this case in the transition from feudalism to capitalism). This section also looks at the debates between Perry Anderson and E.P. Thompson concerning the nature of the English Civil War and to the attempts to apply Gramsci's concept of hegemony to historical developments. Gramsci's ideas can also be applied to economic theory and Chapter 7 concludes by looking at how Gramsci's ideas have led to debates over Fordist production and forms of economic regulation and state intervention. These issues have provoked very important contemporary debate and they raise the question of the relation between the social and the economic that is discussed in the Conclusion.

Some Marxist Categories

The majority of the book is organised according to different schools, but it is also important to consider Marxist social theory according to major themes and concepts. The concluding chapter picks out some main areas of concern – Marxism's theory of history, the focus on the economy, the concept of ideology, Marxist views on class and the state and finally, Marxism's commitment to emancipation. It examines these debates by looking at the different schools of Marxism, but also by employing the critical realist philosophy that is discussed in Chapter 8.

Since Marxism is such a broad school, it is worth outlining some of these major themes at the beginning. Perhaps the Marxist theory of history is the most important issue as this contains all the other issues in it. It starts from our basic need to produce that which is necessary to keep us alive and moves from this material issue to the historical question of how such processes of production are organised. Historical materialism, therefore, is the focus on the reproduction of the material conditions of social life and on the particular historical forms that this takes.

This moves us to Marxism's focus on the economy. Marxism addresses the historical form of the production process through the concept of mode of production. The economic system is particularly important in explaining the mode of production. The capitalist mode of production is explained in terms of generalised commodity production, the ownership and non-ownership of the means of production and the sale of labour-power by the working class. The issue to be addressed throughout this book is the extent to which social and historical explanation can be provided by a focus on these economic conditions and the extent to which we need to bring in other factors.

One such factor is ideology, another key focus of Marxist social theory. Marxist theories of ideology tend to fall into two categories. The first is straightforward – the view that ideology represents a false set of ideas spread by the ruling class. To put this less crudely, we could say that ideology relates to the beliefs of different social groups. However, the second approach to ideology focuses on the notion that such beliefs, rather than coming from any particular social group, are generated by the social system itself. Marx gives us the theory of commodity fetishism or the coming to worship commodities as things in themselves rather than as products of human labour. The wage form also generates ideology in making us believe that we are receiving a fair wage, hiding the real process of exploitation that is taking place. In both these cases it is processes – the labour process and the process of commodity exchange – that creates ideology, rather than any particular individual.

The focus on class is one of the best-known aspects of Marxist theory. Put simply, class is based on the relationship to the means of production. Under capitalism there are two main classes – the bourgeoisie who own the means of production and the working class which does not and therefore has to sell its labour-power to the capitalists in order to survive. But as subsequent debates show, from this starting point all sorts of issues emerge with regard to whether classes can be defined so straightforwardly, or whether further social divisions exist.

The Marxist theory of the state is a controversial topic. Many Marxists follow the view put forward in the *Communist Manifesto* that the state is an instrument of the ruling class and that under capitalism it is used to support the process of economic exploitation. However, other approaches move away from the view of that state as a class instrument and see it instead as a factor of social cohesion both in the sense of it bringing different social groups together, and in co-ordinating the relations between the different parts of the social system.

Finally, Marxism sets out a theory of emancipation. This is a complicated issue and somewhat embarrassing for a book such as this. To what extent is Marxism *merely* a social theory? Is the purpose of Marxism simply to analyse society? Is it possible for non-Marxists to take up the best aspects of Marxist social theory to explain issues that cannot otherwise be explained? Or does Marxist social theory necessarily entail Marxist political practice? Does the fact of describing the world in a certain way compel us to commit ourselves to try to do something to change it? Marx and Engels' own commitment to the revolutionary cause is quite clear even if the commitment of later Marxists is more questionable. For Marx the whole point of interpreting the world is in order to change it. By trying to explain the workings of capitalist society, Marxist theory makes us better equipped to try and bring about social change. Without such a commitment to social change, it is questionable whether we are still discussing Marxism.

The Conclusion, as will be seen, examines these different areas and offers some criticisms of various Marxist assumptions. These criticisms include, in the respective areas, the use of the base-superstructure model, the tendency towards economic determinism, the issue of whether ideology is a necessary social feature, the need for a more stratified conception of social class, as to whether the state can be reduced to its class form, and finally the need to re-examine the relationship between social theory, philosophy and emancipatory action. But despite these difficult questions, the book concludes by affirming the importance of Marxism while advocating a critical approach to Marxist social theory. It rejects the need to move beyond Marxism, but recognises the need for greater flexibility and an openness to new ideas. Marxism attempts to provide a theory of the social world, but is at the same time a product of the very things that it is trying to describe. A critical approach to Marxist social theory is essential if it is to move on and attempt to explain changing socio-historical conditions. In turn, a Marxist approach to the social world is essential if we want to be able to criticise this world and do something to change it.

Further Reading

There are many introductory books on Marxism. The best known and most interesting are Kolakowski's three volume *Main Currents of Marxism* (1981) and MacLellan's *Thought of Karl Marx* (1971) and *Marxism After Marx* (1998). Ralph Miliband's *Marxism and Politics* (1977) is a very good read. Perry Anderson's *Considerations of Western Marxism* (1979) takes a more polemical approach. Alan Swingewood's book *Marx and Modern Social Theory* (1975) is interesting in relating Marxist theory to the broader sociological tradition. *A Dictionary of Marxist Thought* (1991) edited by Tom Bottomore is a very useful resource. The Marxist internet archive http://www.marxists.org has a huge amount of material.

2

Marx and Engels

Introduction: Capital and Class

The two most striking features of Marxist social theory are the focus on the mode of production and the emphasis on the class relations that derive from this. However, Marx is known not just as a social theorist, but as a revolutionary socialist. Flowing from Marx's analysis of production and class relations comes a revolutionary practice. The point of trying to understand the world is to change it (Marx 1975f: 423). But this relationship between theory and practice is complex for in order to change the world, one has to understand it properly. For Marx and Engels, other forms of socialism are simply are not capable of doing this. As Engels was to argue, the choice is between Utopian and scientific socialism with only the analysis of advanced works like *Capital* capable of grasping the world in its complexity.

Although known for their materialist approach, Marx and Engels began their work within the idealism of classical German philosophy, drawn to its strong emphasis upon the problem of human estrangement and alienation. It was only gradually that they moved towards their focus on the economic mode of production and social class relationships. This chapter looks at some of the early concerns of Marx and Engels before considering how the concepts of capital and class become central to their analysis. The concern with human alienation does not go away, but it becomes understood in the context of the relations of capitalist production. The capitalist production process turns the potentially creative and satisfying aspect of human labour into an alien force while the products of this labour (commodities) later confront those who produce them as independent and estranged objects. The only way out of such a situation is to confront the system that produces it. This chapter looks at how Marx and Engels seek to combine their analysis of the production process with an analysis of political struggles and the need to transform society. This requires a complex analysis of the two main protagonists, capital and class, which are at the same time constitutive of each other. Capital may produce human misery and alienation, but it also produces the forces capable of overcoming them.

The Early Work

Marx and Engels began as Young Hegelians, following the German philosopher GWF Hegel and his dialectic as it applied to Mind, Spirit and ideas as well as the relationship between master and slave. The influence of Hegel on Marx is a matter of much dispute, but the struggle between master and slave can be seen as shaping Marx's understanding of the relationship between proletariat and bourgeoisie or capital and labour. The two elements in the master / slave relationship stand in an unstable unity, each depending on the other while in fundamental contradiction. Only the victory of the slave can overcome this contradiction and move history forward.

Hegel's dialectic is idealist rather than materialist because it is concerned with the progress of the Mind, through struggles, towards self-understanding and freedom. Such a view is radical in the sense that it can be applied to the collective understanding of society (or world Spirit) as developing according to a dynamic process. This introduces a historical element into philosophy by linking self-consciousness to historical development. But Hegel's philosophy is also conservative insofar as it posits an end to the process – effectively Hegel's own realisation of this process and the political and social reality of nineteenth-century Prussia. In opposing such conservative tendencies, the school of Young Hegelians, reinterpreted Hegel's philosophy in terms of the alienation of humanity and its struggle towards liberation. In Ludwig Feuerbach this takes the form of a humanist struggle against religion, placing humanity, rather than God, at the centre of the struggle for freedom. But Marx is later to attack Feuerbach for his passive form of materialism which Marx feels does not place enough emphasis on practical human activity and political struggle.

An early expression of Marx's approach can be found in his critique of Hegel's view of the state. Hegel makes an important distinction between the state or political society and civil society which comprises the economic sphere and private relations. Because civil society, as an arena of particular needs and self-interest, is potentially divisive, the state is seen by Hegel as acting to ensure that the general or universal interest prevails. In his *Critique of Hegel's Doctrine of the State* Marx criticises this, arguing that the state is run by a bureaucracy which, rather than defending the universal interest, actually develops its own interests. The Prussian absolutist state, supported by Hegel, actually serves the interests of a small group – the property owning Junker class. So, rather than representing the universal interest, the state bureaucracy represents the particular interests of certain groups, while attempting to disguise these as the universal interest: 'The bureaucracy must therefore protect the *imaginary* universality of particular interests . . . in order to protect the *imaginary* particularity of the universal interest' (Marx 1975b: 107). Therefore the separation of civil society from political society leads to the state playing a mystifying role that disguises the fact that in reality the state represents only the interests of the property owning few. The state claims to represent the interests of the whole community. It does this in an abstract, legalistic way while at the same time excluding most of the population from genuine involvement in social and political life.

In Marx the proletariat comes to take on the universal role that Hegel falsely attributes to the state bureaucracy. Engels talks of Marx combining idealist German philosophy with French political theory and British political economy. As Marx develops his ideas, he sees economic life rather than religion as the root of human alienation. In *On the Jewish Question* Marx writes that: 'Money is the estranged essence of man's work and existence; this alien essence dominates him and he worships it' (Marx 1975c: 239). Here we find Marx becoming a materialist and seeing that it is not ideas or religious views that cause alienation but the material realities of social life. The question of money enters Marx's work for the fist time, while it is argued that the emancipation of social groups (the Jews) can only be achieved through the abolition of private property. Marx asks whether there is a group in society whose needs are such that they will engage in a total social revolution? Is there a group whose suffering is universal and so will engage in a universal revolution? The proletariat begins to appear as an answer to this question. In Marx's *Critique of Hegel's Philosophy of Right* it is stated that: 'Philosophy cannot realize itself without the transcendence of the proletariat, and the proletariat cannot realize itself without the transcendence of philosophy' (Marx 1975e: 257). There is still in these works an idealist tendency to overstate and the importance of the arguments of philosophy. But there is at the same time a recognition of the importance of social struggle. The proletariat will overcome its estrangement and liberate all of humanity. The next stage is to move further towards political economy, something that is done in the 1844 Manuscripts.

Here Marx starts to study the labour process, arguing that

> the object that labour produces, its product, stands opposed to it as *something alien*, as a *power independent* of the producer . . . In the sphere of political economy this realisation of labour appears as a *loss of reality* for the worker, objectification as *loss and bondage to the object*, and appropriation as *estrangement*, as *alienation*. (Marx 1975d: 324)

Workers are alienated from their products and also from themselves. This makes it difficult for them to reflect on the nature of this process for 'this alien character inevitably appears as something *real*' (Marx 1975d: 335). Through estrangement, workers find themselves confronted with the powers of their own essence but in the form of objectified, alien objects. Modern production leads to a situation where labour is external to the worker and 'does not belong to his essential being; that he therefore does not confirm himself in his work, but denies himself' (Marx 1975d: 326). Therefore alienation occurs when human beings become separated from their true essence.

It is argued that it is labour that is the essence of what Marx calls our species-being (our human essence). It is through the fashioning of our

environment that we find human fulfilment. Alienation means that we lose control over this process. What we produce becomes estranged from our creativity.
Relationships between people become like relations between things. The idea
here is that society denies our true species-being, our essence as people living
and producing within nature and alongside each other. The essence of the true
community lies in our activity, however, with the development of private property we become estranged from the products of this activity. The products of
human labour are separated from their producers and gain power over them.

The notion of alienation is present throughout Marx's work, but it is much
stronger in the earlier work where it is contrasted with the idea of a 'true'
human essence or species-being. Through an examination of how the worker
is estranged from their product and from the production process Marx is
developing the basis of an economic analysis although this is based on the role
of private property in a more general sense and not on the specific economic
ideas associated with the production of surplus value (something that is discussed later). But Marx does connect the processes of wage-labour, trade and
exchange to the production of an alienated consciousness. The early work is
also characterised by a particularly strong Hegelian understanding of the
dialectical struggle to overcome alienation. Therefore, '*Communism* is the *positive* supersession of *private property* as *human self-estrangement*, and hence
the true *appropriation* of the *human essence*'. This communism is a humanism
based on 'the *genuine* resolution of the conflict between man and nature, and
between man and man, the true resolution of the conflict between existence
and being, between objectification and self-affirmation, between freedom and
necessity, between individual and species' (Marx 1975d: 348).

Ideology

Alienated forms of consciousness can be said to be forms of ideology. In the
early works Marx is particularly concerned with the role of religion which is
said to justify and reinforce alienation by shifting people's consciousness away
from the problems of everyday life towards higher things while also making a
virtue out of misery and suffering. Religion offers comfort, but not a solution
to social problems. It does not cure but instead deadens the pain. As the well
known saying goes:

> *Religious* suffering is at one and the same time the *expression* of real suffering and a
> protest against real suffering. Religion is the sigh of the oppressed creature, the heart
> of a heartless world and the soul of soulless conditions. It is the *opium* of the people.
> (Marx 1975e: 244)

Marx describes religion as an ideology because it creates a mystifying picture
while leaving the real relations of the world intact. These real relations are in

fact the source of religious ideology for: 'This state and society produce religion, which is an *inverted consciousness of the world*, because they are in an *inverted world*' (Marx 1975e: 244). Ideology, then, has an organic link with real social relations, but it produces a mystifying picture of them. This theme is developed by Marx and Engels in *The German Ideology* where it is argued that the production of ideas and conceptions in our consciousness is interwoven with our material activity. Such things as morality and religion, although they have the semblance of independence, are really the product of (imperfect) material intercourse. Ideology is an illusory representation of our species-being. It is obfuscatory in that it blurs the real conflicts and contradictions of social life. Marx and Engels write that the phantoms formed in the human brain are sublimates of our material life processes (Marx and Engels 1965: 37–38).

In *The German Ideology* Marx and Engels continue to describe ideology as an 'inversion' of material life:

> If in all ideology men and their circumstances appear upside down as in a *camera obscura*, this phenomenon arises just as much from their historical life-processes as the inversion of objects on the retina does from their physical life-process. (Marx and Engels 1965: 37)

There is a danger of this portrayal of ideology as an inversion of the world becoming slightly mechanistic in that the dominant ideology is but an inverted reflection of real economic relations. As we will see, in the 1859 *Preface*, ideology becomes part of the superstructure of society, something that is determined by the economic base. If ideology is presented here as a reflection of the economic base of society, *The German Ideology* also presents ideology as an instrument of the ruling class:

> The ideas of the ruling class are in every epoch the ruling ideas: i.e. the class which is the ruling *material* force of society, is at the same time its ruling *intellectual* force. The class which has the means of material production at its disposal, has control at the same time over the means of mental production ... the ruling ideas are nothing more than the ideal expression of the dominant material relations material relationships. (Marx and Engels 1965: 61)

We must decide whether to read such a passage as an indication that the ruling ideology narrowly reflects material conditions, or whether it simply means that those classes who have control over economic and material resources are better placed to dominate social, cultural and political life. The latter need not mean that the leading ideas in these domains neatly reflect the dominant economic interests. The fact that certain groups have access to economic resources does mean that they can influence the political and cultural sphere (as a study of newspaper proprietorship clearly shows). But although the economic structure of society does tend to produce the ruling ideas, how these ideas are expressed or articulated depends upon many other social, cultural and political factors.

Ideology is seen as a form of consciousness, describing a set of ideas or beliefs, or different theories, outlooks and ways of seeing the world. However, for Marxists it has a negative connotation best expressed in Engels' remark that ideology is false consciousness. At the very least ideology is said to be partial or misleading. Ideology may represent the way that things *appear* to us in our day-to-day interactions, but this appearance may not be the whole picture. Invoking the dialectical distinction between essence and appearance, we can say that while the capitalist system may *appear* to be based on free and fair exchange, the real *essence* of capitalist relations – as we will see, the production of surplus value – remains hidden. In later works like *Capital* Marx strongly ties ideology to a process he calls fetishism whereby things become identified by their appearance rather than true nature.

The concept of estrangement is now given a more a precise definition. It is no longer simply the estrangement of human essence by private property but the way that workers are dominated by social forms that are real and yet hide their true natures. While many workers believe they are doing a fair day's work for a fair day's wage, the wage form hides the real nature of the production process and the extraction of surplus labour from the producer. Marx also talks of the fetishisation of the commodity form which presents the social characteristics of commodities as natural and intrinsic to them:

> The mysterious character of the commodity-form consists therefore simply in the fact that the commodity reflects the social characteristics of men's own labour as objective characteristics of the products of labour themselves, as the socio-natural properties of these things . . . It is nothing but the definite social relation between men themselves which assumes here, for them, the fantastic form of a relation between things. (Marx 1976: 164–65)

Marx's theory of commodity fetishism shows how ideology is produced by the normal workings of the capitalist system. This ideology helps society to function and it is in fulfilling this cohering function that ideology is often conceived of, within the Marxist tradition, as a social cement that holds together the different parts of the social system. Ideology, therefore, is concerned with the unity and reproduction of the social system, generating the necessary beliefs to ensure that humans act in the right ways. Later writers, particularly within the structuralist tradition will look at how this extends to politics and culture, but in Marx the main focus is on economic forms. Social forms like money, capital, the commodity and the wage are real but at the same time mystifying forms that conceal the essence of capitalist relations through their surface appearances and create the illusion of free and equivalent social relations. The generation of such ideology helps ensure the reproduction of the social system by ensuring that human action helps to reproduce society rather than question its real basis.

This leads to a debate within Marxism as to whether these illusory forms are in themselves sufficient to ensure the stability and reproduction of the capitalist system. In their political writings Marx and Engels lay greater stress on the role of ideas that are generated in the course of class struggle. But, as Jorge Larrain points out (Larrain 1983), their account of ideology does tend to emphasise its negative rather than positive effects and it has been left to future Marxists like Lenin and Gramsci to give a more positive account of the processes by which different classes *actively* use ideology to advance their interests.

Economic Analysis

Commenting on his method, Marx writes that:

> My inquiry led me to the conclusion that neither legal relations nor political forms could be comprehended whether by themselves or on the basis of a so-called general development of the human mind, but that on the contrary they originate in the material conditions of life . . . that the anatomy of this civil society, however, has to be sought in political economy. (Marx 1975a: 425)

For Marxism, in order to understand the development of human society it is necessary to understand the fundamental role played by production. Marx talks of the need to study political economy because he recognises that the process of production – the relations both within societies and between societies and nature – has an organised character based on certain economic principles. Through production, the members of society are able to satisfy their basic wants and needs – the need for food, clothing and shelter as well as other, more developed tastes. The reproduction of the basic material conditions necessary to sustain human existence is something fundamental to all societies. The particular form that this takes, however, is a historical matter. Marx therefore examines society and the history of societies from the point of view of the ways in which production is organised, or what is termed the dominant *mode of production*.

Marxists argue that what is particular about the *capitalist* mode of production is that it is based on the generalised production of commodities (goods for exchange) and wage-labour (in contrast, perhaps, to slave labour, feudal bondage or a system of primitive bartering). In *Capital*, Marx embarks on a systematic study of the economic laws of the capitalist mode of production, examining both the workings of capitalist society and its contradictions. Marx begins his work with an analysis of the commodity. The commodity is an item that through its qualities satisfies human needs and in this sense it is said to have a *use value*. However, under capitalism, commodities are produced, primarily, in order to be exchanged for money or other goods. Therefore, when an item assumes the form of a commodity it thereby acquires an *exchange value* based on its relation to other commodities.

As will be argued later, Marx's analysis of commodity production employs a method of dialectical abstraction that is concerned with moving away from the (fetishised) appearance of commodities in their exchange relations in order to examine the social conditions that underlie them. Marx's analysis of the commodity leads to an analysis of the social relation between capital and labour. This is Marx's *labour theory of value*.

The labour theory of value argues that the value of a commodity is equal to the amount of human labour that goes into its production. The value of an item is equal to the amount of labour-time socially necessary for its production (Marx 1976: 129). In return for this labour-time the capitalist pays workers a wage. In fact the payment of wages represents the purchase of a unique commodity – that of labour-power. What is unique about labour-power is that it is the only commodity capable of producing value over and above its own value. What the capitalist is buying is not the actual amount of labour performed by the worker, but the worker's capacity to work for a given period of time. During this time the capitalist must ensure that the worker can produce more value than what is given back in wages. This surplus is based on the difference between the value the workers produce, and what they receive in wages. The extraction of surplus labour forms the basis for capitalist profits.

Capitalist society, like previous societies, is based on a system of class exploitation. Surplus labour exists in other types of society – for example, under the feudal system the peasant performs unpaid labour for the landlord. What is specific about the capitalist system is the production of *surplus value* which is what the capitalist can extract from the labour-power employed above the exchange value of that labour. If a worker is hired for a day we may say that part of this day consists of necessary labour time or that portion of the day used to produce the value equivalent to wages, while the rest of the day consists of surplus labour time where the value of the goods produced goes to the employer. So, in a simple example, the worker may spend four hours producing goods of a value of £50, the same amount as their day's wages. The next four hours of the day (and the next £50) goes to the capitalist. However, because the capitalist is driven by profits (and the need to compete with rival producers) it is necessary to try and increase this rate of exploitation (or amount of surplus value). This can be done most simply by increasing the working day without an increase in pay so that the worker may spend longer producing surplus value for the capitalist. However, it can be done more subtly by increasing the productivity of labour. So, for example, the worker may still work the same hours and receive the same pay, but will produce more in this time. With the introduction of better machinery, the worker may now only take three hours to create £50 worth of value. The capitalist now gets five hours of surplus labour.

What is unique about the capitalist system (as the section on ideology pointed out) is that this relation of exploitation appears as fair or at least free. Unlike previous forms of class exploitation such as direct enslavement or the forcible payment of rent to the feudal lord, capitalism is based on the voluntary sale of the worker's labour power to the capitalist. This voluntary aspect is of course another ideological illusion since the mass of workers are *forced* to sell their labour power to someone or other. That this is necessary is because the capitalist system operates on the basis of the ownership and non-ownership of the means of production. Because the mass of workers do not own the means of production (raw materials, tools, factories and capital) they are forced to sell their labour-power to the capitalist in order to survive. Compared to previous forms of exploitation, this process represents an economic rather than a political compulsion, allowing the representatives of the capitalist class to make the ideological claim that each individual is free to do as they wish and make the best of their particular abilities. The wage-labour process acts in a mystificatory way that conceals the real level of exploitation and generates the feeling that wage-labour is consensual. Again we can see what Marx means when he talks of ideology as being generated by and legitimating the economic process.

The way that capitalism organises the production process brings a new level of intensity. In particular, capitalism constitutes a new stage in the division of labour, destroying the social bonds and feelings between different people, and undermining the free spirit of the individual. With the division of labour comes the routinisation of work, turning the worker into little more than a machine. This is well documented in passages in Marx's *Capital* and in Engels' *Condition of the Working Class in England*. Workers are further divided into those with jobs and those who are unemployed and constitute a 'reserve army of labour'. In the spirit of the market, workers compete against each other for jobs while firms compete against each other for profits. This further adds to the coercive power of the system and adds to the pressure on those who are forced to sell their labour-power in order to survive. According to Marx's theory of *immiseration*, the dynamics of the capitalist system lead to increased misery for the masses and an ever declining standard of wages.

Whether this is true or not is a matter of debate. It might be argued that this is not the case in the advanced capitalist economies, but then this may be so precisely because these economies are advanced at the expense of the poor in the Third World. Then again, this immiseration may be talked of as relative rather than absolute with the gap between the rich and poor continuing to grow. Or else, we may view the theory of immiseration as a general tendency which may be offset by counteracting tendencies like political intervention, state planning and so on. In fact, we may make such a point about Marx's economic theories more generally – that they describe general structural tendencies and causal mechanisms which may be offset by a number of counter-tendencies in the open context of the real world. This does not invalidate

Marx's economic analysis. Rather, we must remember that it is analysis that involves a process of theoretical abstraction and that when analysing a concrete situation a thorough empirical analysis of multiple causal processes must be undertaken.

Historical Materialism

Marx never actually used the terms historical and dialectical materialism, perhaps indicating why his legacy in these areas is so disputed. Part of the problem concerns the degree to which Marx's historical analysis flows from the economic analysis just outlined. Yet it is the study of the production process and the way in which this production is organised that makes the Marxist theory of history distinctively materialist. Unlike Hegel's idealist history as the unfolding of spirit, Marx bases his view of history on our productive capacities. He argues that human history is that of different modes of production. The organisation of the process of production is a necessary feature of all societies, but the way in which these relations are organised assumes a particular historical form. Historically we can point to different modes of production such as the communal system of primitive society, the slave system of ancient society, the serfdom of feudalism and the wage-labour economy of capitalism. This, then, is the most basic principle of the Marxist theory of social organisation – society is organised around the dominant mode of production and that: 'The mode of production in material life determines the general character of the social, political and spiritual processes of life' (Marx 1975a: 425).

To take this matter a little further, we can find in the 1859 *Preface* Marx's most concise statement on the nature of societies:

> In the social production of their existence, men inevitably enter into definite relations, which are independent of their will, namely relations of production appropriate to a given stage in the development of their material relations of production. The totality of these relations of production constitutes the economic structure of society, the real foundation, on which arises a legal and political superstructure and to which correspond definite forms of social consciousness. (Marx 1975a: 425)

The economic base of society is said to comprise of the forces and relations of production. Since this economic aspect of society forms its foundation, the base is ultimately determining of the legal, political and ideological superstructure which stands upon it. Such a view has been criticised for overemphasising the power that the economic base has in determining the rest of the social order. Such a model can certainly be seen as schematic with political, legal, cultural and ideological relations seen as being determined by the economic base. There have been fierce debates within Marxism as to how to interpret the base – superstructure model, whether the different levels of society have any autonomy and how much influence the superstructure can exert over the base. Perhaps the base prescribes the limits and degree of variation. Perhaps the economic is only determinant 'in the last instance'. Perhaps the base – superstructure relationship can be inverted, or maybe rejected altogether. Much of the rest of this book is in fact concerned with these issues.

Marx's distinction between the forces of production and productive relations is equally problematic. The productive forces refers to the technological means of production (like factories and machines) as well as labour power, while the relations of production refers to how these are organised, legally protected and legitimated – through classes and ownership. This again raises the issue of what has primacy, forces or relations? The *Preface* gives primacy to the productive forces suggesting that these shape the development of productive relations which in turn develop the social relations at the level of the superstructure. This deterministic view then assumes a historical character with social development explained in the following way:

> At a certain stage of development, the material productive forces of society come into conflict with the existing relations of production . . . From the forms of development of the productive forces these relations turn into their fetters. Then begins an era of social revolution. The changes in the economic foundation lead sooner or later to the transformation of the whole immense superstructure. (Marx 1975a: 425–26)

Such a statement has encouraged a mechanical version of historical materialism that reduces historical development to stages in economic development. While, for the reasons described above, it may be correct to see the economic structure of society as the main driving force of history, many interpreters of Marx have giving this a particularly one-sided and mechanical emphasis as we shall see in Chapter 3.

Against the mechanical version of historical materialism we might ask what the so-called economic foundation actually consists of? Indeed we might begin by noting that the issue of production is not reducible to the economic sphere but entails a wider array of social relations. For example, law is said to belong to the legal and political superstructure, but equally, a case could be made for it belonging to the base since capitalism is founded upon legally defined property rights. Other important social structures and institutions pose similar problems for surely such things as the family, education and training, welfare, indeed the state itself, play an important role in production (providing skills and support to workers or helping to safeguard private property rights) and yet cannot be reduced to either the economic or the superstructural. All of these could be said to reinforce the 'superstructural' level of politics and culture, but equally, they are important factors in the reproduction of capitalist relations of production.

The forces and relations distinction creates similar problems in terms of deciding how they can be separated. Marx's *Preface* suggests that the productive forces develop to ever-greater degrees until, at a certain stage, they come into conflict with social relations. This supposedly explains why it is that social orders are eventually overthrown. Capitalism creates potentials that are not fulfilled and capitalist relations create obstacles to further human development. This implies that the productive forces develop up until a point where they clash with wider social relations. But surely the productive forces cannot be considered in isolation but only ever in the context of these wider social relations. Rather than returning as fetters to further development, the relations of production are present from the beginning. They do not just constrain development but enable it in the first place. The passage from the *Preface* suggests that we can follow through the process of development to a point where the relations of production become a fetter, hindering further development. This is obviously problematic given that the *Preface* claims that social revolution is dependent on this contradiction. The truth is that this schema has proved to be of no real help to Marxists when analysing actual history, not least the Russian Revolution. Take the following statement from the *Preface*:

> No social order is ever destroyed before all the productive forces for which it is sufficient have been developed, and new superior relations of production never replace older ones before the material conditions for their existence have matured within the framework of the old society. (Marx 1975a: 426)

This mechanical view of history was contradicted by the Russian revolution and led the Italian Marxist Antonio Gramsci to declare the events a 'revolution against Marx's *Capital*'. Yet Gramsci himself continued to operate within such a framework, not least in his comment on social change that 'the old is dying but the new cannot yet be born'.

So how should we understand such passages from Marx? Perhaps the best thing to do is to view them as metaphors which are useful in pointing to general problems but which are no substitute for more careful theoretical and empirical analysis. Too much attention has often been paid to small passages from more popular works like the *Preface* and the *Communist Manifesto* where Marx and Engels attempt to summarise their theories. For a better understanding of historical materialism it is more fruitful to turn to the more substantial works like *Capital* although there remains the issue of the relative weight given to economic analysis. It is still possible to read works like *Capital* as reinforcing economic determinism. But as Engels was to write in his letter to J. Bloch:

> Marx and I are ourselves partly to blame for the fact that the younger people sometimes lay more stress on the economic side than is due to it. We had to emphasise the main principle vis-à-vis our adversaries, who denied it, and we had not always the time, the place or the opportunity to give their due to the other elements involved in the interaction. (Engels 1975: 396)

Later writers like Gramsci and Althusser attempt to give more weight to these other elements. In developing a theory of historical materialism, it is also advisable to pay more attention to Marx and Engels' political writings where, due to the unfolding of actual events, they step out of the determinist view of history. Here there is a focus on the effects of class struggle as a force of history. Indeed, although we could choose to interpret Marx in a one-sided way and declare that the economic basis of society determines class, we could also turn this around and claim that it is class and class struggle that determines society. At least this is the intention of Marx and Engels themselves when they open the *Communist Manifesto* with the declaration: 'The history of all hitherto existing society is the history of class struggles' (Marx and Engels 1973: 67). So we are faced with two competing interpretations of historical materialism, one that sees it in terms of the development of modes of production and one that views history as class struggle. For the latter view we turn to Marx's political writings.

Classes and Class Struggle

In keeping with the approach of historical materialism we can say that different classes are determined on the basis of their place in the mode of production. Therefore, under capitalism classes can be defined on the basis of the ownership or non-ownership of the means of production. In a short chapter in *Capital* the working class is defined as wage-labourers or the owners of mere labour-power while the capitalists, as the owners of capital, derive their income from profit (Marx 1981: 1025). Unfortunately, this is as far as Marx's economic study of class gets before the manuscript breaks off. This brevity has provoked debates over the importance of such issues as productive and unproductive labour, the creation of surplus value and the subjective side of class. However, we can also develop a more social understanding of class derived from the political writings.

We have seen how in his early work Marx makes the proletariat central to his understanding of social change. This theme is further developed in the *Communist Manifesto* which attempts to combine a historical materialist analysis of society with an outline of the necessary tasks facing the working class and its organisations. When this pamphlet was written in 1848, powerful workers' movements were developing across Europe. In Britain the Chartist movement was making headway while the revolutionary socialism of Auguste Blanqui was gaining influence in France, but it was the stirring of the German working class that most interested Marx and Engels. The *Manifesto* should therefore be seen as an agitational work aimed at those who would sweep away the old order. Perhaps for this reason the *Manifesto* is keen to stress the polarity of social classes – those who are the owners of the means of production and the modern wage-labourers who are reduced to selling their labour power.

The first of these classes, the bourgeoisie, is the product of a long course of development resulting from a series of revolutions in the mode of production. Marx and Engels are keen to stress that historically the bourgeoisie has played a progressive role in putting an end to 'feudal, patriarchal, idyllic relations' and bringing together the means of production, collectivising the population and advancing political centralisation and modernisation. Of course it may be speculated as to how much this is a matter of the conscious intent of the bourgeois class and how much this is a matter of the dynamics of the capitalist system. The bourgeoisie cannot afford to stand still but must continually revolutionise the relations of production. In just one hundred years, the *Manifesto* argues, capitalism has created more massive productive forces than all preceding generations put together. The dynamic nature of capitalism combined with the actions of the bourgeois class indicate the coincidence of economic and political factors.

But although the capitalist system is dynamic and the bourgeoisie plays a progressive role, the constant revolutionising of production and the competition for profits generates ever-greater levels of exploitation of the workforce. A fundamental class antagonism exists between capitalists and the workers who are forced to sell their labour-power. The distinctive feature of capitalism is that it has simplified class relations so that 'Society as a whole is more and more splitting up into two great hostile camps, into two great classes directly facing each other: bourgeoisie and proletariat' (Marx and Engels 1973: 68). The constant drive to expand capitalism turns more and more people into proletarians. This includes large sections of the peasantry as well as the lower strata of the middle class which sinks slowly into the ranks of the working class as its members are forced to sell their labour-power to survive. At the same time, this process creates another contradiction for the exploited class is also unified by this process, becoming a collective force that shares common experiences and interests. While the other classes remain bound to the existing order, 'the proletarian movement is the self-conscious, independent movement of the immense majority, in the interest of the immense majority' and ultimately the grave-digger of capitalism (Marx and Engels 1973: 78, 79). Capitalism brings about the collective organisation of those who are destined to overthrow it.

However, this still leaves the problem of whether the working class is really as united and homogenous as the *Manifesto* claims. It is presumed that the development of capitalism will lead to the working class becoming a single revolutionary group standing in opposition to the bourgeoisie. Such a reading understands class on a purely objective basis – that is, in relation to the ownership of the means of production. Even this may produce divisions within classes for some workers will enjoy better working conditions and wages and a higher social status in relation to others. These differentiations need to be dealt with by the notion of *class fractions* as we see in later chapters. But above all, it is necessary to take into account subjective factors that affect social class – above all, the question of consciousness. Objective class relations may be important, but they develop into class consciousness only when the working class realises its position within society. Marx deals with this issue of class as a subjective factor when he talks of a class-in-itself and a class-for-itself.

While a class-in-itself is something given by the relationship to the means of production, a class-for-itself implies an active social relation based on specific interests, actions and consciousness. Class is no longer simply given by a group's economic position but is conditioned and reformed through the political process of class struggle:

> Economic conditions had first transformed the mass of the people of the country into workers. The combination of capital has created for this mass a common situation, common interests. This mass is thus already a class as against capital, but not yet for itself. In the struggle . . . this mass becomes united, and constitutes itself as a class for itself. The interests it defends become class interests. But the struggle of class against class is a political struggle. (Marx 1963: 173)

Therefore, Marx does not view class as a static category, but as something that is continually reproduced through the different socio-economic, political and ideological relations that people are engaged in. Above all, class consciousness is forged through people's struggles and collective experiences. Classes become active 'for themselves' when they form political parties and trades unions and engage in collective struggle in order to improve their position within society. Similarly, the lack of such struggles, may result in people losing their class identity. This may be illustrated by recent events. Current social theory is full of the notion that we have gone beyond class or that class is no longer relevant. What has actually happened is that in the late 1980s and 1990s the working class suffered a series of notable defeats with the collapse of so-called Communism and the triumph of the free market. This has resulted in a serious decline in class consciousness but it does not mean that class no longer matters. A person's relationship to the means of production is still a key factor, but this must be measured against consciousness and the way in which people see their place in society.

Such discussions about class and class struggle raise an age-old problem in social science, that of the relation between structure and agency. A person's class can be seen as being determined by social structure and the various economic relationships that they are engaged in. These social structures enable people to act in a certain way but also impose constraints upon them. Structures therefore confer upon agents certain powers and liabilities. The socialisation of production gives the working class a collective power that the more disparate peasantry and petite bourgeoisie does not have. But how these powers are exercised is a contingent matter. This depends on the interaction political, cultural and ideological factors as well as the consciousness of the actors themselves. Within a given framework and set of circumstances agents can act. But this is always within a given framework best summed up by Marx's expression that people make their own history but under conditions not of their own choosing.

The State

Marx did not develop a systematic view of the state so his various writings have left a disputed legacy. At best we can say that the work of Marx and Engels leads to a view of the state as an institution responsible for or supportive of class domination and rulership. This is why, in the early works Marx criticises Hegel for not seeing that the state represents the interests of the property owning elite and that the state's claim to represent the universal interest is an ideological one. Marx's initial solution was to demand a genuinely democratic society. However, he soon realises that this cannot be achieved without a more far-reaching social transformation including the abolition of private property.

The recognition of the importance of ownership of the means of production leads Marx's position to evolve into the view that the state is an *instrument* of the ruling class that is used to defend their private interests. This position is most clearly expressed in the *Communist Manifesto* where Marx and Engels claim that: 'The executive of the modern state is but a committee for managing the common affairs of the whole bourgeoisie' (Marx and Engels 1973: 69, for a similar expression see also Marx and Engels 1965: 79–80). According to the instrumentalist approach, the state is a political representative of the economically dominant class. This fits neatly into the base-superstructure model whereby the economy represents the basis of society and the state is the main institution of the legal–political superstructure. Where the economy leads the state follows.

The state lends its support to economic exploitation by offering political and military coercion. The *Communist Manifesto* describes the state as an 'armed body of men', a coercive instrument that can be used as a tool by the ruling class to gain political acceptance of its economic power. Such a view might be criticised on two grounds: for an overemphasis of coercion and the way it neatly matches political and economic interests. On the matter of coercion, a more sophisticated approach would examine the importance of consent and more subtle means of social control. It is also the case that economic and political interests often do not coincide and that the state becomes a terrain for the playing out of various struggles between competing groups and their social, economic and political interests. As well as assuming the base-superstructure model, the instrumentalist view of the state also assumes a class model that sees two homogenous classes with clear interests. Both assumptions might be considered to be overly simplistic.

Marx's writings about actual political events are more complex. The workers of Paris rose up in 1870 and established a Commune based on a socialised system of production under the control of a democratically elected government. However, this was bloodily suppressed by the ruling class. Marx's study of these events, *The Civil War in France*, explains that the Commune failed because 'the working class cannot simply lay hold of the ready-made state machinery, and wield it for its own purposes' (Marx 1974a: 206). This indicates that although sections of the capitalist class may seek to use the state as their own instrument, it cannot be used in such a way by the working class. The working class cannot, therefore, use the existing state as an instrument for its own rulership for such a state is designed to maintain the rule of capital and its repressive apparatuses will defend this role rather than allow the state to be used for socialist purposes. So the working class must smash the existing state and establish a new one that is better suited to defending a system of common ownership. There is thus a link between Marx's writings on the Paris Commune and later work by Lenin on the need for a dictatorship of the proletariat.

The argument that the working class cannot just lay hold of the existing state suggests that the state is more than just an instrument of the dominant group or class but has a more deeply inscribed character based on its relation to the economic system. The state is capitalist not simply because it is under the control of the bourgeois class but because of its intrinsic relationship to the capitalist system. In later debates between Marxists over the nature of the capitalist state, Nicos Poulantzas (1978a) took the view that the state has a 'structurual–functional' role based on its intrinsic relation to the mode of production. In a debate conducted in *New Left Review* he opposed what he saw as the more instrumental position of Ralph Miliband (see also Miliband 1973a for an instrumental view of the state). According to Poulantzas, the state cannot be reduced to the decisions of its leading personnel or leading representatives of capital precisely because its role is to transcend any potential differences between these people and to act as a mediator between capital and labour. As an illustration of this more functional aspect of the state we can turn to Marx's writings on the regime of Louis Bonaparte.

Here it is argued that under exceptional circumstances the state displays a degree of autonomy. The warring factions within the ruling class balance each other out with state power attaining a degree of independence. Rather than seeing the state as an instrument of a particular group, this view concentrates on the functions of the state, arguing that whatever the differences within the ruling class, the role of the state must go on. Therefore, according to Marx's *Eighteenth Brumaire of Louis Bonaparte*, the French state rose above class divisions and assumed a more autonomous nature under the authoritarian control of a single dictator. In fact Bonaparte, rather than representing the ruling class was more representative of the small peasant and petite bourgeoisie. This goes against the view that the state is simply the instrument of the economically dominant class. The ruling class had lost its vocation to rule and into the void steps the figure of Bonaparte causing Marx to remark that: 'France therefore seems to have escaped the despotism of a class only to fall back beneath the authority of an individual' (Marx 1973b: 236).

The Bonapartist state became necessary in order to hold things together when conflicts between class fractions could not be resolved. Although the state arose above the different fractions of the ruling class, it was still required to respond to the overall needs of capitalist development. Power fell into the hands of the state executive which assumed a more autonomous role. Although the case of Louis Bonaparte is an exceptional one, this view of the state *as a factor of social cohesion*, to use Bob Jessop's term (Jessop 1985), can be applied more generally to describe the process whereby the state seeks to resolve or contain the conflicts between different groups and interests in order to protect the general needs of the economic system. Therefore the state assumes an importance as a bureaucratic and military organisation with interests of its own. It is less a committee for managing the common affairs of the bourgeoisie than a giant administrative apparatus whose function is to ensure social and economic stability.

In achieving this, the state must act as a mediator between the economic and political spheres. The state becomes historically necessary once society moves beyond a basic subsistence level of production. Its development may well be linked to the rise of class society, however, it might be also argued that, regardless of this fact, the state also has a socially necessary function in relation to such factors as the distribution of surplus product, the regulation of different interests and the mediation of different conflicts. It argues that the state must function in the best interests of the economic mode of production – that is, under capitalism, the state must act in accordance with the demands of private property, the market economy and capital accumulation. Against any mechanical interpretation of this, it is precisely because there is no absolute guarantee of smooth functioning between the economy and the ruling class that the state must play a unifying role. Rather than seeing the state as a superstructural response to the economic base, the state now becomes central to the unity and reproduction of the social system as a whole. However, it is also necessary to see that there is no guarantee that the state can successfully play this unifying role for this is in turn dependent upon various contingent factors including the balance of class forces and the particular interests of those exercising power.

Although this section has concentrated on interpretations of Marx, Engels' book *The Origin of the Family, Private Property and the State* should also be mentioned since this has also been influential in historically situating the rise of the state and linking it to the growth of class society and, importantly, to the development of the family (safeguarding the inheritance of private property). Engels argues that the state has not existed for all eternity and that there have been early societies that did without state power. However, '[a]t a certain stage of economic development, which necessarily involved the split of society into classes, the state became a necessity because of this split' (Engels 1978: 210). This occurs once human labour is able to produce more than is necessary for the maintenance of the producers, so the state is linked to the production, protection and distribution of this surplus. Most generally, the state is an organisation of the possessing class for its protection against the non-possessing class:

> It is as a rule the state of the most powerful, economically dominant class, which, through the medium of the state becomes also the politically dominant class and so acquires a new means of holding down and exploiting the oppressed class. Thus the ancient state was, above all, the state of the slave-owners for holding down the slaves, just as the feudal state was the organ of the nobility for holding down the peasant serfs and bondsmen, and the modern representative state is an instrument for exploiting wage labour by capital. (Engels 1978: 208)

We can see that this is an instrumental perspective but also an institutional and historical approach that links the development of the state to changes in wider society. However, Engels does have a rather mechanical notion of historical development based on the stage of development of the division of labour (Engels 1978: 210).

In *Anti-Dühring* Engels considers what will happen to the state after the Communist revolution. This will be the first genuinely social revolution carried through by a class that does genuinely represent the universal interest. Consequently after the revolution, class differences will begin to fade with the result that the state starts to disappear:

> *The proletariat seizes power and to begin with transforms the means of production into state property.* But it then puts an end to itself as proletariat, it thus puts an end to all state differences and class antagonisms, and thus also to the state as state . . . The government of persons is replaced by the administration of things and the direction of the process of production. The state is not 'abolished', *it withers away.* (Engels 1976: 362–63)

Dialectics and Method

Dialectics has a long history. The meaning of the term comes from 'dia' and 'logos' in Greek philosophy and refers to contradictions in reasoning. In Hegel the concern is with how struggles in thought and consciousness lead to historical progress. Contradictions lead to resolution at a higher level. In Marx and Engels, this dialectical struggle becomes material.

Taking up Hegel's dialectic of Spirit, Marx argues that Hegel's philosophy only transcends the world in thought when this must be done in practice. In *Capital* Marx claims that Hegel's dialectic is standing on its head and that it 'must be inverted, in order to discover the rational kernel within the mystical shell' (Marx 1976: 103). The first problem with Marx's dialectic is in determining the extent to which it has taken over Hegel's dialectic of Spirit. Particularly problematic is Hegel's understanding of the dialectic as teleology – that is to say, a process with a purpose. We have seen with the discussion of historical materialism that seeing history as a process is problematic. Or at least, it is problematic if this process is given a telos or purpose or design so that history is regarded as passing through a number of determined phases before it reaches its culmination in the endpoint of Communism.

Under what becomes known as dialectical materialism the Hegelian approach to the dialectic is combined with the materialism of the Enlightenment such as might be found in evolutionary biology. This finds its strongest expression in the work of Engels who declares dialectics to be 'the science of the general laws of motion and the development of nature, human society and thought' (Engels 1954: 180). For Engels the three main laws of dialectics are the transformation of quantity into quality whereby gradual quantitative developments lead to revolutionary qualitative changes, the interpenetration and unity of opposites whereby things are in a constant state of internal struggle due to their contradictory make-up, and the negation of the negation whereby change is both a break from the past and a continuation or carrying forward of the old into the new (Engels 1954: 62). These can be seen working together in the struggle of opposites, with contradictions leading to development and the movement to a higher stage. The dialectical process is sometimes described as thesis, antithesis, synthesis.

The dialectic in Engels has a wider scope than it does in Marx and is more controversial. As well as being more Hegelian in its nature, it is also more generalised. This is particularly so in Engels' theory of the dialectic of nature which aims to bring historical materialism and natural science together. Drawing on the scienctific ideas of his time, Engels argues that all processes are dialectical, including those of the natural world. Even getting drunk is described by Engels as the transformation of quantity into quality! (Engels 1954: 66).

Maybe such statements indicate the banality of the dialectic of nature. To talk of acorns turning into oak trees in such a way does not really add to science. Engels' treatment of dialectics has led some like Eduard Bernstein to declare that dialectics is nonsense while others like Georg Lukács have argued that dialectics only applies to method or at best, to the social world. Yet despite the problems, what Engels says about the nature of dialectics makes some sense. He divides dialectics into what he calls an objective dialectics which characterises natural and social phenomena, and a subjective dialectics as method or dialectical thought: 'Dialectics, so-called *objective* dialectics, prevails throughout nature, and so-called subjective dialectics, dialectical thought, is only the reflection of the motion through opposites which asserts itself everywhere in nature' (Engels 1954: 211).

There is a problem with this which is that thought does not just reflect reality. The 'Subjective dialectic' of thought is hard work precisely because it does not just reflect reality because reality is not something that is immediately revealed (think of the earlier distinction between appearance and essence).

Rather, 'subjective' dialectics requires a theoretical effort that bases itself on a process of abstracting from the concrete or manifest in order to look at underlying processes and contradictions. We deal with this next. However, Engels is right to distinguish between dialectics as a method and the dialectical reality that it examines. Dialectical thought attempts to reveal the innermost nature of things, their inner tendencies, intrinsic nature, contradictions and conflicts that this engenders. It sees reality as an interconnected process rather than as comprised of isolated entities as mainstream positivist science supposes. This means seeing things as part of a whole. Dialectical theory stresses the importance of the concept of totality. It is necessary to look at the relationship between parts and the whole, to examine the tensions that may exist between them and how they are in a constant state of development and co-determination. The dialectical method must highlight this relationship. It must do so because reality is like this. If method is dialectical it is so because reality is dialectical. But to grasp this reality, a complex process of abstraction must take place.

The Marxist method proceeds by means of hypothesising certain structures and causal mechanisms and attempting to study their operation, initially in isolation, then in combination. Marx explains his method as abstracting from the concrete starting point in order to understand how things work in theory, a process which reveals that the starting point was not as simple as it first seemed, but represents the 'concentration of many determinations'.

> The concrete is concrete because it is the concentration of many determinations, hence the unity of the diverse. It appears in the process of thinking, therefore, as a process of concentration, as a result, not as a point of departure in reality, even though it is the point of departure in reality and hence also the point of departure for observation and conception. (Marx 1973c: 101)

Abstraction necessarily entails a critical stance towards concrete forms like the commodity and wage forms as they appear in their immediacy. Marx's analysis reveals that behind their immediate form lies a more complex social relation. It also reveals how various relations entail other relations and how social mechanisms and structures work in complimentary and contradictory combinations. By revealing the complexity of concrete social forms, such an analysis entails a critique of their immediate appearance.

Therefore developing an analysis of these forms often leads to a negative evaluation of them. This can be described as an explanatory critique. In criticising the form, the explanatory critique suggests that things are other than as they appear and that the process that produces such forms can be other than it is. Revealing the unfairness of wage-labour relations suggests that there may be a fairer alternative that does not involve deception. Unlike other approaches to social science (like positivism and hermeneutics), explanation and understanding are necessarily critical.

Abstraction is a dialectical process as it moves from the concrete to the abstract and returns to the concrete understood in a new way. By contrast, the classical political economy that Marx critiques accepts the concrete as it is found, making its findings natural, rather than looking at its social determination. Political economists are unable to explain the true nature of the economic system. They can explain its appearance but not its essence – another dialectical distinction.

Marx's work is full of such dialectical pairs – essence and appearance, concrete and abstract, base and superstructure, forces and relations, use value and exchange value, working class and bourgeoisie, capital and labour.

Dialectics has a bad reputation. Discussions of such things as the dialectic of nature have led some Marxists to reject dialectics altogether or at least to argue that it is something specific to the social world. But if theory is dialectical, then the reality to which it refers must also be dialectical. Abstraction, for example, is not merely a method but reflects something real (or it is a method for getting at the deeper layers of reality). As Marx says: 'even the most abstract categories . . . are nevertheless, in the specific character of their abstraction, themselves likewise a product of historical relations' (Marx 1973c: 105). Quite simply, Marx's analysis of society reveals the dialectics of social and historical processes and relations, of a society in conflict or in transition, of struggles between classes and between capital and labour. We conclude this chapter with a discussion of the dialectics of social change.

Social Change

With the notion of dialectics we have an approach that sees things in a constant state of change. This section addresses the issue from the point of view of structure and agency. First it addresses the issue of structural contradiction and crisis within the system, then looks at the role of agency in social transformation.

Marx looks at social change from the point of view of conflicts between structures or contradictions within the system. Marx argues that the capitalist system has inherent weaknesses and crisis tendencies that will lead to its downfall. One of the most basic contradictions is the tendency of rate of profit to fall. Capitalism is based on the need for profit which in turn is based on the extraction of surplus value. Marx argues that although labour is the source of surplus value, there is a historical tendency for the amount of labour (or what he calls variable capital) to decline as a proportion of total capital, thus reducing that proportion of capital capable of producing surplus value and hence profit. This is a contradiction because it is actually the desire to extract increasing amounts of surplus value that leads the capitalist to spend more money on machines and other forms of fixed capital that can increase the productivity of labour. In a competitive environment this reduces costs per unit and gives the producer an edge over any rivals. But ultimately, it is not factories or machines that create profit for the capitalist but the exploitation of unpaid labour. While the innovative capitalist may initially benefit from the use of improved technology, the benefits of this soon disappear as the improvements become generalised across the industry.

Such a crisis occurs because of the nature of capitalist competition and the drive to accumulate. The free nature of capitalist production creates unstable or anarchic conditions that undermine the smooth flow of production and circulation. One such theory is that the anarchy of the capitalist system leads to crises of *overproduction* where different capitalists or indeed whole sectors or industries are unable to sell their goods and capitalists are unable to realise their profits. Overproduction is a result of the constant drive to accumulate combined with the archaic nature of capitalism which means that this accumulation is at the mercy of the market.

These crisis tendencies are inherent to the capitalist system. However, they may be offset by counteracting tendencies such as state intervention and planning, increased productivity or technological advance. To some extent these may depend on the actions of particular agents like scientists, politicians or capitalists. Marx's more structural account of conflict and change is also supplemented with a much more agential, creative and dynamic theory of class struggle. The ruling class and bourgeoisie will respond to events and crises in different ways with different strategies. Likewise, the working class may organise to improve its own situation. In *The Poverty of Philosophy* Marx explains how large-scale industry concentrates a group of workers into a class and gives them the potential to resist the power of capital. This potential owes its origin to the structural contradiction between the social nature of production and the private appropriation of capital. Marx argues though that this is not enough and that classes needs to establish themselves on a political level so that the struggle of class against class becomes a political struggle (Marx 1963: 172–73). Marx gives an account of how the bourgeoisie came to power and smashed the old forms of state and civil society. It came to power for two reasons – first because antagonisms were already present in the old feudal order, and also because it was prepared to take political action to overthrow that order and establish its own rule. But on coming to power the bourgeoisie finds itself in a similar position to the old classes that it replaced.

Marx writes that 'revolutions are the locomotives of history' (Marx 1973a: 46). History develops by means of contradictions which give rise to conflicts which give rise to revolutions. Structural conditions give certain groups the potential to act, but how they act is a matter for agency. Social change is a result of both structure and agency best summed up by Marx's statement that: 'Men make their own history, but not of their own free will; not under circumstances they themselves have chosen but under the given and inherited circumstances with which they are directly confronted' (Marx 1973b: 146).

But the legacy of this is far from clear as the existence of the rest of this book testifies. It opens up debates about how much weight to give to social structure and process (structural Marxism) and what emphasis to place on the role of agency (praxis Marxism). It also needs to be resolved at the level of how to achieve social change. Most of Marx and Engels' work suggest this is by revolution. The bourgeoisie will not give up power without a violent struggle while the proletariat cannot just not lay hold of the state machinery and use it for its own purposes. But a dispute emerged as to whether towards the end of their lives Marx and Engels allowed for the possibility of peaceful social change. This leads to another big debate in the Marxist tradition, that between reform and revolution, an issue covered in Chapter 3.

Further Reading

Certainly the *Communist Manifesto* is the place to begin. This is the best introduction to Marx and Engels' revolutionary politics although one must bear in mind the historical context. Other works that are easy to read and contain Marx's main ideas are the deeply problematic 1859 *Preface* which sets out his view of historical development, and political writings like the *Civil War in France* and the *Eighteenth Brumaire of Louis Bonaparte*. Marx's political writings are collected together in the volumes published by Penguin, each of which has a useful introduction. The first section of Marx and Engels' *German Ideology* is important for views on ideology and ideas. Engel's *Origins of the Family, Private Property and the State* provides an interesting account of historical development. Marx's economic writings are more difficult to read and often very long. However, it is worth trying the first chapter of volume one of *Capital* on the commodity. For a very useful summary of the ideas in *Capital* try Marx's pamphlet *Wages, Price and Profit*. The internet archive http://www.marxists.org has online versions of these articles. The first chapter of Bob Jessop's book *The Capitalist State* is very useful for different theories of the state in Marx. Miliband's book *The State in Capitalist Society* is a clear expression of the instrumental view. Andrew Collier's book *Marx* is a very good recent introduction. The most enjoyable biographical work is Francis Wheen's *Karl Marx* (1999).

3

Classical Marxism

Introduction: The Second International and Bolshevism

Classical Marxism, like many such terms, can mean all things to all people. This chapter shows the wide variations between those claiming the mantle. Nevertheless, the period of the Second International from 1889–1914 spans the vital gap between Marx and Engels and Lenin, and therefore all the debates and controversies over the legacy of the 'founders' and the development of Social Democracy (which at this time meant Marxist political parties). This chapter briefly looks at the two chief theorists of this period – Kautsky and later, Plekhanov – as well as the 'revisionist' dispute in the German Social Democratic Party (SPD) and the response of Rosa Luxemburg. The outbreak of the First World War brought about the collapse of the Second International leading Lenin and others to reflect on the 'betrayal' of the Social Democrats. It fell to Lenin and the Russian Bolsheviks to continue the revolutionary Marxist tradition, although some might consider this a departure from the 'classical' understanding of Marxism. This was certainly the attitude of many leaders of the Second International who denounced the actions of the Bolsheviks as premature. Even sympathetic revolutionaries like Gramsci declared the Russian Revolution to be a revolution against the teachings of Marx's *Capital*.

The Second International, based mainly on European workers' parties of which the German SPD was the most significant, might have been the first real embodiment of Marxist principles. But in reality, it was a loose federation whose diverse elements were struggling to come to terms with the Marxist legacy. The problem facing the parties of the Second International was that as they grew in influence they were in a position to win concessions in favour of the working class, but this meant compromising principles and making alliances with bourgeois forces. As these temptations became greater there developed a growing divide between the abstract theoretical Marxism of these parties and their reformist political practice. The abstract Marxism was of no use to practice and the practice bore little resemblance to Marxism. In this context, the success of revisionist ideas is to be understood, not according to their theoretical worth, but due to the fact that they reflected the real practical situation.

No one expected the collapse of the Second International over the war. Although congresses passed resolutions opposing the moves towards war, when it came, the main parties gave their support to their own national governments. Even Lenin found it hard to accept what the German SPD had done in voting for war credits. But in hindsight this does not seem so surprising. The parties of the Second International were caught between an abstract and dogmatic interpretation of Marx's ideas and a practical situation where these parties were making parliamentary gains and increasing their influence on the basis of abandoning Marxism in practice. The reformist practice of the parties of the Second International was aimed, not at overthrowing the capitalist state, but at gaining concessions from it. And since these parties became more and more drawn into state politics so, once those states went to war, the Social Democrats followed with them.

However, the war also brought revolution in Russia and a renewal or reinterpretation of 'classical Marxism'. Already weakened by military defeat against Japan and by the 1905 uprising, the First World War plunged Russia into crisis. The initial revolution of February 1917 was a classical bourgeois revolution which saw the removal of the Tsar and the establishment of a Provisional Government. However, Russia continued to fight the war and, with millions dead and many more millions starving, Lenin was able to oppose the new regime by promising peace, land and bread. Many Soviets or workers councils were already in existence and in October Lenin ordered the Red Guards to storm the Winter Palace, home of the Provisional Government. This revolution seemed to go against the accepted notion that socialist transformation was only possible in the more advanced capitalist countries, while confirming Leon Trotsky's alternative theory of permanent revolution. But Lenin and Trotsky also argued that revolution in a backward country needed the support of other countries. The isolation of the Russian Revolution and the outbreak of the bloody civil war left a terrible toll. Under these conditions the revolution degenerated. With Lenin dead, Stalin seized power, exiled and then murdered Trotsky, and there emerged a new Soviet orthodoxy that extinguished the last embers of revolutionary Bolshevism. With Stalinism, theory reverted back to the dogmatism and mechanical determinism of the earlier Second International. We are left, as has been said, with a highly disputed 'classical' tradition.

Orthodoxy and Revisionism

If the collapse of the Second International owed a lot to opportunist political practice, it was also a product of the wooden orthodoxy of Second International theory. Karl Kautsky was the leading theorist of the German SPD and his reputation was such that he was known as the 'Pope of Marxism'. He owed some of his repute to his friendship with Engels and, along with Eduard Bernstein, was considered to be his heir. For the keenest followers of Marx, he was seen as a defender of the orthodox view against the revisionism of Bernstein and others. But in a sense it was precisely this 'orthodoxy' with its rigid and mechanical understanding of Marxism that allowed more flexible revisionist approaches to gain credence.

Kautsky's Marxism was very much a product of the ideology of his time. Believing Marxism to be a strict science, he saw a unity of method between Marxism and the natural sciences. His view of historical materialism is influenced by an evolutionary naturalism derived from writers like Darwin and Herbert Spencer. The social world is regarded as a continuation of the natural and history is subject to the same laws. This produces a deterministic and mechanical viewpoint with an emphasis on natural necessity and the belief that the transition to socialism is inevitable. The trouble with this mechanical view is that socialist revolution is premised, not on the actions of the working class, but on the breakdown of capitalism and the development of 'objective' laws. As Kautsky says, 'it is just as little in our power to make this revolution as it is in the power of our opponents to prevent it' (quoted in Salvadori 1990: 40).

Kautsky had a crude understanding of philosophical issues and held a broadly positivistic outlook with an emphasis on universal laws and the unity of scientific method. He understood human consciousness to be the product of the historical development of society so that if society is moving towards socialism, or if the breakdown of capitalism is inevitable, then revolutionary awareness will follow. Unfortunately for Kautsky, this was not what happened in the case of Russia where the consciousness of the proletariat ran ahead of economic developments. According to Kautsky's materialism, economic conditions must fully ripen and the historical process must run its course before social revolution is possible. Therefore he opposed the Russian Revolution as something that was premature and criticised the Bolshevik seizure of power and more generally the idea of the dictatorship of the proletariat.

Kautsky's grouping in the SPD, known as the Centrists, took the middle position between the revisionists on the right, and Luxemburg's revolutionary wing of the SPD. But both other groups might claim that Kautsky's brand of Marxism stood in opposition to the very thing it should be – a guide to action. It is illuminating to note the two very different sections of the SPD's Erfurt Programme, the first based on the orthodox Marxist theory of Kautsky, the second on practice being written by Bernstein. With Kautsky's knowledge being confined to abstract theory, he was clearly in no position to resist the drive towards revisionism in his party.

Eduard Bernstein rejected the deterministic and outdated ideas of the Marxism of the Second International. He opposed the idea of the inevitability of capitalist crises, arguing that capitalism was able to adapt itself through such things as credit and cartels. Against the idea of the polarisation of classes, he maintained the significance of the middle class. Extolling the gradualism he learned from the British Fabians, he favoured the peaceful transformation of society and placed hope in the role of parliament. Socialism would come about, not through crisis, but through the working class gradually winning economic and political rights. This led him to make the infamous claim that the ultimate goal of socialism is nothing, the movement is everything.

Rosa Luxemburg

Although initially active in the Polish revolutionary movement Rosa Luxemburg moved to Germany in 1898 and was immediately drawn into the controversy over revisionism. Her pamphlet *Reform or Revolution* argues that if Bernstein is right that capitalism has stabilised then socialism ceases to be objectively necessary. But Bernstein is wrong to think of credit as overcoming problems of the system, on the contrary it accentuates them, separates production from ownership and increases the contradiction between property relations and relations of production. Likewise cartels only increase the antagonism between producers and consumers. Marx, she argues, remains fundamentally right on the essential contradiction between the anarchy of the market and the socialised form of the production process.

Luxemburg argues that revisionism wants to try and lessen capitalist contradictions. Bernstein's approach is not the conquest of political power but the gradual improvement of the condition of the working class through trade union and parliamentary activity (Howard 1971: 86). But, Luxemburg argues, Bernstein is wrong to place faith in the trade union struggle since the trade unions are simply trying to achieve a larger share of the wealth for the working class, something that will eventually come up against the limits of the system. Trade union activity is essentially limited to wage struggle and a reduction in labour time. The real problem lies deeper than this in the process of production itself (Howard 1971: 74).

Further, it is argued that the political institutions of bourgeois democracy are dependent on capitalist development but cannot overcome the fundamental question of property relations. Bourgeois institutions on the one hand allow greater freedom of expression and organisation for defending working class interests, and, on the other, they can undermine or derail such demands. The bourgeoisie can in fact use democracy to arrest the revolutionary process. Luxemburg writes that as soon as democracy shows signs of representing the true interests of the working class, the democratic forms are sacrificed by the bourgeoisie (Howard 1971: 83). Luxemburg, we can see, holds a rather crude instrumentalist view of political institutions as aids of bourgeois development. However, she did see democratic rights as instruments that could be used to some degree by the working class for its emancipation and she was also worried that in Russia the Bolsheviks curtailed too many democratic liberties.

So although Luxemburg took a revolutionary approach, she was critical of Lenin and the Bolsheviks, and in particular, the idea of a tightly disciplined vanguard party of professional revolutionaries. She accused the Bolsheviks of fetishising organisational issues and adopting 'Blanquist' conspiratorial organisation that separated the party from the masses. Against this, she stressed the independent activity of the proletariat and the importance of learning through experience. In overstressing organisation the Bolsheviks underestimate the maturity of the working class, narrowing the struggle rather than developing it (Howard 1971: 295). She praises the revolutionary spontaneity of the Russian working class and states: 'Finally, we must frankly admit to ourselves that errors made by a truly revolutionary labor movement are historically infinitely more fruitful and more valuable than the infallibility of the best of all possible "central committees" ' (Howard 1971: 306).

Luxemburg advocated the mass strike as a spontaneous expression of revolutionary working class consciousness that will overcome the inertia of party bureaucracy and allow creative expression. Such struggle will transform the consciousness of the masses. This is not something that can be conjured up by the revolutionary party, but is a real expression of the masses who learn through their actions, raise their own demands and address their own needs. The mass strike is not an isolated action but an indication of heightened class struggle in a particular period. It is not something that is artificially made, but an historical phenomenon (Howard 1971: 231). The strike, she writes, 'is the living pulse-beat of the revolution and at the same time its most powerful driving wheel' (Howard 1971: 237). The mass strike is not a tactic or method, but the proletarian struggle itself. From the mass strike would emerge the necessary forms of proletarian democracy.

Such views lead to the accusation that Luxemburg embraced the view that the working class will spontaneously radicalise. There is an amount of truth in this although she does write:

> It is not true that socialism will arise automatically and under all circumstances from the daily struggle of the working class. Socialism will be the consequence only of the ever-growing contradictions of capitalist economy and the comprehension by the working class of the unavoidability of the suppression of these contradictions through a social transformation. (Howard 1971: 88)

This leads to new problems, however. Like Kautsky and others, Luxemburg accepts the inevitability of capitalist breakdown. Her way of arguing this is novel. In *The Accumulation of Capital* it is claimed that imperialism is necessitated by inherent laws of capitalism that cause competition between the capitalist powers for the non-capitalist markets. She argues that surplus value cannot be realised by the sale of goods to workers or capitalists, so the capitalist system requires a non-capitalist market to exploit. Imperialism is explained in terms of the fight for these new markets, but eventually this non-capitalist sphere will be exhausted and the system will collapse.

Socialism is made possible by the laws of capitalism, but its realisation depends on the subjective factor. But there is an economic determinism to this in that Luxemburg believes capitalism will inevitably collapse, leading to a choice between socialism or barbarism. Barbarism is the collapse of capitalism as manifested in militarism, world wars and the destruction of modern culture and society. Still, Luxemburg appears to have an unshakable belief in the inherent radicality of the working class. Her position can be described as workerist in the sense that capitalism brings about increased class polarisation and radicalises the masses. She is also a catastrophist in the sense that capitalist laws will bring about stagnation and crisis, political reaction and war. With the issue of working class power so pressing, she has no time for such 'secondary' issues as the national question or the struggle of the peasantry.

Such an approach would have serious difficulty in explaining post-war economic stabilisation but at the time would have had much resonance. Although still critical of the Bolsheviks on the issue of democracy and on the national question, Luxemburg took their side against the betrayal of Social Democracy. The Left opposition become more coherent and united around ideas on imperialism and the mass strike. Initially Luxemburg did not form a separate party, fearing the creation of a 'purist' group cut off from the masses. But the expulsion of Luxemburg's Sparticist group and Kautsky's Centrists led to the formation of the USPD (Independent German Socialist Party). When Luxemburg's group became the German Communist Party in 1919, the split with Social Democracy was complete. So much so that her opposition to the new SPD government cost Luxemburg her life (she was murdered by socialists turned barbarians).

Lenin and Imperialism

Lenin is regarded as a great political leader rather than as a great theorist, yet his work is important given the collapse of orthodox Marxism and the need for a new emphasis on revolutionary action. Lenin rescues the idea of Marxism as a guide to action and makes an important break from determinism. Of particular importance is Lenin's theory of imperialism or a new capitalist epoch based on the dominance of monopoly and finance capital. By contrast, Lenin's theories of organisation and the dictatorship of the proletariat seem mundane, but they too have important theoretical implications.

Lenin's early work develops the ideas of his mentor Plekhanov arguing that the working class struggle must initially take place within a bourgeois-democratic context. Plekhanov, considered to be the 'father of Russian Marxism', argued that the Russian revolution would have two stages. First, the democratic revolution would remove the feudal Tsarist residues with the working class playing a leading role in this struggle. Russia would then go through a capitalist phase of development before being ready for socialism. Thus Lenin argues that the role of the working class is limited by the backward stage of the Russian economy and society. But, despite its small size, the working class can play an active role in extending the boundaries of political debate and struggle. So although it is not possible to 'jump out of the bourgeois-democratic boundaries of the Russian revolution . . . we can vastly extend these boundaries, and within these boundaries we can and must fight for the interests of the proletariat' (Lenin 1975a: 47).

However, Lenin developed the view that the struggle around national-democratic demands grows over into a struggle for political independence and working class forms of democracy. His idea of class leadership, based on the vanguard of the working class (the most class-conscious elements), gets more closely attached to the struggle for state power and the application of the leading role of the proletariat through the state. By contrast, Plekhanov remained trapped in the deterministic approach of the Second International, arguing that the productive forces must be further developed before any such struggle for power is possible. Such a schematic view of history led Plekhanov to oppose the Bolshevik revolution and even to support the First World War.

The Social Democrats' response to war, as was said, took Lenin a little by surprise. But he quickly developed his theory of imperialism to explain such events and to outline a Marxist response. He writes that

> capitalism only became imperialism at a definite and very high stage of its development . . . when the features of the epoch of transition from capitalism to a higher social and economic system had taken shape . . . Economically, the main thing in this process is the displacement of capitalist free competition by capitalist monopoly. (Lenin 1975b: 104)

The basic features of imperialism are the concentration of production and capital, the merging of bank capital with industrial capital, the export of capital rather than commodities and the formation of cartels. Above all, though, it is about the division of the world. This leads to disaster, for:

> what means other than war could there be *under capitalism* of removing the disparity between the development of productive forces and the accumulation of capital on the one side, and the division of colonies and 'spheres of influence' for finance capital on the other? (Lenin 1975b: 118)

Yet Lenin suggests that the basis for a higher system is being created, that monopoly and the concentration of capital makes centralisation and socialisation of the means of production possible.

Lenin's main ideas are hastily taken from other sources (Hobson, Hilferding and Bukharin in particular). But these ideas are used to draw more radical conclusions. First, Lenin explains the treachery of the leaders of the Second International in terms of imperialism producing enough spoils to bribe the layer he calls the labour aristocracy or the best off sections of the working class. This may make revolution in the advanced countries more difficult since workers and their representatives develop an interest in the spoils of the system. But instead, countries like Russia become the weakest link in the imperialist chain. Because capitalism now operates on a world scale, countries like Russia are subject to immense contradictions and are more likely to produce a socialist revolution led by a radicalised layer of the working class.

Proletarian Dictatorship and the Party

Lenin became convinced that a proletarian revolution was possible in Russia. In fact, following the February Revolution he came to the conclusion that a situation of dual power already existed. Alongside the bourgeois government stood what effectively amounted to a workers' government based on the soviets or workers' councils. These bodies sprang up from below, developing their own forms of proletarian democracy. For Lenin, power could either go towards the bourgeoisie, or towards the working class. However, for the latter to be successful, a period of proletarian dictatorship was necessary.

In Lenin's view, the proletariat must overthrow the bourgeoisie and take state power. Once this is achieved, state power can be used to win the sympathy of wider layers. Lenin makes a distinction between the masses and the more class-conscious members of the working class that he calls the vanguard. The revolutionary party must direct itself, first of all, at this most conscious and politically advanced section of society. The task, then, is to organise the vanguard, and, through them, appeal to the wider masses. In order to play this leading role, it is argued that the party must be disciplined and centralised. Lenin's ideas on democratic centralism set out how this disciplined party is to be organised, and how the greatest freedom of discussion must be balanced with the maximum unity of action.

Lenin's views on party organisation as outlined in *What is to be Done?* have been criticised as excessive, or as the product of an extreme situation. This booklet also contains a passage on consciousness that has achieved notoriety:

> Class political consciousness can be brought to the workers *only from without*, that is, only from outside the economic struggle, from outside the sphere of relations between workers and employers. The sphere from which alone it is possible to obtain this knowledge is the sphere of relationships of *all* classes and strata to the state and the government. (Lenin 1947: 75)

Along with Lenin's views on organisation, this seems to confirm the critics' view that Lenin was an elitist who believed that revolution would be brought to the masses by a band of professional revolutionaries; in effect, he was substituting the actions of the party for those of the class. However, what is often overlooked is that fact that this passage is directed against the tendency to adapt to spontaneous class consciousness, and in particular, is a warning

against economism and trade union syndicalism. Lenin argues that class political consciousness needs organisation and leadership, that spontaneous struggles are not enough. So Lenin is rejecting the spontaneist tendencies that are to
be found in Luxemburg and some anarchists, for example, and arguing that,
particularly under the difficult conditions revolutionaries were facing in
Russia, clear direction and leadership are required.

Lenin's emphasis on direction and leadership indicates how the concepts of
democratic centralism and proletarian dictatorship are linked and flow into
one another. Both recognise that spontaneous action is not enough and that
organisation and leadership is required. Both, however, also reflect the particularly difficult conditions the Bolsheviks found themselves in with the severity
of the discipline imposed fluctuating according to circumstances. Despite
friend and foe alike concentrating on *What is to be Done?* as the definitive
work on party organisation, Lenin himself recognised that it reflected the difficult circumstances at the time of writing. Likewise, the dictatorship of the
proletariat is conceived of as an emergency measure that is necessary in times
of transition from capitalism to socialism when state power is required to
repress the counter-revolutionary bourgeoisie and to stabilise the new regime.
Yet, according to Lenin's *State and Revolution*, perhaps due to the influence of
debating with the anarchists, not only the dictatorship, but the state itself will,
in time, begin to wither away. Sadly, this clearly did not occur in Russia, and
with the Bolsheviks confronted with crisis conditions, civil war and international isolation, increased repression was used. The dictatorship became ever
stronger, and towards the end of his life, and in his last testament, Lenin shows
signs of despair with the growing bureaucracy, both within the revolutionary
party, and in the Soviet state.

Permanent Revolution

Before looking at Leon Trotsky's analysis of this growing bureaucracy within
the USSR let us return to the question of why the revolution occurred in Russia.
Trotsky explains this in terms of his theory of uneven and combined development, arguing that less developed nations are subjected to a peculiar combination of different stages of the historical process. Under pressure from external
influences these countries develop modern capitalist features, leading to the
creation of a small but significant working class. By contrast, the bourgeoisie
is in a weak and compromised position, being almost entirely dependent on
foreign capital and investment, and unable to establish strong national roots.
Consequently, as Lenin argued, the bourgeoisie is unable to carry through the
tasks of the democratic revolution, while the peasantry, despite forming the
majority of the population, is incapable of playing any kind of independent
role. It therefore falls upon the working class to play the leadership role, and in
doing so, the struggle moves beyond the limits of the bourgeois revolution.

Trotsky's theory of permanent revolution, developed from the ideas of Parvus, supports the idea that a working class revolution is possible given the weakness of the bourgeoisie and the contradictory social and economic conditions caused by the rapid development of capitalism in a backward agrarian country. However, the 'permanency' of the revolution is dependent upon the stronger proletariat of the advanced capitalist countries. Therefore, the revolution must not just be permanent in the sense of extending beyond the unsolved national and democratic demands, but it must extend beyond the nation itself.

Therefore, although the conditions of uneven and combined development and an under-developed civil society make the capture of state power easier in the East, it also makes the subsequent task of maintaining this state power more difficult. By contrast, in the West, the working class faces a more difficult initial struggle for power, but once power is won, the more developed civil society will make it easier to build a socialist society. As Trotsky says:

> The ease with which we conquered power on November 7, 1917, was paid for by the countless sacrifices of the Civil War. In countries that are older in the capitalist sense, and with a higher culture, the situation will, without doubt, differ profoundly. In these countries the popular masses will enter the revolution far more fully formed in political respects. (Trotsky 1974: 221)

Such views, we will later see, are also developed in the work of Antonio Gramsci.

Socialist Culture

Trotsky was the most sophisticated of the Bolsheviks when it came to matters of art and culture. Even on the issue of permanent revolution he is aware of the cultural dimension when he writes that '[r]evolutions in economy, technique, science, the family, morals and everyday life develop in complex reciprocal action and do not allow society to achieve equilibrium. Therein lies the permanent character of the socialist revolution as such' (Trotsky 1969: 132–33).

Trotsky opposed attempts, common in the USSR at this time, to try and impose a working class culture on society. He argued that a true socialist culture must be allowed to evolve through new social structures and material conditions. Until this process is well under way, the dictatorship of the proletariat is seen as an abnormal period for art in which it has difficulty in finding roots. Trotsky criticises the Proletkult movement which, under the influence of Bogdanov, was arguing for the development of an authentic proletarian culture. The Proletkult movement established educational and cultural groups throughout the country, giving those involved a fair degree of autonomy. Ultimately this aroused the suspicions of Lenin who believed that Bogdanov was trying to build himself a power base, although Trotsky was more critical of the mistaken ideas behind the movement, arguing that:

> It is fundamentally incorrect to contrast bourgeois culture and bourgeois art with proletarian culture and proletarian art. The latter will never exist, because the proletarian regime is temporary and transient. The historic significance and the moral grandeur of the proletarian revolution consists in the fact that it is laying the foundations of a culture which is above classes and which will be the first culture that is truly human. (Trotsky 1991: 50)

The working class, by nature, is culturally disenfranchised and alienated. It cannot be compared to the bourgeoisie who enjoyed a degree of cultural autonomy many years before assuming political power. Whereas the 'bourgeoisie came to power fully armed with the culture of its time [t]he proletariat . . . comes into power fully armed only with the acute need of mastering culture' (Trotsky 1991: 220–21). Only when a firm material base has been established can the matter of a socialist culture fully emerge.

Fascism and the United Front

Trotsky has provided probably the foremost Marxist analysis of fascism. Analysing the situation in Germany, he argues that fascism arises as a mass movement as a result of a deep structural crisis along national and economic lines. There is also a political crisis with the traditional political parties unable to offer leadership. Fascism assumes a political significance due to a paralysis on both sides of the class struggle. The ruling class maintains control at the economic level, but in the political sphere it suffers a crisis of political representation of these interests. The working class is also beset by internal differences, a weakness that gives the petite bourgeoisie an elevated importance.

Trotsky argues that the fascist programme is a product of the frustration of the petite bourgeoisie with the social and economic order. However, the fact that fascism can only come to power with the support of the big bourgeoisie means that this programme, as a programme aspiring to political independence, can never be fully implemented as intended and becomes reduced to ritualistic acts. The illusions are reduced to a naked bureaucratic masquerade as fascism descends into bonapartism (Trotsky 1971: 406). Because of this, Trotsky concludes that ultimately '[f]ascism is a specific means of mobilising and organising the petit bourgeoisie in the social interests of finance capital' (Trotsky 1971: 441). This is not something willingly chosen, but is a last ditch attempt by the bourgeoisie to maintain power over the working class when all other means have failed.

Trotsky's strategy to confront fascism is a cautious one that recognises that the anti-fascist struggle is principally defensive. He acknowledges that an offensive by the Communist Party would come up against the bloc between the state and the fascists and would lead to defeat. It is necessary to strengthen the defences built up by the working class such as the trade unions and political parties, and it becomes necessary to unite with the reformist social democratic forces in a common struggle for the defence of these bodies. This leads to the policy of the united front which closes ranks with other forces against the common enemy, while at the same allowing the communists freedom to organise themselves and put their own demands. For Trotsky, the united front tactic is about pushing the social democrats as far as they can go in the struggle against fascism while recognising that to fully remove the threat of fascism it is necessary to go beyond reformism and overthrow capitalism itself. This means that the united front tactic must allow for both unity of action and the political independence of the forces concerned, or as Trotsky puts it: 'March separately, but strike together!'

Trotsky's analysis of fascism is a sophisticated version of Marx's theory of Bonapartism. However, it has its instrumental dangers, particularly if fascism comes to be seen simply as a tool of the ruling class to be used as a last resort in order to mobilise the petite bourgeoisie and the declassed layers against the organised working class. But this pales in comparison with the stupidity of the Stalinists who, instead of forming a united front against fascism decided there was no qualitative difference between the fascists and the social democrats.

The Degeneration of the Revolution

In writing about permanent revolution, Trotsky notes the possibilities for revolution in a country like Russia, and also the dangers this poses. Revolution in such a country requires the support of subsequent revolutions in the more advanced capitalist countries. Otherwise, as he argues:

> The maintenance of the proletarian revolution within a national framework can only be a provisional state of affairs, even though, as the experience of the Soviet Union shows, one of long duration. In an isolated proletarian dictatorship, the internal and external contradictions grow inevitably along with the successes achieved. If it remains isolated, the proletarian state must fall victim to these contradictions. The way out for it lies only in the victory of the proletariat of the advanced countries. (Trotsky 1969: 133)

Falling victim to these contradictions means, for Trotsky, the degeneration of the workers' state and the development of a counter-revolutionary parasitic caste. Trotsky notes that the development of such a situation had not really entered into the heads of many Marxist theorists. Marx, for example, had not reckoned with a revolution in a backward country, while Lenin could not have foreseen such a prolonged isolation of the Soviet state. Trotsky, however, was confronted with such a situation in a very real sense. Following Lenin's death, the leading

Bolshevik fell victim to the bureaucratic degeneration of the revolution and Stalin's rise to power. Today's history books focus on the personal rivalries between Trotsky and Stalin. But for Trotsky himself, the force behind the Soviet bureaucracy was not Stalin or any other figure but the conditions of social and material isolation, of scarcity in objects of consumption (Trotsky 1972: 112), of unproductive labour, of civil war and foreign intervention. As with the emergence of fascism in Germany, Stalin arose as a Bonaparte, rising above a politically atomised society, personifying social and material degeneration.

In his influential critique, *The Revolution Betrayed*, Trotsky states that: 'In no other regime has a bureaucracy ever achieved such a degree of independence from the dominating class' (Trotsky 1972: 248). The bureaucracy rises above society and imposes its own rule through the political apparatus. Its rule is based on the defence of privilege, however, it is not class rule and the bureaucracy has no independent economic role or property rights. Rather, the bureaucracy feeds off the working class in parasitic fashion. As Trotsky says: 'The means of production belong to the state. But the state, so to speak, "belongs" to the bureaucracy' (Trotsky 1972: 249). The state is still a workers' state in the sense that it is based on collectivised property relations, but should this situation solidify, the gains of the revolution will be lost.

Because the state is still a workers' state, albeit a degenerated one, Trotsky argues that to overthrow the bureaucracy a political rather than a social revolution is necessary. He defines the Soviet Union as a degenerated workers' state according to the material basis of that state and its relation to the dominant property relations, rather than according to its leadership whose own degeneration is a product of material isolation and economic backwardness. In this sense, Trotsky's analysis has some similarities with Weber's account of bureaucracy – that the bureaucracy is not an economic class, but is defined politically and represents a social caste or status group. As Trotsky says: 'The bureaucracy has neither stocks nor bonds. It is recruited, supplemented and renewed in the manner of an administrative hierarchy, independent of any special property relations of its own' (Trotsky 1972: 249).

Conclusion

There emerged among the heirs of Marx and Engels a kind of objectivist materialism drawn from evolutionary science, and applied to the social world in a crude and mechanical way. A new science of dialectical materialism was born, with Marxists like Plekhanov objectifying the philosophies of Hegel and Feuerbach and drawing heavily on the empirical generalisations of Engels' philosophical work. Dialectical materialism could be applied to all knowledge, with Marxism regarded as a complete theory, its philosophy a total and integrated world view. Classical Marxism, in the shape of Kautsky and Plekhanov, embraces the most schematic and mechanical interpretation of

Marx's view of historical development. For example, according to Plekhanov, 'the properties of the geographical environment determine the development of the productive forces, which in its turn determines the development of the economic forces, and therefore all other social relations' (Plekhanov 1920: 49). The model of determination is linear and reductionist with each layer being determined by the preceding one.

It is not surprising that most of the mechanical determinists of the Second International abandoned revolutionary practice. The faith that they placed in the development of the productive forces offered such reassurance about the socialist future that the parties of the Second International could get on with the day-to-day business of reformism. As Kautsky argued: 'Our task is not to organise the revolution, but to organise ourselves *for* the revolution; it is not to *make* the revolution, but *to take advantage of it*' (quoted in Salvadori 1990: 21). There emerges a theory / practice spit, with Marxism explaining the future and reformism dealing with the everyday.

The First World War interrupted this pleasant situation and threw the whole movement into crisis. Then the Bolsheviks went and led a coup against the laws of history. The orthodox mantle shifted Eastwards, with Lenin and the Bolsheviks offering a much more dynamic Marxism in which the role of agency and the place of action is restored. Following the degeneration of the revolution and the consolidation of Stalinism, Lenin's views have come to be seen as the orthodox approach, even though he is clearly responding to the supposed orthodoxy of Kautsky and other 'renegades'. In addition, Stalinism has added its own certainties and mechanical laws of motion, turning Leninism into a crude apology for the actions of the Soviet leadership.

Despite their many differences, all the writers of this period can be said to accept a degree of determinism. In Kautsky and Plekhanov it is obvious, in Luxemburg, despite her spontaneism, it takes the form of the belief in the inevitable breakdown of capitalism leaving the working class no choice but to fight for socialism. Even in Trotsky there is a lot of schematism and catastrophism, particularly in his writings on the West and his predictions for forthcoming revolution. In *The Transitional Programme* he tries to rally the troops of the newly formed Fourth International (the Third having become the degenerate Comintern) with the claim that '[t]he economic prerequisite for the proletarian revolution has already in general achieved the highest point of fruition that can be reached under capitalism,' allowing his followers to describe the phenomenal growth of the post-war period by means of his claim that 'Mankind's productive forces stagnate'! (Trotsky 1977: 111). The Trotskyists, like most other classical Marxists, ended up replacing analysis with schemas. With religiosity they embraced the ideas of these thinkers without consideration of the turbulent historical context.

Betrayal seems to be an important word in classical Marxism – the betrayal of Marxism, the betrayal of the Second International, the betrayal of Lenin. This suggests that there might be something wrong with orthodox, classical

Marxism itself. In all of this there is a fairly schematic understanding of the historical process that needs to be questioned. Lenin, Luxemburg and Trotsky were creative thinkers who emphasised the role of human action and understanding. The tragedy is that subsequent generations of classical Marxists have turned this legacy into sacred dogma, rather than embracing its critical spirit.

Further Reading

Salvadori's book *Karl Kautsky and the Socialist Revolution* (1990) gives a good account of Second International Marxist orthodoxy. Howard (1971) is the best edited collection of Luxemburg's work. Some of her polemics like 'Reform or Revolution' are available in pamphlet form. A good introduction to Luxemburg is Geras's *The Legacy of Rosa Luxemburg* (1976). The work of Lenin and Trotsky ranges over a lot of areas, some of which are of limited interest today. The most interesting of Lenin's books are *Imperialism: The Highest Stage of Capitalism* which deals with the relationship between capitalism and foreign intervention, and his main work on the state – *State and Revolution*. Lenin's pamphlet on party organisation, *What is to be Done?* has a more limited appeal. Trotsky's main books are *The Permanent Revolution and Results and Prospects* (1969) which sets out his theory of social revolution and *The Revolution Betrayed: What is the Soviet Union and Where is it Going?* (1972). Good but long introductions to Lenin and Trotsky are Harding's two volume *Lenin's Political Thought* (1977 and 1980) and Knei-Paz's *The Social and Political Thought of Leon Trotsky* (1978). Lots of work from the writers of this period is available online at http://www.marxists. org/archive/index.htm.

4

Praxis Marxism

Introduction: The Meaning of Praxis

Praxis is a word of Greek origin and in the most general sense refers to human activity and action. The concept has a long philosophical history from Aristotle through to Hegel. Marx develops the concept in two works in particular – the *Economic and Philosophical Manuscripts* and the *Theses on Feuerbach*. This inspires what is often termed a praxis Marxism that emphasises such things as free action, creative activity, class consciousness and revolutionary change. Praxis is above all transformative and concerns the way we act upon and transform our environment. Put in the most general sense, Marx writes that nature is our inorganic body, the matter, object and tool of our life activity (Marx 1975d: 328). We make our life activity an object of our will and consciousness and therefore it is '[c]onscious life activity directly [that] distinguishes man from animal life activity. Only because of that is he a species being . . . Only because of this is his activity free activity' (Marx 1975d: 328).

The *Manuscripts* argue that we become alienated from our essential species-being through such things as private property and the way the production process is organised. Labour becomes objectified as something external to the worker. Marx therefore looks to the transformation of this type of human labour through praxis and genuine self-conscious activity. Marx argues that all social life is essentially practical and that therefore: 'All mysteries which lead theory to mysticism find their rational solution in human practice and in the comprehension of this practice' (Marx 1975f: 423). He argues that:

> The chief defect of all hitherto existing materialism (that of Feuerbach included) is that the thing, reality, sensuousness, is conceived only in the form of the *object or of contemplation*, but not of *sensuous human activity, practice*, not subjectively. (Marx 1975f: 421)

The famous last thesis on Feuerbach is Marx's answer to the problem of philosophy, namely, that: 'The philosophers have only *interpreted* the world, in various ways; the point is to *change it*' (Marx 1975f: 423).

These early works of Marx form what some have called a more humanist form of Marxism focusing on what it is to be a human being, how we become alienated from our true selves, and how we can re-find ourselves through human praxis. This appears to fit well with some of the views of the writers covered in this chapter although it must be noted that Marx's early work was not available until the middle of the twentieth century. The works of praxis Marxism are generally more philosophical. Their emphasis is on human consciousness, and the fact that our activity takes place within a human environment. Such an emphasis on the human reflects the problems of the time. These writers were responding to issues such as the degeneration of the Second International and Comintern, the growth of Stalinism and the mechanical nature of orthodox Marxist theory. The question of freedom becomes important. Attention is paid to the subject and their actions and thought. There is a rejection of 'scientific' Marxism in favour of Marxism as a theory of action. As Soviet Marxism grew increasingly Stalinist, critical thought shifted westwards and led to the formation of what became know as Western Marxism.

This chapter looks at a group of Marxists who can be categorised as praxis Marxists although they are certainly not a unified school. Although the positions of Korsch and Lukács are similar, the existentialists have very different influences. Gramsci, who is often bracketed with Korsch and Lukács because of his philosophical statements is, in fact, the one writer to resist the temptations of speculative philosophy and develop a systematic social theory. As Perry Anderson notes (1979), Gramsci's concept of hegemony is the one non-speculative Western Marxist concept. We will therefore spend more time outlining his oeuvre, while we conclude by stating how Gramsci differs from the other praxis Marxists.

The Philosopher of Praxis

Antonio Gramsci is famous for his concept of hegemony which stresses that leadership in society cannot be based solely on coercion but also requires a large degree of consent. For a group to assume a position of leadership, the support of the masses is essential. At a time when Marxist theory was dominated by economic determinism, Gramsci's work shifts the emphasis away from a narrow focus on the economic basis of society and emphasises the importance of 'superstructural' factors – like politics, culture and ideology. And in shifting focus to this terrain, Gramsci is placing more emphasis on the human factor and stressing the importance of people's actions and ideas.

Therefore Gramsci attempts to avoid the mechanical materialism prevalent in Marxist approaches of the time, by focusing on the concept of praxis, or human action and will. It was the fellow Italian Antonio Labriola who first used the term 'philosophy of praxis' to describe Marxism. Because he was a Communist, Gramsci was arrested by Mussolini's fascists and wrote most of his work while in prison. Thus the term 'philosophy of praxis' is used as code for Marxism in order to avoid the prison sensor. However, the term also captures the spirit of Gramsci's approach which is to reject the mechanical or 'scientific' aspect of Marxism in favour of an emphasis on historical actions and human will. The term 'philosophy of praxis' conveys this dynamic aspect.

To understand why Gramsci is a praxis philosopher, it is necessary to examine his influences. In particular, his philosophy of praxis in inherited from the political writings of Machiavelli. The work of Machiavelli is concerned with the matter of how to rule, govern and win influence, and Machiavelli's conception of the world is based on a philosophy of praxis which emphasises the role of purposeful action – whether this be wit, cunning or the art of statecraft. Gramsci describes Machiavelli's approach as a form of 'neo-humanism' that 'bases itself entirely on the concrete action of man, who, impelled by historical necessity, works and transforms reality' (Gramsci 1971: 249). Machiavelli's work can therefore be seen as the work of a practical realist who is concerned with purposeful human action within a specific social and historical context.

The practical realism Gramsci inherits from Machiavelli is deepened by the influence of the Hegelian philosopher Benedetto Croce who emphasises a view of history as the development of human will and therefore action. Through Croce and Hegel, Gramsci comes to develop a position that can be described as historicism, as emphasising Marxism as historical rather than scientific. This is made clear in Gramsci's claim that:

> It has been forgotten that in the case of historical materialism one should put the accent on the first term – 'historical' – and not on the second – which is of metaphysical origin. The philosophy of praxis is absolute 'historicism', the absolute secularisation and earthliness of thought, an absolute humanism of history. (Gramsci 1971: 465)

The other main non-Marxist influence on Gramsci is Georges Sorel who greatly influenced the Italian syndicalist movement that Gramsci encountered at the Turin car factory. Sorel's conception of revolutionary activity is based on a rejection of 'scientific Marxism' in favour of the spontaneous action of the masses. Sorel also emphasises the importance of myth which can be interpreted as a sort of political ideology capable of galvanising the masses. Sorel's myth comes together with Machiavelli's action and Croce's will in the following passage:

> Machiavelli's *Prince* could be studied as an historical exemplification of the Sorelian myth – i.e. of a political ideology expressed neither in the form of a cold utopia nor as learned theorising, but rather by the creation of a concrete fantasy which acts on a dispersed and shattered people to arouse and organise its collective will. (Gramsci 1971: 125–26)

Thus Gramsci rejects the cold theorising of 'scientific' Marxism in favour of the view that Marxism is the philosophy of human action and will. Ideology, usually regarded by Marxists as 'false consciousness' or a misleading force, is understood here as a positive and galvanising influence that can lead people to action. Such a view is never clearer than in Gramsci's reaction to the Russian Revolution which the young Gramsci declared was a 'revolution against *Capital*', or in other words, was the triumph of human will and action over those scientific schemas that believed historical development had to follow a particular course:

> In Russia, Marx's *Capital* was more the book of the bourgeoisie than of the proletariat. It stood as the critical demonstration of how events should follow a pre-determined course: how in Russia a bourgeoisie had to develop, and a capitalist era had to open, with the setting up of a Western-type civilisation, before the proletariat could even think in terms of its own revolt, its own demands, its own revolution. But events have overcome ideologies. Events have exploded the critical schemas determining how the history of Russia would unfold according to the cannons of historical materialism. (Gramsci 1977: 34)

Instead of a pre-determined schema, Gramsci stresses an active conception of history that 'sees as the dominant factor in history, not raw economic facts, but man, men in societies, men in relation to one another, reaching agreements with one another, developing through these contacts (civilisation) a collective, social will' (Gramsci 1977: 34–35). Like Lenin and the Bolsheviks, Gramsci is concerned to return the active element to Marxist theory. His comments on the Russian revolution shift emphasis away from 'objective' economic or historical developments towards a study of human praxis.

Such a position places emphasis on the importance of moral, cultural and intellectual leadership. Likewise, the problems in Italy – the significance of the Italian *Risorgimento* (the nineteenth movement for Italian unification) the struggles of the new bourgeois class, and ultimately, the rise of populist movements and fascism – all indicate the weakness of leadership. Now it is possible that such a stress on the need for leadership and human will can lead to a voluntarist position, which is to say, to a particular understanding of history that sees it above all as the product of the human will. This is a common problem with praxis philosophy and it tends to minimise the importance of such things as social conditions or social structures. However, it will be argued here (see also Joseph 2002) that Gramsci is not like other 'praxis' Marxists in that his concept of society is not wholly based on human actions, but also concerns the particular context within which these actions take place. The next section will look at how Gramsci's concept of hegemony combines human action with socio-structural context.

Hegemony and the Historical Bloc

Although Gramsci wants to maintain the importance of social conditions, he also wants to create room within Marxism for human praxis. Likewise, although he wants to maintain the importance of the economy, he also wants Marxism to pay attention to politics, culture and ideology. He wants to emphasise consent as well as coercion. And he wants to look at the realm of civil society as well as the state. This is the way in which we should understand the importance of the concept of hegemony.

If we go back to the case of the Russian Revolution, here was a situation where the economy was not developed, yet a revolution still occurred. This was also a situation where civil society was weak and most power lay with a repressive form of state. Gramsci compares this with the situation in the West where the institutions of civil society are much stronger. He writes that:

> In the East the State was everything, civil society was primordial and gelatinous; in the West, there was a proper relation between State and civil society, and when the State trembled a sturdy structure of civil society was at once revealed. The state was only an outer ditch, behind which there stood a powerful system of fortresses and earthworks. (Gramsci 1971: 238)

Gramsci's point is that in Russia, civil society was weak and power largely depended on coercion. Thus the task for revolutionaries in the East was to muster enough force to take state power. However, in the West it is necessary for revolutionaries to gain consent within civil society in order to confront the powerful fortresses and earthworks that the bourgeoisie has at its disposal. This points to the importance of the battle for hegemony and the struggle of ideas. Although power may be more difficult to obtain in the West, once won, it is easier to maintain social cohesion and consensus because of the influence of the institutions of civil society. By contrast, in Russia it may have been easier to take power, but it is more difficult to maintain it because social hegemony is 'primordial' and weak.

In a more developed society, therefore, the brute force of the state gives way to the more subtle mechanisms of social control and consensus formation. Hegemony corresponds to the construction, organisation and distribution of this consensus through and beyond the state and civil society. By taking this approach, Gramsci is opposing the view that social cohesion flows largely from the workings of the economic system and is arguing that social cohesion and consensus are things that have to be actively constructed. However, he is also resisting the instrumentalist view that rulership in society is simply given by one's economic position and that the state is no more than a committee for managing the common affairs of the bourgeoisie. For Gramsci, hegemonic power does not flow automatically from the economic position of the dominant group, rather it has to be constructed and negotiated. The hegemonic bloc has to take into account the interests of those groups over which hegemony is to be exercised. Certain concessions have to be made, consent has to be won, some groups may be brought into the ruling bloc itself. This ruling bloc also has to take into account the social conditions under which it is to operate.

These place real material and structural limits on what can be done, but also enable certain groups to play a more important role than others. It must be remembered, therefore, that although many commentators wish to highlight Gramsci's emphasis on human agency, he does also take account of the importance of social structure, and in particular the role of the economy in determining the way hegemony develops. He argues, for example, that 'though hegemony is ethical-political, it must also be economic, must necessarily be based on the decisive function exercised by the leading group in the decisive nucleus of economic activity' (Gramsci 1971: 161).

Such a view also comes across in Gramsci's understanding of what he calls the historical bloc. The historical bloc might be seen as the way in which a dominant group constructs a ruling alliance that incorporates some groups into the ruling bloc while offering concessions and incentives to others. Still, he sees the importance of social structures when he writes that:

> Structures and superstructures form an 'historical bloc'. That is to say the complex, contradictory and discordant *ensemble* of the superstructures is the reflection of the *ensemble* of the social relations of production. (Gramsci 1971: 366)

So although the historical bloc concerns the relation between different social agents, and the way that some groups achieve a hegemonic position, this must be seen within the context of the relationship between what Gramsci calls the economic structure and the politico-ethical superstructure. By relating the historical bloc to the question of hegemony, Gramsci is attempting to give the base-superstructure relation a more dynamic character. Social hegemony is not given but must be constantly reproduced and developed through human actions. The historical bloc represents the complex interaction of various social and historical forces, ideas and social relations.

Strategy, Alliances and Intellectuals

Gramsci's concepts of hegemony and the historical bloc present us with a dynamic and complex theory of society. It can be seen that Gramsci regards social reality as a complex terrain of fortresses and earthworks, involving different economic, political and cultural factors. Likewise, the social classes that operate on this terrain are also a complex arrangement, comprised of different strata and fractions. This is in direct contrast to the view of Marx and Engels in the *Communist Manifesto* that claims that society is homogenising into two great social groups, bourgeoisie and proletariat. For Gramsci, classes are not homogenous blocs, but are determined by a range of social, cultural, political and economic factors, creating various fractions and strata within classes. It is for this reason that social rulership or hegemony is something that is constructed rather than given. Ruling blocs must be put together from a range of different class strata. The organisation of different fractions of classes and their interests around a hegemonic project makes strategy a vital aspect of social and political processes.

Different hegemonic projects will enjoy varying degrees of achievement, but real success will only be achieved when the hegemonic project is realised through the state. Conversely, those groups that do not enjoy state power are destined to be fragmented, subaltern and subject to domination. Control of the state and implementation of the hegemonic project are therefore crucial hegemonic struggles. The struggle for power takes place across a wide terrain since Gramsci has argued that the state is only an outer ditch and that beyond it stand the various earthworks of civil society. These defences can also be used to protect the dominant hegemony. Those forces attempting to win power must therefore engage in a complex battle. To make this point Gramsci distinguishes between two types of strategy, the war of positions and the war of manoeuvre.

The war of manoeuvre is like a frontal assault, an example of which would be the seizure of power by the Bolsheviks in Russia. Such a straightforward attack was possible because, as Gramsci says, the state was primordial and civil society was weak. However, in the West, a more prolonged and tactical battle is necessary which must be conducted through the various institutions of civil society. In the West there is a better balance between the state and civil society and between the economy and the state and so there is a greater level of social cohesion and integration. The complexity of civil society means that ideological struggle becomes important. Those forces that hope to win state power must already play a leading role in civil society and must already be culturally, politically and ideologically influential: 'A social group can, and indeed must, already exercise "leadership" before winning governmental power' (Gramsci 1971: 57). The war of positions is like siege warfare, or like a slow war of colonisation and territorial conquest. It requires 'exceptional qualities of patience and inventiveness'. But once won it is 'decisive definitively' (Gramsci 1971: 239).

To win power it is necessary to forge a new will out of a diverse range of forces. Initially, under the influence of Sorel, Gramsci had thought that this might occur spontaneously. However, following the failure of the Turin Council movement, Gramsci comes to the view that this collective will can only be forged through the leadership of the Communist Party. In honour of Machiavelli, Gramsci calls the Communist Party the Modern Prince and writes that such a party

> can only be an organisation, a complex element of society in which a collective will, which has already been recognised, and has to some extent asserted itself in action, begins to take concrete form. History has already provided this organism, and it is the political party. (Gramsci 1971: 129)

For Gramsci, the counter-hegemonic alliance is not an alliance of equals – the different component parts of the alliance must be led and directed by the working class and the Party. However, this is not a top-down process. The Party's relationship to the class must be an organic one so that 'the essential task is that of systematically and patiently ensuring that this force is formed, developed and rendered ever more homogenous, compact, and self-aware' (Gramsci 1971: 185). The Party should be an expression of the real experiences of the masses and for this reason Gramsci places great emphasis on the role of those he calls organic intellectuals who are a part of the masses, but can play a leading and directing role. He writes that:

> Every social group, coming into existence on the original terrain of an essential function in the world of economic production, creates together with itself, organically, one or more strata of intellectuals which give it homogeneity and an awareness of its own function not only in the economic but also in the social and political fields. (Gramsci 1971: 5)

These intellectuals are organic because they are closely tied to class positions and practices. The distinction between traditional and organic intellectuals is based on the importance of social function. The role of the intellectual has as much to do with organisation as does with ideas. As Gramsci says: 'By "intellectuals" must be understood not those strata commonly described by this term, but in general the entire social stratum which exercises an organisational function in the wide sense – whether in the field of production, or in that of culture, or in that of political administration' (Gramsci 1971: 97n.). The functioning of the intellectual is bound up with the process of hegemony and the need to transmit ideas and cement and unify the hegemonic alliance or bloc. The intellectual is also crucial to the development of the outlook of this alliance and its philosophy or world-view.

For Gramsci, and for most praxis Marxists, Marxism is more like a philosophy than a science. First, like other philosophical and ideological positions, Marxism is a guide to action and a means of mobilising people. Second, it is a philosophy in the sense of being a world-view of a particular group. Across the social terrain there are a number of different philosophies, and different social groups have their own conceptions of the world which are manifested in their actions. Philosophy and politics are thus linked together in that 'philosophies', for Gramsci, are tied up with the leading role of intellectuals in shaping organic blocs and normative action. Above all, they are a particular elaboration of world-views, derived from hegemony in the sense that they are the expression of groups seeking domination or moral leadership. There is an important link between these conceptions or world-views and hegemonic position. Those groups lacking independence and autonomy will be ideologically subordinate to the hegemonic group and will adopt their world-view as their own. Marxism needs to go beyond its scientific analysis and go among the masses to win over hearts and minds. For Gramsci, Marxism is a philosophy, and philosophy is history in action.

Lukács and Class Consciousness

We have seen how Gramsci is influenced by the philosophy of Hegel via the work of Croce. Other praxis Marxists are also heavily influenced by Hegel's work – none more so than the Hungarian philosopher Georg Lukács. This is because Hegel's work can be used to oppose the rigid, 'scientific' Marxism prevalent at that time. It places emphasis on questions of consciousness, shifts attention to the role of the subject, looks at the actions of a class 'for itself', and emphasises the importance of totality and dialectical method. Lukács combines the theory of Marxism as praxis with the Hegelian dialectic, and attempts a synthesis of philosophy and theory.

Lukács came late to Marxism and his early influences were provided by his friendships with Weber, Bloch and Simmel. His earlier work was concerned with aesthetics and literary criticism. The experience of the First World War led Lukács to join the Hungarian Communist Party following its foundation in 1918 and he held a post in the short-lived revolutionary government of 1919. It was shortly after this that Lukács published his most famous work, *History and Class Consciousness*. However, the Stalinisation of the Communist movement was to force Lukács to abandon the positions outlined in his work and he turned back to the literary criticism of his earlier years. Much of Lukács's later work bears the stamp of Stalinism and so, like most others, we concentrate on *History and Class Consciousness*, the work Lukács was later forced to recant.

This work, as we have said, was inspired by Hegel and is an attempt to unite revolutionary subject and material object and make history and class consciousness one and the same thing. This led the Stalinists and many others to denounce the book as Hegelian idealism. However, the book is not simply a product of Hegel, it is also influenced by the anti-naturalism prevalent in the German philosophy (phenomenology and hermeneutics) of this time. As Callinicos notes, this leads Lukács to emphasise the historicity of knowledge, to examine the outlooks of particular social classes, and to emphasise particular experiences rather than universal causal laws. This gives rise to three problems in relation to Marxist social theory – the questions of the relations between thought and reality, between theory and practice, and between economic base and political / ideological superstructure (Callinicos 1983: 72). Lukács's answers to these problems provoke strong reactions. Some, like Callinicos argue that Lukács's work presents an idealist view of history with a utopian and messianic view of the proletariat as the negation of bourgeois society (Callinicos 1983: 74). Others welcome Lukács's focus on human consciousness and actions and regard his work as a brilliant anticipation of the yet to be published early works of Marx which are more Hegelian and humanist in their approach.

What was certainly available to Lukács at this time were Marx's mature economic writings, and it is in part from these that he develops his central concept of reification. Marx's theory of commodity fetishism explains how commodities take on the appearance of independent things, and we do not therefore recognise the social relations involved in the production of these objects. This aspect of capitalism is further emphasised in Lukács's theory of reification which is said to affect all human relations. We are all subject to fetishistic illusions whereby our world is made up of 'things' which appear to be independent of us. In this world of things, we ourselves become passive objects and society seems independent of our actions.

Lukács argues that social relations become reified because we fail to recognise that these social relations are relations between people. As capitalism develops, reification sinks more deeply into our consciousness and soul:

> The transformation of the commodity relation into a thing of 'ghostly objectivity' cannot therefore content itself with the reduction of all objects for the gratification of human needs to commodities. It stamps its imprint upon the whole consciousness of man . . . This rationalisation of the world appears to be complete, it seems to penetrate the very depths of man's physical and psychic nature. (Lukács 1971: 100–01)

This passage also indicates how Marx's theories of alienation and commodity fetishism are combined with Weber's theory of rationalisation. Reification is about the rationalisation of social life, the domination of technology, the increased division of labour, and an ever-increasing degree of specialisation leading to a partial and fragmented social life. Because of this we can no longer conceive of the unity of the social world. Reification makes the world unintelligible to us. We can no longer comprehend it in its totality. It also appears to us as frozen and static – we can no longer see the world as comprised of processes.

Reification is like the 'thingification' of social relations and it would seem that Lukács shares Weber's misery about the all-encompassing nature of rationalisation. But whereas Weber retreats into despair, Lukács, as a Marxist, must try to find a solution. *History and Class Consciousness* is an optimistic work that argues that despite reification, it is possible to develop a 'true' consciousness and understanding. Or at least the working class can.

Lukács picks up on Marx's point in *Capital* that the consciousness of the bourgeoisie and the consciousness of the proletariat are affected by the same process of human self-alienation. The difference is that the bourgeoisie feels at home in this alienation and recognises this alienation as its own, whereas the working class feels destroyed by this inhuman existence (Lukács 1971: 149). The bourgeoisie is cursed with a contradictory consciousness which means that it will never be able to overcome its reified outlook. Ultimately it is the role that each class plays in the process of production and the particular interests that this generates that determines which class can become revolutionary. It is the proletariat that is given this unique historical role. The emancipation of society depends upon the working class acquiring a self-consciousness and self-understanding which, because of its role in the production process (the most fundamental of social relations), simultaneously means an understanding of society as a whole.

The Working Class as Subject–Object

Lukács argues that knowledge of reality can only arise from the point of view of a class and the struggles that it is engaged in. Thus the theory of praxis links knowledge to the unfolding of history through human action. This leads to Lukács's view that the proletariat is both the subject and object of history. He writes that

> the unity of theory and practice is only the reverse side of the social and historical position of the proletariat. From its own point of view self-knowledge coincides with knowledge of the whole so that the proletariat is at one and the same time the subject and object of its own knowledge. (Lukács 1971: 20)

The proletariat represents the universal class and the fate of the revolution, and hence of society, and is determined by its maturity and level of self-understanding. Lukács stresses the importance of the unity of theory and practice. The essence of historical materialism is inseparable from the practical and critical activity of the working class. Marxism is about overcoming reification. If the working class becomes aware of its exploitation and reification, social life starts to become intelligible, class consciousness is awakened, and this increased self-knowledge can lead to social action and emancipation.

For praxis Marxism the process of social change is no longer conceived of in terms of mechanical laws, but develops through action and conflict. We must become aware of ourselves as socio-historical beings who must act in order to change things. However, Lukács does require some guarantee that human praxis can be effective. Thus the Communist Party emerges as '*the bearer of the class consciousness of the proletariat and the conscience of its historical vocation*' (Lukács 1971: 41). The Party plays a crucial role without which the proletariat cannot overcome its reification and ideological crisis. The Party makes people aware of their experience, reflects and develops the consciousness of the proletariat, and links our theory to practice. Ironically, though, it was the Party that was later to partly silence Lukács.

A criticism of Lukács's attack on the 'scientism' of orthodox Marxism is that his own theory relativises knowledge by tying it to social context and making it relative to the experience of a particular class. 'True' knowledge is said to be that expressed by the working class, but why should this be so? Against the accusation of relativism it might be said that Lukács explains the superior knowledge of the working class in relation to its position in the process of production. Thus the superiority of one class viewpoint is grounded, not in the mind, but in real social relations. Unfortunately, as the name suggests, *History and Class Consciousness* is overwhelmingly a work about consciousness that says very little about the social structures that might help generate such an understanding. It is very much a work of philosophy, not a social scientific study of the structure of society.

In keeping with the influence of Hegelian philosophy, Lukács argues against relativism by claiming that there is good and bad knowledge and that good knowledge is that which can grasp the whole or the totality and which can therefore resist the fragmented view of reified thought. For Lukács, then, the most important aspect of Marxism is not its economic analysis or its focus on the mode of production, but its emphasis on the concept of totality. The reification of society and therefore consciousness means that we often do not see things as interconnected and we struggle to see the totality of things. Lukács argues for a dialectical method that sees the supremacy of the whole over the parts. His view of the totality is that it is an expressive totality in that 'the essence of the dialectical method lies in the fact that in every aspect correctly grasped by the dialectic the whole totality is comprehended and that the whole method can be unravelled from every single aspect' (Lukács 1971: 170). Whereas bourgeois thought is fragmented, reified and lacking in dialectical method, the Marxist viewpoint is a total viewpoint that sees everything.

This emphasis on dialectics is shared with other praxis Marxists like Korsch and Sartre. It must be stressed that their approach to dialectics is in stark contrast to what they regard as the mechanical viewpoint of orthodox dialectical materialism. Engels is a particular target, for it is suggested in his 'dialectics of nature' that the dialectic is something that is 'out there' in the world. Lukács argues against this by stating that dialectics is not something that is imported into Marxist theory from the outside, but is derived from history and human praxis (Lukács 1971: 177). The dialectic does not exist separately from the revolutionary praxis of the proletariat, but is the way in which the working class becomes aware of society as a whole and its place within it. Thus:

> the dialectical method as the true historical method was reserved for the class which was able to discover within itself on the basis of its life-experience the identical subject–object, the subject of action; the 'we' of the genesis: namely the proletariat. . . . The self-understanding of the proletariat is therefore simultaneously the objective understanding of the nature of society. When the proletariat furthers its own class aims it simultaneously achieves the conscious realisation of the – objective – aims of society. (Lukács 1971: 148–49)

Thus dialectics links to history and to praxis. 'Truth' is based on the viewpoint of the subject–object of history. Marxism, rather than being a scientific study of society becomes the consciousness, experience and actions of the working class as it moves towards a revolutionary position. Therefore, praxis Marxism, for Lukács is not passive reflection, but the active self-knowledge of the working class and its awareness of a society that it is in the act of transforming.

Karl Korsch

Korsch is often bracketed with Lukács and comes to similar conclusions regarding the role of the subjective factor, the development of working class consciousness, the unity of theory and practice and the role of (Hegelian inspired) dialectics. Active in the German Communist Party in the 1920s, Korsch, like Lukács, was briefly a minister in a short-lived revolutionary government (Thuringia). While he was a professor at Jena University he became a Communist member of the Reichstag and edited the Party's journal *Die Internationale*, But he was regarded as an ultra-leftist and idealist and was condemned along with Lukács at the 1924 Comintern Congress. Unlike Lukács he refused to engage in self-criticism and was expelled from the Communist Party in 1926. Thereafter he continued to write as an independent Marxist, becoming increasingly critical of Leninism, finding it little different to the mechanical materialism of the Second International. Korsch eventually came to the view that the Comintern was counter-revolutionary and that the USSR was a dictatorship.

Lukács reconciled himself with the Party, wrote a book on Lenin and embraced Lenin's *realpolitik*. Korsch, by contrast, argued that the Party cannot substitute for the self-activity of the working class. This understanding of the importance of working class activity is inspired by writers like Sorel. It also comes from Korsch's experience of the failure of the 1918–20 German uprising which, he believed, was an example of the Party substituting itself for the class and acting without the necessary cultural and theoretical preconditions. So like Gramsci and Lukács, Korsch emphasises the importance of ideological struggle. But unlike them, he places less emphasis on Party organisation, and argues that subjective preconditions are more important than Party organisation.

Therefore, Marxism becomes something like the revolutionary expression of the working class. In Korsch's view, the 'emergence of Marxist theory is, in Hegelian-Marxist terms, only the "other side" of the emergence of the real proletarian movement' (Korsch 1970: 42). The revolutionary class finds its theoretical expression in dialectical materialism and the unity of theory and revolutionary practice. Theory is an essential part of the revolutionary movement, while Marxism is the practical interpretation of human consciousness.

Marxism, it is claimed, is not a science because it does not seek 'objective' knowledge of society. Nor is Marxism a philosophy. Korsch believes he is following Marx's claim that revolutionary socialism in fact represents the abolition of philosophy. For if philosophy is an expression of the historical process then a revolutionary movement will ultimately do away with it. Korsch claims that '*Marxian theory constitutes neither a positive materialistic philosophy nor a positive science.* From the beginning to end, it is a theoretical as well as a practical *critique* of existing society' (Korsch 1971: 65). From this it can also be seen that Korsch regards Marxism, not as a positive force, but as something that is primarily *critical*. Marxism, as praxis, is neither a science nor a philosophy but a critique of society and an attempt to change it.

This obviously put Korsch in opposition to writers like Kautsky and Hilferding who argue that Marxism can provide a theory of laws of development of society without necessarily entailing any critique, or commitment to value judgements. Likewise, the separation of theory and practice is also evident in the Soviet Union where the specific and revolutionary character of Marxism has been abandoned in favour of general and universally valid doctrines. Against this abstract theorising, Korsch argues for a Marxism based on concrete revolutionary praxis and states that: 'Marxist "theory" does not strive to achieve objective knowledge of reality out of an independent, theoretical interest. It is driven to acquire this knowledge by the practical necessities of struggle' (Korsch 1971: 68).

But again, as with other praxis Marxists, the charge of relativism arises. It seems that in Korsch, the understanding of society is reduced to the expression of the practical activity of a particular group – the working class. Truth is seen as the instrument of practical action. Even natural science is regarded as no more than an expression of certain class-interests; nature too is a human creation. Opponents of Korsch's approach will argue that by claiming that 'the Marxist system is the theoretical expression of the revolutionary movement of the proletariat' (Korsch 1970: 42), he is *reducing* Marxism to the philosophical viewpoint or world-outlook of a particular social group. Supporters will claim that Korsch is simply expressing what is contained in Marx's *Theses on Feuerbach*, that Marxism's 'primary purpose is not *contemplative enjoyment* of the existing world but its active transformation' (Korsch 1971: 61).

Existentialist Marxism

Existentialism can be summarised as a philosophical outlook that emphasises the importance of human existence as opposed to the existence of mere objects. In particular, what is important about human existence is consciousness and praxis. We are not pre-formed, but are self-creating, decision making creatures, and our actions are marked by intentionality. Existentialism is concerned with the condition that we find ourselves in, our place in the world and our relations with others.

In post-war France, existentialism took a rather strange journey towards Marxism, driven by the two main thinkers, Jean-Paul Sartre and Maurice Merleau-Ponty. These two thinkers share much in common, but while Sartre moved closer to Marxism, Merleau-Ponty became increasingly critical both of Marxism and of Sartre himself. In part, the breakdown in relations between the two was due to Sartre's closeness to the French Communist Party, an organisation which exerted an important influence in post-war France. Merleau-Ponty was also critical of Sartre's *Being and Nothingness*, arguing that by emphasising freedom as nothingness, the work came close to nihilism. Merleau-Ponty's critique also complains that Sartre places too much emphasis on individual projects, and his own work attempts to provide existentialist Marxism with a firmer social and historical grounding. His most important book, *Phenomenology of Perception*, criticises what he calls Sartre's Cartesian dualism or over-emphasis of the individual, and argues that existentialism needs a more socio-historical approach. Merleau-Ponty's view is that freedom lies, not with the individual, but with the proletariat. Like Lukács he argues that workers must authenticate their subjectivity. But Merleau-Ponty later comes to the view that the proletariat had failed to become the universal class. His book *Adventures of the Dialectic* is a work of disenchantment, arguing the difficulty of joining history and freedom, and criticising Lukács, Trotsky, and, of course, Sartre.

It is left to Simone de Beauvoir to respond to this attack. De Beauvoir continued to believe in Sartre's version of existentialism which informs her writings on feminism. She also maintains a socialist position, although no longer believing her initial view that it can resolve the question of women's liberation. Although chiefly regarded as a feminist writer, de Beauvoir's work can also be seen as an attempt to bring together existentialism and socialism. *The Second Sex* is heavily influenced by the existentialist viewpoint, arguing that women have been reduced to objects for men. Women internalise this objectification and, by enacting patriarchal roles, live in state of inauthenticity. Women are denied their own subjectivity and praxis.

We now concentrate on Sartre's *Critique of Dialectical Reason* to see how he attempts to blend existentialism with Marxism. Sartre's move towards Marxism in the 1960s is itself an example of the importance of praxis. Sartre had already been radicalised by the experience of French resistance against the Nazis and his time in a prisoner of war camp. Then came Algeria and the Vietnam war, the growth of the radical left and the events of May 1968. Despite this, and despite Merleau-Ponty's accusations, Sartre was critical of the Communist Party. Events in the Soviet Union, the invasions of Eastern Europe, and the stagnation of orthodox Marxist theory pushed Sartre to avow a humanist form of Marxism. This stressed the importance of human being, argued that people are the creators of society, and that history is an active and creative process.

Sartre developed core themes from his earlier existentialism and incorporated them into a Marxist outlook. Most important are the concepts of freedom and contingency. This means we ourselves are the source of our morals and values and an essential part of our being is our being-free. But while the earlier existentialism is individualistic, Sartre now attempts to develop more of a conception of history and collective action. Marxism injects history into Sartre's existentialism which becomes concerned with the question of our practical freedom in the world around us. The importance of Marxism, for Sartre, lies in its historicity. Marxism is in fact the historical reality of our age, a kind of world-view or world spirit. Marxism, Sartre says, 'is History itself becoming conscious of itself' (Sartre 1991a: 40).

But Sartre's understanding of Marxism is lacking a number of characteristic features, notably the emphasis on economic relations and the dynamics of capitalist society. His approach, like that of many praxis Marxists, is more philosophical. Marxism is not a study of economic laws but a philosophy of the human condition. Sartre still maintains an emphasis on the concept of mode of production, but in a different sort of way – there is not an economic emphasis but a focus on production as human praxis. Because of this notion of praxis, there is, like Lukács and the early Marx, a strong emphasis on alienation. A key question is how this alienation is to be overcome, how consciousness or authenticity is to be reached. This is not an automatic thing but requires effort.

This effort raises the issue of dialectics. Like other Marxists, particularly those influenced by Hegel, Sartre is keen to stress the importance of the dialectic. But Sartre is against Engels's attempt to naturalise the dialectic because this implies that the dialectic is out there in nature when in fact dialectics should be about the way humans appropriate nature through praxis. Sartre's dialectical rationality is a reflexive process based on the interaction of human praxis and matter, or what is called the practico-inert. The concept of the practico-inert functions to explain how, although the world is based on our praxis, we come to experience it as alienation, as brute matter.

The dialectic of subject and object is also the dialectic of human actions and material things. This is not so much a case of opposition as mediation. In Sartre's terminology, the Hegelian-Marxist in-itself becomes the practico-inert and the for-itself becomes human praxis. The in-itself is brute, undifferentiated being, while praxis concerns the dialectic of human activity. This looks at how consciousness is embedded in the world around us so that through praxis the material world becomes meaningful to us. Existentialism can help in the attempt to develop 'a comprehensive knowing which will rediscover man in the social world and which will follow him in his praxis – or, if you prefer, in the project which throws him towards the social possibles in terms of a defined situation' (Sartre 1963: 68). Meaningful human action is seen as a totalising and active process that opposes itself to the practico-inert.

The process of mediation means the internalisation of the external and the externalisation of the internal. We in fact produce the practico-inert – it is a product of human praxis. Why then should the practico-inert come to confront us as an alien force? Sartre's answer is that praxis becomes alienated under conditions of scarcity. It is through the misery of scarcity that the practico-inert makes itself felt. Scarcity is the primordial determination of human relations by matter. Scarcity is the main reason why humans become mediated by things and why our praxis is turned back against us. Our praxis has been worked into an inert mass that embodies its alienation. Praxis is made the other. It is absorbed and loses its meaning. Social relations are rendered passive. Scarcity becomes a driving force of history and the main determining feature of different types of society. It is scarcity that generates the division of labour and the struggle between classes.

Scarcity produces objectification and history is the way in which praxis has been alienated and people set against each other. Alienation occurs when people become other than themselves or when they incorporate into themselves the otherness of inert matter. As Sartre puts it,

> as soon as man begins to designate himself not as the mere reproduction of his life, but as the ensemble of products which reproduce his life, he discovers himself as *Other* in the world of objectivity; totalised matter, as inert objectification perpetuated by inertia, is in effect *non-human* or even *anti-human*. (Sartre 1991a: 227)

An example of this objectification can be seen in the way that market relations alienate people from each other, from their products, and indeed from themselves. However, the practico-inert, in objectifying us and presenting us with a common condition or situation, also offers a common solution. Our productive activity – both physical and mental – underlies the structure of the social world. Through our praxis we are able to come to an understanding of this totality. Knowledge need not be based on external observation or reflection but can be dialectical knowledge of the totality as gained through our practical relationship with it. Because it is the human project that underlies the structure of the social world, it is through a dialectical understanding of society from within history, within experience, within human society, that we can know our situation.

Human praxis totalises. Sartre's account moves from the individual to the totality and back again. It looks at how different conditions affect different people in different ways, but argues that moving towards a single historical meaning for all is a progressive thing so that: 'Our historical task, at the heart of this polyvalent world, is to bring closer the moment when History will have *only one meaning*, when it will tend to be dissolved in the concrete men who will make it in common' (Sartre 1963: 90). This seems a somewhat teleological viewpoint and can be compared to Lukács's view of the historical destiny of the proletariat, or Gramsci's view that history asymptotically approaches a certain end-point. Praxis Marxists tend to share this teleological view because of the influence of Hegel and the dialectic of telos, praxis and totalisation. It might be wondered whether it is so desirable to reach this single world-view? Sartre suggests that a unified world-view is a progressive thing when he writes:

> This means that History is intelligible if the different practices which can be found and located at a given moment of the historical temporalisation finally appear as partially totalising and as connected and merged in their very oppositions and diversities by an intelligible totalisation from which there is no appeal. (Sartre 1991a: 817)

For Sartre, human relations are those between one praxis and another. This has consequences for a theory of class. Whereas for Marx class has an objective basis in the social relations of production, for Sartre, class is about lived experience. The working class is a historical group formed by organised praxis. We make ourselves workers or bourgeois through our activity and on the basis of this we totalise our worldview. Classes unite themselves in relation to the other and thus collective action and the class struggle are important in defining what class is.

Sartre has two categories of human collectivity – the group and the series. Groups are seen as sharing common bonds of reciprocity. The group is seen as based on the unity of constitutive individuals and their praxis. The fused group comes together in the context of scarcity and develops a common project to overcome this scarcity. Praxis forms a common unity which is continually reformed. The group may form itself into an organisation in order to gain greater control over our material conditions. This again indicates how the practico-inert and conditions of scarcity may act to bring people together in a common situation. We act against forms of alienation as might be found in social institutions or in economic relations. In the fused group the individual recognises in the other not an other but himself/herself. We come to see our own project of freedom in the other, a project that is recognised and confirmed by the other. This is freedom as mutual recognition. Sartre again tries to combine individual freedom with collectivity so that although freedom is individualistic, it finds its confirmation in the fused group. It is only with others, engaged in common struggle against scarcity, that individual freedom can be fulfilled. Common praxis has a common aim and purpose and is reciprocal. The group is based on common needs, common praxis and a common threat.

But in the institution or the organisation praxis may again become other. It may become machine like or be burdened with inertia. Authority may force individuals to conform to the goals of the collective. The apparatus becomes hierarchical. This would account for the role of the state which, like other social institutions, acts to manipulate and control people. Thus as well as seeing the group as an active collective, Sartre sees other collectives of people as inert. The pressure of the practico-inert brings people together in what Sartre calls a series. People still engage in praxis, but this is passive activity. The unity of the series comes, not from our own projects, but from the conditions imposed by the object. The working class in the main is defined as seriality. Sartre's illustrations of seriality include our position in the market place and the role of racism.

History can therefore be understood as follows. Our praxis produces, but this product is turned against as the practico-inert. Our aim must therefore be to recover this through the common praxis of the group. Sartre's existential project attempts to restore to historical materialism the key concepts of action, struggle and understanding. This highlights the importance of Marxism as a dialectical critique that is related to the human condition. As Sartre says:

The entire historical dialectic rests on individual praxis in so far as it is already dialectical, that is to say, to the extent that action is itself the negating transcendence of contradiction, the determination of a present totalisation in the name of a future totality, and the real effective working of matter. (Sartre 1991a: 80)

The problem with Sartre's account, as this passage also indicates, is that there remains a heavy emphasis on the individual. Such passages rightly emphasise the subjective side of social change, but is this perhaps at the cost of founding the conception of social ontology itself on the actions of individuals? The criticism remains that Sartre's notion of praxis is little more than the radical freedom of the subject and that, as with his early existentialism, the individual remains the key motivating force.

Conclusion

Praxis Marxism is important in the context of twentieth-century developments. With Sartre we saw how his work develops in response to post-war French society. Praxis Marxism is also a response to orthodox Marxism, Stalinism and developments in the USSR although it became mainly a Western movement. One exception was the *Praxis* group in Yugoslavia. Petrovic, for example, writes:

> One of the basic achievements of our postwar philosophical development is the discovery that man, who was excluded from the Stalinistic version of Marxist philosophy as an obstruction, is in the centre of authentic Marxist philosophical thought. (MacLellan 1998: 163, *Praxis* vol1 1967: 64)

What the praxis Marxists have in common is a shared humanist emphasis. They are also keen to restate the importance of history. Against the 'scientific' approach, they argue for an active historical and human element. Their emphasis is on creativity and subjectivity, human will, consciousness and action. This indicates the importance of Hegel and concepts like dialectic, alienation and totality.

However, although praxis Marxism sees itself as rebelling against the mechanical viewpoint of orthodox Marxism, more often than not it imposes its own teleological schema where history becomes the process of confirmation of subjective knowledge or class consciousness. In other words, the praxis Marxists confront objectivist teleology with their own subjectivist teleology. The common error is to *impose* a philosophical framework onto historical materialism thereby pre-judging and undermining an actual scientific investigation of real historical relations.

These views tend to reduce Marxism to the theoretical expression of the working class, or the subject. Marxism is regarded by Gramsci, Lukács and Korsch as a self-sufficient, comprehensive and totalising standpoint. For Lukács the proletariat is at one and the same time the subject and object of its knowledge while Gramsci argues that '[o]bjective always means "humanly objective" which can be held to correspond exactly to "historically subjective" ' (Gramsci 1971: 445). Instead of being a science, Marxism becomes a perspective, or world-view. This immediately poses the danger of relativism as Marxism is no longer defined in relation to knowledge of the real world. This explains why, in order to avoid the conclusion that there is no objective truth and that one group's view of the world is as good as another's, the praxis philosophers seek to give certain groups a prominent historical place and purpose and so adopt a teleology.

Further, the idea that Marxism is simply the expression of the working class presupposes that the revolutionary subject is unified. A serious omission in Korsch's work is the lack of any sense of the unevenness of working class consciousness. He assumed that the majority of workers were always revolutionary and that Marxism is their theory. Lukács, by contrast, does understand that class consciousness is uneven. The problem with Lukács, however, is that his Hegelian philosophy leads him to see everything in terms of consciousness (uneven or otherwise), which again, like Korsch, ignores the question of objective social structures. For Lukács, any differences in class consciousness will be overcome through a process of self-realisation. What this ignores is the fact that differentiations within the working class are not due to consciousness alone, but are the product of real social relations.

Roy Bhaskar writes of praxis Marxism that: 'Marxism is now fundamentally the expression of a subject, rather than the knowledge of an object' (Bhaskar 1991: 173). However, Bhaskar is somewhat unfair to Gramsci in bracketing him Lukács and Korsch for Gramsci does pay attention to objective social relations. Gramsci's writings are not just philosophical, but raise important political, cultural and sociological issues. His concept of hegemony indicates how society is stratified and how different social groups have their basis in the social divisions caused by material relations. That Gramsci emphasises the question of the tactics and strategy necessary for uniting diverse layers around a hegemonic project shows that he rejects the Lukácsian or humanist notion of a universal class subject in favour of the view that the working class is a product of complex social relations. Furthermore, Gramsci makes claims about society more generally. His concept of hegemony contrasts with the Russian usage of the term which applies to the struggle of the proletariat and its need for alliances, and looks at the question of leadership in society generally. This contrasts with Lukács and Korsch who only concern themselves with the role of the proletariat, reduce their analysis to the proletarian world-view, and consequently fail to provide a broader social theory. Unlike these theorists, Gramsci does not impose such a burdensome philosophical framework on his analysis and he allows the political element to dominate in his work. Of all the praxis Marxists, therefore, it is Gramsci who offers the best prospects of developing a substantial Marxist social theory.

Further Reading

The philosophical nature of much of this work makes reading quite difficult. Gramsci is probably easier than the rest although his writing is often disjointed and sometimes obscure. His *Selections from the Prison Notebooks* (1971) is the best work to read, especially the sections 'The Modern Prince' and 'State and Civil Society'. This volume also contains a very good introduction. Other good introductions to Gramsci include Boggs's *Gramsci's Marxism* (1978), Joll's *Gramsci* (1977) and Ransome's *Antonio Gramsci: A New Introduction*. An interesting but critical article is Perry Anderson's 'The Antimonies of Antonio Gramsci', in *New Left Review*, 100 (1976) which is available online at www.newleftreview.co.uk. Lukács's main book is *History and Class Consciousness* (1968). An interesting analysis of his work is Michael Löwy's *Georg Lukács: From Romanticism to Bolshevism* (1979). Sartre's work is notoriously difficult and it is better to start with an introductory book, the best of which is *Sartre's Marxism* by Mark Poster (1979). Marx's *Economic and Philosophical Manuscripts* and *Theses on Feuerbach* are both in the Penguin collection *Early Writings* and are well worth reading as an introduction to the theory–practice issue. More general coverage of praxis Marxism is provided by Hoffman's *Marxism and the Theory of Praxis* (1975).

5
Structuralism

Introduction: Origins

The label 'structural Marxism' is rejected by those considered to be its chief proponents – Althusser, Balibar and Poulantzas. Nevertheless, their version of Marxism is strongly influenced by the structuralism that dominated France in the mid 1960s as well as being a reaction against the humanist and existential Marxism discussed in Chapter 4.

Structuralism has its origins in the linguistics of Saussure and Jacobson which places its emphasis on the general underlying structure that makes language possible. It is argued that the linguistic sign is made up of a signified and signifier. The signifier (e.g. word) is arbitrary in relation to that which it signifies (object) – its use is a matter of convention. Signs derive their meaning through their relations with other elements (words) and are products of a system of internal differences. This points to the unstable, arbitrary nature of meaning which is not to be sought in the intentions of the subject, but in the system of signs.

In the work of Levi-Strauss we see the application of this to anthropology and such things as kinship or mythology. Levi-Strauss looks at the rules of a code within a culture. Within these cultural systems the subject has little freedom. People are located within rule-systems and it is the system rather than the subject that provides meaning. Likewise the psychoanalysis of Jacques Lacan places its emphasis, not on the active ego, but on the structure of the unconscious and the means by which the individual is subjected to what is termed the symbolic order (or system of represenation).

The ideas of Lacan (in psychoanalysis), Bachelard (in the philosophy of social science) and others influenced Louis Althusser's attempt to critique orthodox Marxism. As a critical member, he could see how the French Communist Party used theory as a means of legitimising its own practice. Stalinist orthodoxy was based on the same naturalistic and evolutionary determinism that dominated the Second International. Its economic determinism – in particular the idea of the development of means of production – is used to legitimise the aims of the Soviet state. This leaves little room for creative human action and no room for critical philosophy. We saw in Chapter 4 how Sartre and other French Marxists employed existentialism to emphasise human creativity and the importance of lived experience. Sartre rejected the scienticism of Stalinist theory in favour of a historicist approach that situates theory within the historical process.

But Althusser, although opposed to the economism of Stalinist orthodoxy, is equally opposed to Sartre's humanist, praxis based approach. For Althusser, both humanism and Stalinism embrace a teleological viewpoint that assigns to historical development some sort of purpose or destiny. The structuralism that Althusser draws on rejects the idea that there is a universal human essence. In a study of Marx's development, Althusser argues that Marx moved away from his early focus on human essence to create a theory of history based on the development of social structures and the mode of production. In contrast to praxis Marxism and its focus on the role of human action and consciousness, it is structures rather than agents that dominate Althusser's theory of society. This chapter looks at Althusser's structuralist view of society, his conception of theory and his work on ideology. It then looks at how some of this is developed in the work of the Greek Marxist Nicos Poulantzas, as well as exploring Poulantzas's use of Gramsci and his views on social classes and the state.

Althusser – Knowledge and Theoretical Practice

Althusser argues that his work constitutes an attempt to draw a line between what he claims is Marxist theory and approaches that are overly subjectivist, voluntarist, historicist, pragmatic and, above all, empiricist (Althusser 1977: 12). In opposition to these errors, Althusser attempts to establish the 'scientific' credentials of Marxism. An important notion in the construction of this argument is that of the *epistemological break*. This effectively allows Althusser to claim that there are two Marx's, an early humanist one, and a later scientific one.

The notion of the epistemological break is taken from the French philosopher Gaston Bachelard and is somewhat similar to Thomas Kuhn's notion of paradigms. According to Bachelard, science does not have a smooth evolution, but is marked by discontinuities and ruptures. Althusser argues that there is an important epistemological break in Marx's work. This is the point at which Marx breaks from his early humanist notions and starts to establish the science of historical materialism. Whereas Marx's early work emphasises the question of human alienation, his mature work – *Capital* in particular – represents an entirely different problematic or theoretical formation. As Althusser claims:

> This 'epistemological break' concerns conjointly *two distinct theoretical disciplines*. By founding the theory of history (historical materialism), Marx simultaneously broke with his erstwhile ideological philosophy and established a new philosophy (dialectical materialism). (Althusser 1977: 33)

However, this break in Marx was not necessarily a conscious thing. In keeping with structuralism, Althusser argues that theory develops, not according to the author's intentions but through the structure that determines which questions emerge in what form (this structure is called the problematic). In keeping with a structuralist reading of the text, it is necessary to employ a *symptomatic reading*, recognising that symptoms on the surface are indicative of an underlying structural basis. In attempting to focus on the later 'scientific' Marx, Althusser employs a symptomatic reading to rid Marx of any humanist and Hegelian influences. Hegel was of course a very real influence on Marx, but Althusser's approach is to read between the lines and focus on the less obvious emergence of a very different problematic.

As has been mentioned, Althusser is opposed to the teleological notion of historical purpose and so is opposed to Hegel's idea of the development of spirit. Likewise, he is opposed to attempts to bring this into Marxism by turning Hegel's *Geist* into some sort of human spirit or even into some working class or communist movement (of self-conscious actors). For Althusser, then, history is a process without a subject, while conversely, Marxism is not historicism, but a structural analysis of a system.

Not surprisingly, this 'discovery' of a scientific Marxist problematic raised the ire of humanists and historians, best represented in E.P. Thompson's outpouring, *The Poverty of Theory*. Here Thompson argues that Althusser reduces active historical processes to static theoretical categories. Thompson criticises Althusser's 'self-generating conceptual universe' (Thompson 1978: 13), and structuralism's self-regulating, self-validating systems, arguing that Althusser de-historicises and de-socialises social relations whereas 'all these "instances" and "levels" are in fact human activities, institutions and ideas' (Thompson 1978: 97). The biggest danger with Althusser's structuralism is the elimination of the role of agency with agents regarded merely as the 'bearers' of social relations. With agents given such a passive role, Thompson is able to argue that 'Althusser's constructions of the "theory of history" afford no terms for *experience*, nor for process when it is considered as human *practice* . . . Althusser's structuralism is, like all structuralisms, a system of *closure*' (Thompson 1978: 98).

But actually, Althusser's approach does focus on the idea of social practice even if it does not do this in the humanist way. We will later see how practice relates to such things as ideology and class positions; here we briefly note the idea of theoretical practice. For Althusser, theoretical practice is responsible for the transformation of what he calls Generalities I, or the raw materials of the discipline (like concepts and ideas). Generalities II refers to the process of theoretical production while Generalities III refers to the product of this process.

However, Althusser's conception of scientific practice has been criticised for regarding the criteria of scientificity as internal to the scientific practice itself. The production of scientific knowledge tends to get separated from the socio-historical conditions within which this takes place. Science, in effect, becomes epistemologically and historically autonomous. The problem, then, if scientificity is internally determined, is how we can step back and decide on the status of a practice, in particular, how we can make the distinction between science and ideology that Althusser is so keen to maintain. It might be said that Althusser's mistake is to regard science and ideology as entirely separate domains, rather than as different *aspects* of the same practice (Collier 1989: 28). A further problem with Althusser's approach to science arises from his distinction between real object and thought object. The thought object is that which is worked on by science in the process of theoretical production. In contrast to this concrete-in-thought is the concrete-reality which is its object. The problem with this distinction is that there is again the idealist tendency to say that the development of science takes place entirely within thought and that the real object plays no role in the development of this process.

The Structure of the Totality

Althusser's opposition to Hegel allows him to develop a radically new view of the social whole. Hegel's position is described as that of an 'expressive totality' where each of the elements of the whole expresses a single inner essence. Against this position, Althusser argues that: 'There is no longer any simple unity, only a structured, complex unity. There is no longer any original simple unity (in any form whatsoever), but instead, *the ever-pre-givenness of a structural complex unity*' (Althusser 1977: 199).

Althusser's argument is that there are different levels of the social totality and that each level is relatively autonomous and has its own particular development. Most forms of Marxism adopt the Hegelian dialectic in assuming that all instances of the totality are a reflection of a basic contradiction at the level of production. By contrast, structural Marxism breaks from this crude base-superstructure model, arguing that the economy is only determinant 'in the last instance'. This allows weight to be given to political, cultural and ideological factors and moves away from economic determinism. The conjuncture is to be understood as a complex combination of these different levels. As an example, Althusser discusses how Lenin was able to analyse the structure of the conjuncture, its various displacements, condensations and contradictions all in a paradoxical unity, the basis on which political action was to take place (Althusser 1977: 179).

Althusser borrows from psychoanalysis the term overdetermination in order to emphasise how the social body is 'determined by the various *levels* and *instances* of the social formation it animates' (Althusser 1977: 101). Overdetermination is Althusser's way of understanding the Marxist dialectic as a focus on complex contradictions, where different instances do not reflect the whole but are relatively independent and distinct. Thus: *'the specific difference of Marxist contradiction is its "unevenness", or "overdetermination", which reflects in its conditions of existence, that is, the specific structure of unevenness (in dominance) of the ever-pre-given complex whole which is its existence'* (Althusser 1977: 217).

However, this does raise problems as to how to deal with Marxism's traditional insistence on the importance of the economy. According to Althusser, overdetermination means: 'that a revolution in the *structure* does not *ipso facto* modify the existing superstructures at one blow (as it would if the economic was the *sole determinant factor*)' (Althusser 1977: 115–16). Rather, as we have noted, the different levels enjoy relative autonomy while the economy is only determinant in the last instance. But this determinance in the last instance means that the economy determines which element is to be dominant in any given social formation. Therefore, the system is described as a structure in dominance where the dominant element is not fixed, but is a product of the relations of overdetermination, determined by the economy in the last instance. Therefore the economy displaces the dominant role within a social formation to a particular instance. Under Feudalism it was the political that was the dominant instance, but this dominance of the political was ultimately determined by the economy. The trouble is that this position tries to have it both ways. It quite rightly allows the different levels of the social formation to have some degree of autonomy, but then goes back to the traditional Marxist instance that it is the economy that is determinate – albeit in the last instance. But then, just when this has been established, we are informed again that: 'From the first moment to the last, the lonely hour of the "last instance" never comes' (Althusser 1977: 113).

Ideology

Whereas ideology has a largely negative character in the work of Marx and Engels and a more political role in the work of Lenin and Gramsci (including mobilising popular movements), in Althusser, ideology has a more structural–functional role in equipping people for social existence. It is argued that ideology is required in all societies if people are to be equipped to respond to the demands of their conditions of existence. Consequently, 'ideology is not an aberration or a contingent excrescence of History: it is a structure essential to the historical life of societies' (Althusser 1977: 232). Thus, Althusser rejects the commonly held view that ideology is simply a negative product of class society, claiming that it is a necessary feature of all societies. Even a communist society will have ideology, but whereas the ideology of class society has negative effects, ideology in communist society will represent our relation to our conditions of existence for the benefit of all of us.

Althusser suggests that ideology is an organic part of all societies and that it is basic to their functioning and continued existence:

> So ideology is as such an organic part of every social totality. It is as if human societies could not survive without these *specific formations*, these systems of representations (at various levels), their ideologies. Human societies secrete ideology as

the very element and atmosphere indispensable to their historical respiration and life. (Althusser 1977: 232)

Ideology is produced wherever there is social practice and 'there is no practice except by and in ideology' (Althusser 1984: 44). As we have said, Althusser's notion of practice is a non-humanist one and so if ideology is essential to the social practices of everyday life, then it has a largely unconscious nature in that it is in the background in a taken-for-granted or unrecognised way. As Althusser says:

> So ideology is a matter of the *lived* relation between men and their world. This rela-
> tion, that only appears as '*conscious*' on condition that it is *unconscious* . . . In ide-
> ology men do indeed express, not the relation between them and their conditions of
> existence, but *the way* they live the relation between them and their conditions of
> existence: this presupposes both a real relation and an '*imaginary*', '*lived*' relation.
> (Althusser 1977: 233)

So Althusser develops a critical understanding of ideology based on the fact that ideology somehow generates an *imaginary* relation between people and their real conditions of existence and that this somehow obscures the *real* basis of the relationship. Althusser is also critical of ideology as a system of repre-sentations that imposes itself upon us. This can be seen in his notion of inter-pellation which attempts to explain how it is that ideology constitutes us as subjects. People are recruited into identity positions by being interpellated or hailed. This is a process whereby people recognise themselves in a particular identity and think 'that's me'. Ideology hails or interpellates concrete individu-als as concrete subjects (Althusser 1984: 47).

Ideology works by 'recruiting' subjects, or 'transforming' individuals into subjects by '*interpellation* or hailing . . . which can be imagined along the lines of the most commonplace everyday police (or other) hailing: "Hey, you there!"' ' (Althusser 1984: 48). So although ideology is often unconscious it involves this act of recognition. A very obvious example of this is the role of advertising which appeals to our sense of who we are. But this is a recognition of an identity and situation that we have limited choice over. The irony is that ideology presents this imposition as a free choice, or as Althusser puts it, 'the individual is *interpellated as a (free) subject in order that he shall submit freely to the commandments of the Subject*' (Althusser 1984: 56). There are no sub-jects except through their subjection, but this process of subjection is such that it seems to be done all by oneself.

Althusser's other major contribution to the Marxist conception of ideology is his notion of ideological state apparatuses (ISAs). The ISAs are those state institutions that assist in the reproduction of the social formation. Althusser divides the state institutions into Repressive State Apparatuses like the police, army and prison system and those like education, the church, the family, the media and various cultural bodies, political organisations, trade unions and so on which he considers to be primarily ideological in their nature. Of course, the issue arises as to whether such things as the family or the church should be classified as state institutions at all. It tends to be that the ISAs are overwhelmingly of the private domain. A looser definition is also required in order to comprehend the repressive and ideological aspects of these institutions. While Althusser states that 'the Repressive State apparatus functions "by violence", whereas the Ideological State Apparatuses *function "by ideology"* ' (Althusser 1984: 19) a modification is required since 'repressive' institutions like the police also reply upon and produce ideology (such as the language of law and order) while ISAs may also depend upon repression as a secondary aspect.

Behind Althusser's theory is the view that the reproduction of society is as much an ideological affair as an economic one. As Althusser argues, 'the reproduction of labour power requires not only a reproduction of its skills, but also, at the same time, a reproduction of its submission to the rules of the established order' (Althusser 1984: 6). As with the theory of interpellation, the issue of subjection arises – in this case, through a series of specialised institutions that reinforce the ruling ideology. The issue of the institutionalisation of the ruling ideology also relates to the question of hegemony: '*no class can hold State power over a long period without at the same time exercising its hegemony over and in the State Ideological Apparatuses*' (Althusser 1984: 20).

Despite criticising Gramsci for his humanism and historicism, Althusser is influenced by the Italian's work. So too is Nicos Poulantzas who relates hegemony to the way that leadership is exercised through government apparatuses and private institutions. For Poulantzas the ISAs are responsible for the ideological articulation of the ruling bloc. They are also the site of battle between competing factions of the different classes as they attempt to assert their control over society. But to get to these we need to first examine Poulantzas's ideas on social classes and class fractions and then the nature of the state.

Poulantzas on Fractions

Like Althusser, Poulantzas tries to break from economic reductionism. This can be seen in his work on classes where he argues that social classes are not only defined in relation to the economic means of production, but are also determined by political, ideological and other social practices. The effect of these different practices is to produce differentiations within classes. Classes are not homogenous but are composed of different class *fractions* based on different social, economic and political factors (e.g. sections like the military elite, finance capitalists, manufacturers and so on). Thus the bourgeoisie is not a single united group, but contains within it various competing fractions with different, conflicting interests. Since classes are divided into different fractions, the rule of the dominant class must be constructed through the building of a complex set of alliances. In fact, the hegemonic class may not even be the economically dominant one, but that which can best unify what Poulantzas calls the power bloc. This talk of hegemonic blocs indicates that Poulantzas is drawing, not only on structuralist ideas, but also on the work of Gramsci. Like Gramsci, Poulantzas is concerned with how a ruling bloc is created out of various social groups, although Poulantzas does place more emphasis on the structural–functional aspect of hegemony – an issue to be explored in the next section.

Poulantzas's discussion of the structural basis of the different class fractions becomes rather complex. In particular, he tries to distinguish between different types of fraction according to economic or political factors (Poulantzas 1973: 84–85). These are:

Autonomous fractions which correspond to different interests, powers and relations within classes. These differences are related to socio-economic structures – for example, fractions exist within the bourgeois class based upon finance capital and industrial capital.

Social categories do not have the same autonomy as class fractions and are comprised of various classes and fractions, but are unified by their structural relations and functions. The most notable examples of social categories are the bureaucracy and the intelligentsia.

Social strata are the secondary effect of the combination of modes of production in a social formation. Poulantzas here specifically refers to the labour aristocracy. Unlike fractions and social categories, these groups cannot themselves constitute a social force, but they can exert an important political influence – such as the influence of the labour aristocracy in the development of revisionism or reformist political practice.

Because classes and social groups have different economic, political and ideological determinations, the construction and maintenance of political blocs through a negotiation of interests is important. An economically dominant class is thus not immediately assured of political power. This must be achieved through a power bloc which 'constitutes a contradictory unity of *politically dominant* classes and fractions *under the protection of the hegemonic fraction*' (Poulantzas 1973: 239). This unity is never assured since the class struggle and the particular rivalry of interests is constantly present. Against economic determinism Poulantzas's analysis allows a genuine role to be given to political processes.

Poulantzas and the State

Given the various different class fractions within society, the state assumes a vital role in bringing them together. Poulantzas writes of the state as 'the dominant classes' political power centre' and as their 'organising agent' (Poulantzas 1973: 190). But Poulantzas expresses this in a decidedly non-agential way when he argues that:

> The principal role of the state apparatuses is to maintain the unity and cohesion of a social formation by concentrating and sanctioning class domination, and in this way reproducing social relations, i.e. class relations. Political and ideological relations are materialized and embodied, as material practices, in the state apparatuses. (Poulantzas 1978a: 24–25)

The state must act as a factor of social cohesion in bringing together the different groups and securing the unity of the power bloc. Poulantzas argues against the instrumentalist view that the state is the tool of a particular class, arguing that the state is capitalist, not because it is controlled and used by the capitalist classes, but rather because of its objective place or function in the reproduction of the economic mode of production. Poulantzas refers to Marx's analysis of Bonapartism in France to argue that the state, rather than being the instrument of any one class, is relatively autonomous and that this autonomy allows it to play the role of organising the different classes and class fractions. The state therefore has a general function in managing class contradictions and maintaining social cohesion.

The best known expression of Poulantzas's views on the state is his debate with Ralph Miliband in the pages of *New Left Review*. He argues that Miliband's work tends to reduce the state to the issue of its control by sections of the bourgeoisie. For Poulantzas the state has a more objective place in capitalist society. It is necessary to comprehend both social classes and the state as objective structures and as part of an objective system of regular connections. As Poulantzas puts it, there is 'a structure and a system whose agents, "men" are in the words of Marx, "bearers" of it – *träger*' (Poulantzas 1969: 70). Miliband, by contrast, is critiqued for reducing social classes to inter-personal relations. His is a problematic of social actors (Poulantzas 1969: 70). Miliband is therefore wrong to concentrate on the role of elites and state personnel since what matters are not the relations between people, but relations between fractions of capital. The relation between the bourgeois class and the state is an objective relation with the functions of the state and the interests of the dominant class coinciding. Miliband, it is claimed, reduces the role of the state to the conduct and behaviour of members of the state apparatus. Instead, as we have seen, it is necessary to view the state as a factor of cohesion within the social formation and a factor in reproducing the conditions of production (Poulantzas 1969: 72).

The factor of cohesion approach is founded on the argument that because capitalism separates the worker from the means of production, the political sphere can become autonomous. In contrast to previous modes of production, under capitalism it is no longer necessary to secure exploitation by political means and the state is not *directly* implicated in organising economic production. This relative autonomy in fact allows the state to present itself as the representative of the 'general interest'. It is able to stand above competing and divergent economic interests, or, if necessary, to present these interests as the popular will. This is important ideologically as 'the state assumes a specific autonomy vis-à-vis these [socio-economic] relations, in putting itself forward as the representative of the unity of the people/nation' (Poulantzas 1973: 135).

The autonomy of the state apparatus from the economic class struggle is also important because it means that the politically dominant class does not have to correspond to the economically dominant class. Political domination does not flow automatically from the economic situation. The state must act as the cohesive factor in the unity of a social formation, but how this is achieved is a political rather than merely an economic matter. The state becomes crucial as a site where hegemony is established:

> The capitalist state and the specific characteristics of the class struggle in a capitalist formation *make it possible* for a 'power bloc', composed of several *politically dominant* classes or fractions to function. Amongst these *dominant* classes and fractions one of them holds a particular *dominant role*, which can be characterized as a *hegemonic role*. (Poulantzas 1973: 141)

Once the unity of the dominant class fractions has been achieved, the consent of the broader masses must be mobilised. The capitalist state is seen as an 'institutional ensemble' with the function of organising hegemony within the power bloc and mobilising active consent.

The power bloc is a long-term unity across economic, political and ideological domains and the role of the state is to ensure its survival by keeping social struggles within the limits of the mode of production. However, it is inevitable that divisions and fractures occur within the complex of state institutions, reflecting the effect of class struggle and the nature of the different alliances within the power bloc. The capitalist state is based on hegemonic class leadership and democratic institutions. It is argued that when hegemony is stable, normal states predominate, but that during hegemonic crises, exceptional states emerge.

Poulantzas's later work emphasises the tendency towards exceptional forms of the capitalist state. He argues that this period of what he calls monopoly capitalism requires an interventionist state with a strong or authoritarian character. Under monopoly capitalism the state assumes an increasingly interventionist economic role resulting in the irresistible rise of administration and the decline of democratic institutions. There is a change in the role of state apparatuses and political parties and a breakdown of the boundaries between public and private spheres. However, this comes at a cost for while state power is strengthened, the threat to parliamentary democracy undermines social hegemony. Poulantzas terms this process 'authoritarian statism' based on 'intensified state control over every sphere of socio-economic life' (Poulantzas 1978b: 203). He talks of the irresistible rise of state administration which takes over from multi-party democracy. The administration itself becomes politicised and an anti-democratic technocratic discourse emerges.

Poulantzas's analysis of authoritarian statism is particularly concerned with the rise of the dictatorships in Spain, Portugal and Greece, but interestingly, some of this analysis is later applied to the Thatcherite project in Britain as Chapter 7 shall explore. Poulantzas's analysis leads to a concern with democracy and the democratic transition to socialism. The democratic road to socialism involves a protracted struggle to exploit the contradictions within the state. The idea is not to oppose the state from the outside as might be the traditional strategy of Marxism, but to break into the state apparatus itself exploiting the contradictions within it. We study some of these ideas next, followed by an overall assessment of Poulantzas's work.

State, Power, Socialism

Going back to the Poulantzas–Miliband debate, Miliband targets what he calls Poulantzas's structural determinism (which is clearly evident in Poulantzas's reduction of agents to the bearers of structures) (Miliband 1970: 57). Miliband argues that while the government and bureaucracy are indeed subject to structural constraints, what the state does is not wholly determined by 'objective relations'. Those who run the state are not mere functionaries. In particular, Miliband argues that Poulantzas's structural determinism leaves little space for the role of active class struggle. This is something that Poulantzas tries to grapple with in his final work.

Poulantzas is torn between the view that the state has a structural–functional role in securing the cohesiveness of a social formation and the relational view that the state and its institutions are the effect of the class struggle. Poulantzas gradually abandons structuralism so that in his final book, *State, Power, Socialism* the state comes to be regarded as embodying class positions and class practices, thus allowing the dominated classes to build up centres of resistance within the relatively independent apparatuses of the state itself. The state and the ISAs are regarded as a strategic terrain where struggle takes place. Poulantzas moves from a view of ideology as a form of social cement with a functional role for the capitalist system to a view of ideology as a terrain of struggle. Under the influence of Eurocommunism (a reformist tendency within the Communist Parties), and concerned with the rise of authoritarian states, Poulantzas starts to advocate a democratic socialist position, arguing the need to radically transform the state and deepen political freedoms and the institutions of representative democracy while allowing new forms of direct democracy to flourish (Poulantzas 1978b: 256).

Poulantzas's advocacy of democratic socialism coincides with his relational view that the state 'should not be regarded as an intrinsic entity: like "capital", *it is rather a relationship of forces, or more precisely the material condensation of such a relationship between classes and class fractions*' (1978b: 128). State policy is the result of class contradictions inscribed into the state. The state is both constituted and divided by these class contradictions (Poulantzas 1978b: 132). We can see how Poulantzas has shifted from a structural approach influenced by Althusser (and criticised by Miliband) to a more relational approach. We briefly look at how this is influenced by Foucault's theory of power, before looking at how this relational approach is taken up and developed by Bob Jessop.

Poulantzas engages with Foucault to show how disciplines operate to establish social norms and behaviour. In exploring the relation between strategy and power, Foucault focuses on the micro-sites of power and the process of individualisation and normalisation. Poulantzas extends this to argue that it is the state that plays a leading role in forging individuality through techniques of knowledge (disciplines) (Poulantzas 1978b: 66). By drawing on Foucault in this way Poulantzas can show how the exercise of power is much subtler than overt violence and repression. But against Foucault, it is argued that the state monopoly of physical force always underlies techniques of power and mechanisms of consent, shaping the materiality of the social body even when not directly exercised (Poulantzas 1978b: 81). Likewise, power must always relate back to the relations of production. Power may be relational, but at the same time has a base in relations of production and the state apparatus.

This helps illustrate Poulantzas's turn to a more relational approach to power and the state, yet despite these moves and assurances, there is still something unsatisfactory about the relational turn. His work as a whole is either structuralist or relational, but at no point is able to combine the insights of both approaches. Consequently, the insights of his later work are not grounded in the strengths of his earlier structural accounts, something that is noted by Bob Jessop in his book on Poulantzas. By way of conclusion, we look at how Jessop tries to bring Poulantzas's two approaches together.

As noted, the state is not an instrument or a subject but a social relation, more specifically, a material condensation of the balance among class forces. As Jessop puts it, the 'power of the state is the power of the class forces which act in and through the state' (Jessop 1985: 337). The state is a complex institutional ensemble characterised by what Jessop, following Claus Offe, calls a 'structural selectivity' that reflects and modifies the balance of class forces (Jessop 1985: 338). Jessop writes that the key to moving beyond Poulantzas is a focus on strategy. Class contradictions are reproduced inside the state and these contradictions must be linked to class strategies. Strategy acts as an intermediary between structural determination and class positions (Jessop 1985: 342). Putting this in the context of Marxist thinking, Jessop talks of a divide between 'class-theoretical' and 'capital-theoretical' approaches with Marxists either emphasising an abstract logic of capital or the concrete forms of class struggle (Jessop 1985: 343) (something well illustrated by the Poulantzas–Miliband debate). The idea behind 'strategic-theoretical' concepts is to link these modes of analysis, providing middle-range concepts that bridge the gap. This would examine different logics of capital in terms of different accumulation strategies and class struggle in terms of competing hegemonic projects (Jessop 1985: 344). With Jessop's approach we have the 'dual perspective of structural determination and class position' (Jessop 1985: 344–45). Structural determination should be seen in terms of the crystalisation of past strategies, while class strategies should be related to the constraints of class domination and the balance of forces (Jessop 1985: 345). We will see later how this informs Jessop's analysis of Thatcherism as well as his regulationist approach more generally.

Conclusion

It should be clear that the structuralist tradition is useful in two ways. First, it challenges economic determinism and other forms of reductionism, arguing for the complexity of society and the importance of other social domains like the political and cultural. Second, it argues the importance of social structures as against those approaches that err towards voluntarism in their conception of social activity. However, there are many problems with bringing a structuralist analysis to Marxism. This is reflected in the big shifts undergone by Althusser and Poulantzas. Two will be drawn out here. First, in Althusser the theoreticism or scientism of his approach, gives way to the idea that philosophy is the class struggle in theory. Then, in Poulantzas it is evident how a structural–functional account of the state gives way to a relational one that emphasises class struggle. In both cases, structuralist theory is struggling to get to grips with the role of class struggle.

The problem with Althusser's early conception of science is that science gets separated from the socio-historical conditions of its production. There is an absolute separation from ideology which is regarded as something produced in the outside world. However, if as Althusser suggests, ideology is secreted by human practices, then surely this is the case for theoretical practices too? If ideology is everywhere, then surely it is in Marxist theory too. Marxism cannot stand outside the social conditions of its production.

Althusser's theoreticist understanding of Marxism is reflected in his description of philosophy as 'the theory of theoretical practice'. However, Althusser later revised this position in order to take into account Marxism's location in the social world. Philosophy now becomes 'the class struggle in theory'. But if this is so, how are we to understand the relationship between historical materialism and the working class? Is there not a danger of relativism in linking philosophy to the class struggle? Why should working class theory necessarily be superior, particularly given the subordinate position the working class is in? Throughout this shift in understanding Althusser is unable to answer the basic question, how is the scientific and philosophical basis of Marxism determined?

The biggest problem with structuralism is the tendency to undermine the role of agency. This is especially so in Althusser and Balibar, but is also clear in

Poulantzas's view of hegemony where it is defined less in relation to social groups and more in terms of the structural–functional requirements of the social system (securing its unity). Poulantzas later tries to resolve this with a strategic-relational approach, but at the expense of bringing in much contradiction. A dualism emerges in Poulantzas's work so that his main writings contain an overly structural account of the social world with little room for agency, while his later work adopts a relational approach. If in his early work the effects of class struggle are missing, they return later on as a replacement for, rather than a complement to, a structural account. With Poulantzas we either get a structural or a relational approach to hegemony, but he never manages to properly combine the two – that is, that hegemony might be *both* that which secures the cohesion of the social formation *and* that which is a strategic relation between different class fractions. Likewise, the state is seen either in a structural–functional way as a factor of social cohesion, or in a relational way as the embodiment of class positions.

These problems led to critics, particularly those from the praxis side of Marxism, claiming that structuralism was unable to account for the role of class struggle and human agency. Unfortunately this meant that many of the structuralist insights were ignored. Later we will see how the recent work of critical realism attempts to develop an emphasis on social structures, while maintaining the importance of agency and class struggle through the idea that social structures are reproduced and occasionally transformed through human actions.

Further Reading

Structural Marxism, like praxis Marxism, can be a difficult read because of its philosophical nature. Althusser's two main books *For Marx* (1977) and *Reading Capital* (1979) are both difficult. However, the final section of *For Marx*, 'Marxism and Humanism' summarises Althusser's approach nicely. His essay 'Ideology and Ideological State Apparatuses' in Althusser (1984) is easier and very interesting. Poulantzas's main books are *Political Power and Social Classes* (1973), *Classes in Contemporary Capitalism* (1978a) and *State, Power, Socialism* (1978b) which is more critical of the early work. For the Poulantzas–Miliband debate, read *New Left Review* numbers 58, 59, 82, 95 and 138 (Miliband's articles in 82 and 138 are available online at www.newleftreview. co.uk). Good introductions are Callinicos's *Althusser's Marxism* (1976) and Jessop's *Nicos Poulantzas* (1985). E.P. Thompson's critique of Althusser is in *The Poverty of Theory* (1978). An excellent overview is provided by Benton's *The Rise and Fall of Structural Marxism* (1984). Elliott's *Althusser: The Detour of Theory* (1987) is also worth reading.

6

Critical Theory

Introduction: Origins of the Frankfurt School

Despite his critique of modern society, Marx is considered to be a philosopher of the Enlightenment. That is, he believes in the Enlightenment notion of progress in relation to historical development and in a project of universal human emancipation. Expressing the sentiment that humans can gradually take control of their own destiny he writes that freedom 'can consist only in this, that socialized man, the associated producers, govern the human metabolism with nature in a rational way, bringing it under collective control instead of being dominated by it as a blind power' (Marx 1981: 959).

By contrast, the critical theorists Theodor Adorno and Max Horkheimer turn against the Enlightenment claiming that rather than bringing nature under our control we have become more alienated from it: 'Myth turns into enlightenment, and nature into mere objectivity. Men pay for the increase in their power with alienation from that over which they exercise their power' (Adorno and Horkheimer 1986: 9). The anti-authoritarian impulse of the Enlightenment turns into its opposite, another form of domination. This chapter examines the process they call the 'dialectic of Enlightenment'.

Adorno and Horkheimer draw on Marx's theories of alienation and commodity fetishism but these are combined with Max Weber's theory of the rationalisation of the world. They argue that as society becomes ever more rationalised, bureaucratic and authoritarian, the emancipatory project of Marxism becomes increasingly Utopian. Despite claiming allegiance to Marxism, the Frankfurt school moves away from some of the main emancipatory ideas of Marx, and in particular rejects the idea of the working class as a revolutionary subject.

In order to explain such pessimism, it is necessary to take into account the fact that the early Frankfurt theorists were writing at a time of extreme social crisis. The Institute of Social Research was established in 1923 and affiliated to the University of Frankfurt. When the Nazis came to power it was forced into exile. During this period it came under the directorship of Horkheimer who now gave the work of the school a more philosophical orientation. The school also developed an interest in psychoanalysis which was concerned with the manipulation of desire and the fate of the individual. By the time of its return to Germany the school had come to influence the New Left developing in Europe and was an integral part of a new 'Western Marxism' whose hidden hallmark, according to Perry Anderson, was that it was a product of defeat (Anderson 1979: 42).

The fascist state, the product of a particular historical period of social crisis, tends to be seen by the Frankfurt theorists as representing the general direction of late capitalist society. They see fascism and war as products of monopoly capitalism, bureaucratisation and the spread of technological rationalisation. Their experience in exile in the United States led Adorno and Horkheimer to believe that this process was not confined to the openly fascist or Stalinist states, but was a general historical trend. Seeing no way out of this, their work becomes increasingly bleak and pessimistic. This chapter looks at some of the work of the school during this period before considering the more optimistic approach of the leading second generation Frankfurt theorist Jürgen Habermas.

Late Capitalism and the Dialectic of Enlightenment

Adorno's view of late capitalism suggests that the world has become so dominated by technology that the social relations analysed by Marx have started to lose their significance. Even if Marxist theories of crisis are not untrue, the capitalist system has proved resilient enough to indefinitely postpone any anticipated collapse. Marx's economic theory was supposed to provide the basis for understanding class conflict, but this analysis belongs to a previous era of liberal capitalism. With mass production, mass consumption, monopolisation, rationalisation, bureaucratisation, militarisation, totalitarianism and the growth of the culture industry, the world had become a different place. For Adorno and Horkheimer late capitalism represents the integration of the economic and the political. Production and distribution are collectively administered with the state acting like a 'general capitalist'. Humans are still dominated by the economic process, but this now takes place through political state management. The state plays a commanding role so that 'the telos of state intervention is direct political domination independent of market mechanisms' (Adorno 1987: 245).

Whereas Marx suggested that the masses will suffer privation, the critical theorists argued that mass production means that people can be bought off through the ample supply of material goods and entertainment. The immiseration of the masses does take place, but this is an intellectual rather than material process. Seduced by material goods but unable to control their own lives and unable to develop a critical consciousness, people experience the world as blind fate (Adorno 1987: 237). As Adorno and Horkheimer argue:

> The over-maturity of society lives by the immaturity of the dominated. The more complicated and precise the social, economic, and scientific apparatus with whose

service the production system has long harmonised the body, the more impoverished the experiences which it can offer. (Adorno and Horkheimer 1986: 36)

As will be discussed in the next two sections, this alienation or reification is not just an economic phenomenon, but has important cultural, political and epistemological dimensions affecting our very ways of thinking and knowing: 'Through the countless agencies of mass production and its culture the conventionalised modes of behaviour are impressed on the individual as the only natural, respectable, and rational ones' (Adorno and Horkheimer 1986: 28).

Thus, for Adorno and Horkheimer our estrangement runs deeps. They further discuss this estrangement in relation to the dialectic between society and nature. The more society comes to dominate nature, the more society becomes alienated from itself. As Horkheimer puts it: 'The history of man's efforts to subjugate nature is also the history of man's subjugation by man' (Horkheimer 1987: 105). As humanity tries to free itself from nature and bring nature under its control, so, at the same time it degrades itself and destroys its own basis. In *Dialectic of Enlightenment* Adorno and Horkheimer write:

> As soon as man discards his awareness that he himself is nature, all the aims for which he keeps himself alive – social progress, the intensification of all his material and spiritual powers, even consciousness itself – are nullified . . . Man's domination over himself, which grounds his selfhood, is almost always the destruction of the subject in whose service it is undertaken. (Adorno and Horkheimer 1986: 54)

It is argued that nature becomes a mere tool of humanity, something to be dominated, but humanity itself, though this process, loses sight of itself. Our relationship towards nature and towards each other and ourselves becomes manipulative and instrumental. The dialectic of Enlightenment leads to self-destruction and alienation from nature and ourselves.

Adorno and Horkheimer argue that the Enlightenment aimed at liberating us from fear through reason: 'The spirit of enlightenment replaced the fire and the rack by the stigma it attached to all irrationality' (Adorno and Horkheimer 1986: 31). However, the dialectic of Enlightenment is such that it brings in new forms of domination which become so overpowering that they filter through to every level of society, every institution and indeed our very ways of thinking. Enlightenment thinking extinguishes the traces of its own self-consciousness. Thought loses its element of self-reflection and becomes alienated, reified and ritualised.

Reason lacks the ability to make critical judgement or comment on the desirability of any goal. As Horkheimer says, with the American and French revolutions reason becomes harnessed to social process as an instrument. As a result, meaning is supplanted by social function (Horkheimer 1987: 22). Late capitalism represents the subordination of reason to commerce and industry while critical and reflective thought is transformed into instrumental reason.

Justice, equality, happiness and tolerance, all of which are supposed to be inherent in or sanctioned by reason, have lost their intellectual roots. Yet this is something that is willingly given up in the name of progress. The history of civilisation is the introversion of sacrifice, the history of renunciation.

Critical Theory and Negative Dialectics

Adorno and Horkheimer develop a critique of scientific and technological rationality and instrumental reason. They extend this into the realms of philosophy and knowledge to argue how the logic of late capitalism is reflected in the then dominant ideas of the positivist approach to science and in the idealist illusion, put forth in much social theory, of the autonomous thinking subject. In 'Traditional and Critical Theory,' Horkheimer criticises the dominant positivist approach to social science for treating individuals as mere facts and conceiving of the world as it appears to us in its immediacy. It does not register contradictions, and refuses to see the social world as a process of development and change. Positivism claims that philosophy is merely concerned with the classification and formalisation of scientific methods, while it reduces modern science to statements about facts. Therefore, Horkheimer claims that positivism is a form of fetishism in theory. Its rigid concepts presuppose the reification of life in general and our perception in particular (Horkheimer 1987: 81). The celebration of 'facts' is a reification which critical reflection must see through by recognising them as historical products. Horkheimer's alternative approach is therefore to stress how everything is connected together and how reality must be seen as a dynamic totality rather than as a set of individual elements.

Adorno and Horkheimer argue that late capitalism is dominated by what they call identity thinking which (as we mentioned in relation to positivism) is the belief that things are as they appear in their immediacy. Against identity thinking, they put forward an ideology critique. The aim is to show that what exists does not have to be as it is. Things are not given and it is not possible to understand them simply through a process of classification. Rather, things are contradictory and can be other than what they are. Therefore: 'The task of cognition does not consist in mere apprehension, classification and calculation, but in the determinate negation of each immediacy' (Adorno and Horkheimer 1986: 27).

Talk of determinate negation leads to Adorno's notion of negative dialectics. He tries to show how we cannot develop the kind of detached classificatory schema positivists advocate since concepts and objects are mutually implicated. If we want to develop a social critique, we have to do so from within theory using a dialectical method that can develop the implications of context insofar as '[d]ialectics is the self-consciousness of the objective context of delusion; it does not mean to have escaped from that context. Its objective goal is to break out of the context from within' (Adorno 1973: 406). Adorno develops a metacritique of theories of knowledge like positivism and of classificatory and closed systems of thought. Rather than establishing an alternative system of thought, he attempts to undermine these from within in a creative way. This can be seen through his essays and aphorisms such as in his book *Minima Moralia* where the aim is to encourage the reader to engage in creative criticism.

Adorno's aim is to critique identity thinking and the reification of thought and its context. Identity, Adorno argues, is the primary form of ideology (Adorno 1973: 148), while his dialectical ideology critique bases itself on the consistent sense of non-identity (Adorno 1973: 5) so that no object or statement ever remains identical with itself. By making these insights, Adorno is ahead of his time and prefigures many of the arguments made by poststructuralists. As we shall see, Adorno's insights are similar to those of Jacques Derrida, and his critique of identity thinking might be compared to Derrida's critique of presence.

The Culture Industry and the Working Class

Whereas Marx emphasises the role of economic production, Adorno and Horkheimer are keen to stress the role of cultural reproduction. However, their notion of the culture industry likens the production of culture to an industrial process. Late capitalism encourages standardisation and conformity and the development of culture is no different to any other branch of industry. Films, music and other entertainments are mass produced to a standard formula so that all culture becomes the same.

> Under monopoly all mass culture is identical, and the lines of its artificial framework begin to show through. The people at the top are no longer so interested in concealing monopoly . . . Movies and radio need no longer pretend to be art. The truth that they are just business is made into an ideology in order to justify the rubbish they deliberately produce. (Adorno and Horkheimer 1986: 121)

Commercialisation brings about the fusion of culture and entertainment. Culture is measured by its exchange value. The culture industry openly celebrates the fact that social rating becomes the new measure of artistic status: 'the work's social rating (misinterpreted as its artistic status) becomes its use value – the only quality which is enjoyed' (Adorno and Horkheimer 1986: 158). This can clearly be linked to the Marxist idea of fetishism. Films are measured in terms of their box office success, records by their position in the charts and this becomes the main means for differentiating products given their standardised character. The culture industry holds a monopoly over what is to be produced and promoted, and this in turn becomes a form of social control and means of eliminating dissension and originality. The cultural product loses its innovativeness and uniqueness. The stereotypes of the culture industry encourage pathological forms of collectivity. People prefer what is familiar to them so that they no longer need to think for themselves.

> Pleasure always means not to think about anything, to forget suffering even where it is shown. Basically it is helplessness. It is flight; not as is asserted, flight from a wretched reality, but from the last remaining thought of resistance. The liberation which amusement promises is freedom from thought and from negation. (Adorno and Horkheimer 1986: 144)

Products are made easy to digest so that they fit in with the intensive demands of modern society, 'occupying men's senses from the time they leave the factory in the evening to the time they clock in again the next morning with matter that bears the impress of the labour process they themselves have to sustain throughout the day' (Adorno and Horkheimer 1986: 131). The product of the culture industry also plays a pacifying role: 'It comforts all with the thought that a tough, genuine human fate is still possible' (Adorno and Horkheimer 1986: 151). As with Marx's theory of religion, so for Adorno and Horkheimer the culture industry stands in for the missing human ties and relations. Morality is now to be found in the heroes and villains of children's books. Tragic film becomes an institution for moral improvement. The institutions of the cultural sphere provide us with our reasoning, morality and world-outlooks. These relate to deeper psychological needs which the culture industry skilfully manipulates. The industry fills the gap between modern economic activity and moral, ethical and cultural life.

This moral and ethical side is developed further in the work of Herbert Marcuse. He examines how the domination of the system becomes internalised and how these processes shape the development of the individual. As with the other critical theorists, his view of the human individual is rather pessimistic as is indicated by his term 'one-dimensional man'. Marcuse argues that the development of modern society has obliterated our metal faculties. The goods and services that people buy control their needs and petrify their faculties. We are satisfied by the provision of material goods, but we do not realise that our desires and needs have been shaped for us and that we have lost our critical and reflexive understanding.

> The ideology of today lies in that production and consumption reproduce and justify domination. . . . The individual pays by sacrificing his time, his consciousness, his dreams; civilisation pays by sacrificing its own promises of liberty, justice and peace for all. (Marcuse 1969: 80)

Individuals also pay through a repression of their instincts. Society's domination of nature becomes 'internalised' so that it becomes domination over our own nature. Marcuse develops his critique of instrumental reason in the direction of psychology, sexuality and repression. In his social-psychoanalytic work *Eros and Civilisation* he writes that: 'Even at the beginning of Western civilisation, long before this principle was institutionalised, reason was defined as an instrument of constraint, of instinctual suppression; the domain of the instincts, sensuousness, was considered eternally hostile and detrimental to reason' (Marcuse 1969: 132). Whereas Marxism emphasises the alienation of labour, Marcuse is now concerned with the repression of our erotic and aesthetic needs and impulses.

Drawing on Freud, it is argued that human history is the history of repression. Culture constrains our societal and biological existence and controls our instincts. History becomes that of the denial of pleasure and civilised morality is the morality of repressed instincts. Marcuse sees this in terms of the transformation of the pleasure principle into the reality principle which is based on renunciation and restraint. The main function of the ego is to control the instinctual impulses of the id, it is the mediator between the id and the external world and it acts to minimise conflicts with reality. The conflict between the ego and id indicates the contradiction between the individual and society and the struggle against or conformity with repressive forces and objective reason. Thus, the reality principle sustains the organism in the external world through imposing constraint. However, the reality principle is not purely a psychological process. It is embodied in social institutions and has to be reproduced in social life. The dominance of the reality principle over the pleasure principle is never complete and has to be socially secured (Marcuse 1969: 32). In this sense civilisation can still be seen as organised and institutionalised domination. Subjection brings with it certain rewards: 'What started as subjection by force soon became "voluntary servitude," collaboration in reproducing a society which made servitude increasingly rewarding and palatable' (Marcuse 1969: 12).

Like Adorno and Horkheimer, Marcuse argues that the working class has been so integrated into capitalist society that it no longer has a revolutionary potential. Instead, 'An overriding interest in the preservation of the institutional status quo unites the former antagonists in the most advanced areas of contemporary society' (Marcuse 1966: xii–xiii). The working class as conceived by Marx is no longer the majority of the population and it no longer seeks to change the system. It sees its interests as within the system and it has neither the consciousness nor the need for a revolution. It may be a class 'in itself' but not 'for itself'. In any case, the new majority within society are the specialists, technicians and white-collar workers who are a product of the development of the state, political domination and the bureaucratisation of society. Late industrial society increases the number of parasitic and alienated functionaries who lack any sense of social solidarity or class consciousness.

However, Marcuse does maintain hope of revolutionary change. Revolutionary agents are not defined according to economic conditions, but according to political forms of oppression. In the totally integrated society they are those on the margins. They are the outsiders and outcasts, the underprivileged and the intellectuals, all those who carry with them an extra awareness, who have not been totally integrated into society. Marcuse is particularly interested in the student movement, the black movement, third world liberation struggles, the hippies and those engaged in moral and sexual rebellion. These groups, he believes, are concerned with more than just narrow economic or political issues, their outlook is concerned with the system as a whole. The traditional working class is part of the passive majority which needs to be rescued by this active minority who act as potential catalysts of rebellion.

Habermas's Early Work

Jürgen Habermas is the foremost theorist of the second generation of Frankfurt theorists. He is also a theorist trying to overcome the pessimism of his predecessors. One issue he raises early on in his work is that of instrumental reason. In his early work *Knowledge and Human Interests*, Habermas argues that Marx tends to reduce the reproduction of the human species to the realm of labour and instrumental action. Consequently, the Marxist tradition has inherited a restricted notion of philosophical self-reflection seen through the activities of labour and production – something that in turn shapes early critical theory's focus on instrumental reason. Habermas argues that we need to move away from Marxism's production paradigm and look at such things as symbolic interaction and the role of cultural tradition (Habermas 1978: 54). Symbolic interaction exists between societal subjects who reciprocally know and recognise each other. Habermas draws on hermeneutic philosophy to argue for the intersubjectivity of action-oriented mutual understanding. A corresponding notion of human interests represents our basic orientations rooted in the conditions of the reproduction and self-constitution of the human species (Habermas 1978: 196).

Knowledge and Human Interests asks how reliable knowledge is possible. Habermas attempts to answer this by relating the foundations of knowledge to three basic interests of the human species. The three types of knowledge constitutive interests are: (1) *technical* interest grounded in material needs and labour, control of the environment, and empirical analytical science; (2) *practical* interest based on the mutual communicative understanding between individuals and social groups grounded in the species-universal character of knowledge (historical-hermeneutic knowledge); and (3) *emancipatory* interest grounded in our desire to overcome the distorted actions and utterances that result from the exercise of power.

However, Habermas wants to get away from instrumental rationality by showing the universal basis for human rationality and in a self-criticism he argues that his theory of reflection has been limited to the human subject. In his later work, he moves away from trying to ground critical theory in a theory of knowledge and shifts attention from human consciousness to a theory of communicative action. Here the aim is not to disclose some sort of correct consciousness or reliable knowledge, but to examine the structures of mutual understanding. This places much more emphasis on the role of consensus formation within society and shifts focus from the subjective to inter-subjective relations between people.

Habermas looks at how consensus is formed in the public sphere. As power shifted from the aristocracy to the new bourgeoisie, eighteenth century Europe saw the growth of public participation in political life, a widening concept of citizenship, increasing demands for representative government and constitutional and legal freedoms. Accompanying this was the development of new social, cultural and political discourses and new bodies like literary societies, cafes, public lectures, journals and newspapers. This was a particular phase in history when private individuals became increasingly concerned with the government of society. The new bourgeoisie saw itself as the reasoning public, as those charged with fighting absolutism and defending the public interest. Such contestation threw up new legitimating ideologies and universalistic doctrines.

However, as capitalism develops so the classical liberal public sphere declines as the market undermines the legitimacy of its institutions and erodes its independence. The independence of the public sphere is lost when private institutions increasingly assume public power, and when the state begins to penetrate the public realm. State and civil society become increasingly entwined and the distinction between public and private realms becomes blurred: 'this dialectic of a progressive "societalisation" of the state simultaneously with an increasing "statification" of society gradually destroyed the basis of the bourgeois public sphere – the separation of state and society' (Habermas 1989: 142). This transformation takes place due to the development of electronic mass media, advertising, the entertainment industry, the growth of information and bureaucratic centralisation. Two crosscutting processes occur – the communicative generation of legitimate power and the manipulative deployment of media power to promote mass loyalty, consumer demand and compliance with systemic imperatives.

Habermas looks at how the state comes to intervene in the public sphere and also how it intervenes into the economic sphere to safeguard capital accumulation. In this way, the state aims to control the tendencies towards economic crisis through increased intervention and regulation. The state plays the leading role in the maintenance of the cohesion of the socio-economic system. However, closer relation also means that the crisis of the economy may be transferred to other spheres of social and political life. Because the economic system is no longer independent of the state, any manifestations of economic crisis become a social issue affecting a range of different spheres. This means a transformation and displacement of inherent contradictions in one part of the system onto another. The measures taken by the state to avoid economic crisis may precipitate a crisis of rationality and legitimacy in the political and socio-cultural system. Habermas calls this potential problem a *legitimation crisis* which can only be contained for as long as economic growth is achieved.

The problem faced is that 'the state apparatus must fulfil its tasks in the economic system under the limiting condition that mass loyalty be simultaneously secured within the framework of a formal democracy and in accord with ruling universalistic value systems' (Habermas 1988: 58). As well as the possibility that economic crisis may be shifted onto the political system, there is also a problematic relation between the state and the private sphere. The increasing intervention of the state into the private realm may alter patterns of motivation formation, and lead to a motivation crisis. This may be linked to the process of rationalisation and the loss meaning in social life.

Crises come from what Habermas calls unresolved steering problems. Threats towards legitimacy can be averted if the state can credibly present itself to the public – for example, as a social welfare state – and intercept the dysfunctional side-effects of the economic process. But if it cannot do this then manifestations of disequilibrium are unavoidable and a steering crisis emerges whereby the credibility of the state is called into question. The state may act as a factor of social cohesion, but if a crisis in the economic sphere undermines this role, then a crisis of legitimacy develops and spreads across a range of political, cultural, public and private domains.

Communication

Habermas believes that Marx reduces social life to instrumental action by focusing on the economic sphere and thereby ignoring the processes of communicative interaction. It is in this latter sphere that Habermas believes we can retrieve more progressive and emancipatory theories of modernity and rationality. The process of reaching understanding occurs through communicative interaction and our ability to communicate has a universal basis. This process is dialogical and mutual, based on discussion, negotiation and agreement. Habermas invokes the notion of an ideal speech situation in which a rationally motivated consensus or agreement is achieved. The ideal speech situation presupposes rationality, justice and freedom and therefore acts as a measure against which historical forms of communicative distortion can be understood. Discursive communication implies consensual rationality and, in order for communication to be possible at all, these communicative forms of reason are necessarily prior to any instrumental or strategic ones. In other words, communicative rationality is a necessary condition for meaningful social life.

What is made explicit in our communicative action is our shared, historically structured lifeworld. It represents a set of background resources that make human interaction and communication meaningful:

> it both forms a *context* and furnishes *resources* for the process of mutual understanding. The lifeworld forms a horizon and at the same time offers a store of things

taken for granted in the given culture from which communicative participants draw consensual interpretive patterns in their efforts at interpretation. The solidarities of groups integrated by values and the competences of socialised individuals belong, as do culturally ingrained background assumptions, to the components of the life-world. (Habermas 1987b: 298)

Habermas replaces the Marxist notion of base and superstructure with the system–lifeworld distinction. Instead of a model of economic base and cultural, political and ideological superstructure, we have a model based on systemic functioning and communicative interaction. This emphasises the fact that societies reproduce themselves both materially and symbolically. If Marx's error is said to be his overemphasis on the productive paradigm of labour, then Habermas makes the distinction between labour and interaction so that labour belongs to the system and is purposive-rational, instrumental and strategic, while interaction belongs to the lifeworld and involves communicative action, consensual norms and mutual understanding. The system requires the integration of diverse activities in accordance with adaptive goals of the market economy and the political – administrative system. The problem is that systemic integration needs to be institutionalised and anchored in the lifeworld, requiring laws and institutions. The danger here is that of the system overextending itself so that the lifeworld is subject to colonisation by economy and state, power and bureaucracy. The dominance of instrumental reason is indicative of this process of colonisation.

So the theme of legitimation crisis is now developed within a new framework of system – lifeworld disjuncture. The legitimation crisis is now represented by the colonisation of the lifeworld by the system, and in particular, colonisation by the steering media of power and money. It may be that citizens are rewarded with a more efficient market that provides consumer affluence and a more developed and co-ordinated state system that is able to provide such things as education and welfare. But the price to be paid is a loss of individual autonomy and a lack of genuine social consensus. As the system is uncoupled from the lifeworld, spheres of action are taken over by power and money and are no longer integrated into the process of mutual understanding and consensus formation. The problem of modern capitalism is the selective process of rationalisation and the technical and instrumental use of reason. But, versus the pessimism of Weber and the early Frankfurt School members, Habermas argues that this particular development of rationalisation is only one of a number of possibilities. The colonisation of the lifeworld represents the domination and control by instrumental rather than communicative rationality. The problem is not rationality generally, but the domination of technical rationality over communicative rationality. Habermas seeks to return to inter-human relations to find an optimistic solution to the problem of modernity.

For Habermas, rationalisation has a positive aspect in that it rids society of dogma, mysticism and religion and opens up the possibility of critical debate and discussion. It also requires political power to be legitimated and provides the basis for rational consensus. Habermas optimistically believes that there is an inherent human interest in emancipation. His focus shifts from the sphere of production to the lifeworld. He looks to such activities as democratic debate, protest, civil rights campaigning, identity politics, lifestyle politics and any activities that show resistance to the colonisation of the lifeworld. His aim is not to overthrow the system but to safeguard it and to protect the public spheres of communication and identity. In keeping with this perspective, Habermas, like other critical theorists, looks not to any one privileged agent, but to many diverse actors. Habermas's focus is not on the economy but on culture, the aesthetic, the psychological and the lifeworld. Marx's ideal of a free society of producers is replaced with the idea of a fully rationalised life-world. In his latest work he conceives of this taking shape on a global scale through the spread of cosmopolitan democracy (a conception going back to Kant) and global civil society. Others writing about international relations like Linklater and Held have drawn on these ideas to deal with questions of global justice and international society.

Conclusion

Whereas Marx tends to see history and society in terms of the mode of production, Adorno and Horkheimer focus on the cultural and political sphere while Habermas shifts attention to forms of language and communication. Habermas's aim is to examine the structures of mutual understanding derived from our inter-subjective activities. We can see how Marx's focus on production shifts to structures of power and domination and then again to structures of communication and agreement. Habermas's work has moved a long way from Marx's focus on class conflict and its main emphasis is on the role of consensus formation within society.

This may be a more optimistic project, but does it work? Big questions remain about the viability of Habermas's theory. His is an attempt to provide a normative foundation for critical theory based on open and equal discussion and consensus. But maybe Habermas's account contains too much consensus. As Rick Roderick notes, the process of reaching mutual understanding is given so much emphasis that misunderstanding is somehow derivative; there is an assumption that understanding is prior to misunderstanding (Roderick 1986: 159). Against correspondence theory which argues that truth is based on the relation between subjective knowledge and the real object, Habermas advocates a consensus theory of truth where truth derives from inter-subjective agreement within communities. But how do we test validity claims, how do we choose theories, how is agreement reached?

The focus on normative foundations leads to a more harmonious account of capitalist social relations that underplays the problems of state and economy. Because these normative foundations are seen as transcendental and universal rather than historical and specific, Habermas's theory of social consensus turns us away from an analysis of concrete social and political forms. Instead of engaging in concrete historical analysis, Habermas looks for general human conditions. It is in giving this general account of human societies that Habermas's assumptions become problematic. In contrast to an approach such as Gramsci's theory of hegemony, social consensus is not seen as something that is a product of a complex historical struggle involving multiple actors with varying interests and beliefs. Habermas's account cannot adequately account for variations in consciousness or interest. His transcendental approach overemphasises rationality and there is an absence of the sensuous or non-rational. Because his theory is inter-subjective, no account is given of how social agents interact with objective social structures. In short, Habermas's evolutionary account of human communicative capacity is transcendental at the expense of being historical.

Tom Bottomore argues that the Frankfurt School became preoccupied with immediate developments without putting them into historical context. They were thus preoccupied with National Socialism and anti-Semitism in the 1930s and 1940s, the culture industry in the 1950s and, in Marcuse's case, the social movements of the 1960s (Bottomore 1984: 72). He complains that the Frankfurt school did not attempt to engage with Marx's theory of history and that they largely ignored Marx's economic analysis (Bottomore 1984: 73). With Habermas this goes a stage further with focus shifted from mode of production and social structure to forms of communication and normative rules. Historical conditions have been replaced by universal conditions for speech acts. It is therefore very debatable as to whether late critical theory can really be considered to be Marxism at all.

Further Reading

The best known work of Adorno and Horkheimer is *Dialectic of Enlightenment* (1986). The chapter on the culture industry is the most readable. The chapter 'The Concept of Enlightenment' is also important. A collection of Adorno's work has been published as *The Culture Industry* (1991). A collection of Horkheimer's work *Critical Theory: Selected Essays* (1972) is more methodological. His essay 'Critical and Traditional Theory' should definitely be read. Compared to Adorno and Horkheimer, Marcuse's work is more readable. Recommended books are *One-Dimensional Man* (2002) and *Eros and Civilisation* (1969). Habermas's books can be a bit of a struggle due to the technical language. *The Philosophical Discourse of Modernity* (1987b) is probably the best place to start. *Legimtimation Crisis* (1988) is short but not easy. David Held's book (1980) is the best introduction to critical theory, but does not cover the later Habermas. Outhwaite's book on Habermas (1994) is good. Alan How's book *Critical Theory* in this Palgrave series is an excellent new introduction to this school. For an application of these ideas to international relations see Linklater's *The Transformation of Political Community* (1997).

7

Applications

Introduction

Having looked at different schools of Marxism, this chapter looks at various debates within Marxism and some areas that have presented particular challenges to a Marxist analysis. Marxism has contributed to such a wide range of social theories that we have to be very selective in terms of coverage. Four areas of particular importance, but also difficulty, have been chosen. Many other areas could have been chosen instead of these ones. Even within the different fields, the discussion is not meant to be comprehensive. The aim here is to give a taste of some of the historical and contemporary debates around issues of particular complexity. Writings on feminism and nationalism are interesting as they cover areas that are potentially in conflict with Marxism. They also produce social movements that have their own distinct agendas. Feminism raises questions about how to fit gender exploitation together with a class-based analysis. Similar questions emerge in relation to nationalism. How should national movements be understood in relation to socialist movements? These issues continue to prove very problematic for socialist theory and practice.

The chapter then goes on to consider the Marxist understanding of history. This has also produced a large amount of disagreement. Some approaches see history in terms of the development of the productive forces while others emphasise the interaction between different economic, political and cultural forces and, crucially, social classes. This section also looks at the debates concerning the nature of the English Civil War as well as attempts to explain history through a Gramscian approach. We then look at how Gramsci's ideas have also been applied to economic theory through debates over Fordist production and forms of economic regulation. The work of the regulation school has been effective in providing social theory with a non-reductionist account of economic processes. Through the work of Bob Jessop, this is applied to British conditions. This section ends by looking at Jessop's debate with Stuart Hall over the nature of Thatcherism.

We conclude with some general comments on Marxist social theory and its application. Through these debates we can see how applying Marxist theory to social issues raises the question of how much weight to give to economic

factors and how to understand these factors in relation to social, cultural and
political processes. The regulation approach indicates how this might be done
without losing Marxism's distinctive focus on the role of production.

Marxism and Feminism

Marxism defines relations of exploitation as they occur at the point of
production. It shows society to be divided according to social class. But what
about other forms of oppression such as those based on race / ethnicity, sexual
orientation or gender? Are such forms of exploitation dependent on relations
of production, or is there some other basis to these forms of oppression? Such
a question is fundamental to the relation between Marxist and feminist
approaches.

Essentially the relationship between Marxism and feminism depends on how
we conceive of the system of production and the system of patriarchy. Heidi
Hartmann gives a Marxist–feminist definition of patriarchy as a set of social
relations that have a material base in men's control over women's labour
power. This includes women's exclusion from productive resources and the
restricting of their sexuality. Patriarchy has a hierarchical nature which
establishes an interdependence and solidarity among men that allows them to
dominate women (1981: 14–15).

We might simplify the problematic relationship between Marxism and feminism to the following three positions:

1. the exploitation of women is independent of the capitalist system.
    Patriarchy goes back a long way
2. the exploitation of women is entirely bound up with capitalist production.
    The struggle for women's liberation is the same as the struggle against
    capitalism
3. the exploitation of women is not reducible to capitalism but it takes a
    particular social and historical form under capitalist society.

The following will largely explore this last position.

Classical Writings

Marx and Engels briefly discuss the issue of the family in the *Communist
Manifesto* where it is rather glibly argued that the bourgeois family will disappear once private property is abolished (Marx and Engels 1973: 83). From the
classical writings it is Engels rather than Marx who has most to say about
the role of the family and the exploitation of women. His book, *The Origin of
the Family, Private Property and the State*, despite flaws, has been hugely

influential. Under the influence of the anthropologist L.H. Morgan, Engels analyses the subordination of women from the point of view of a general history of social development. He looks at how the family has developed in relation to private property and how societies shifted from the matriarchal to the patriarchal: 'The overthrow of mother right was the *world historical defeat of the female sex*' (Engels 1978: 65). Engels goes on to argue that monogamous marriage cements the subjugation of one sex by another and as a result, the bourgeois family is based on a fundamental inequality between husband and wife. Household management has lost its public character and the division of labour within the family is such that the 'modern individual family is founded on the open or concealed domestic slavery of women' so that 'within the family he is the bourgeois and the wife represents the proletariat' (Engels 1978: 85). The liberation of women from this situation requires the abolition of the monogamous family as the economic unit of society and the bringing of women back into public industry (Engels 1978: 86). The emancipation of women is impossible 'so long as the woman is shut out from social productive labour and restricted to private domestic labour' (Engels 1978: 195). The answer to this problem is therefore strongly bound up with the production process so that

> With the transfer of the means of production into common ownership, the monogamous family ceases to be the economic unit of society. Private housekeeping is transformed into a social industry. The care and education of the children becomes a public affair. (Engels 1978: 87–88)

Clearly this view is open to the accusation of being economistic. It underestimates the ideological factors that must be overcome if women are to gain equality. For Engels, social divisions can be overcome if women can be drawn into the labour process. Hartmann argues that Engels never really questions how and why women are oppressed as women (Hartmann 1981: 5). It is ironic then to note that Marx and Engels write in the *Communist Manifesto* that 'the bourgeois sees in his wife a mere instrument of production' (Marx and Engels 1973: 84), yet it might be said that they themselves hold an instrumental viewpoint. As Lise Vogel suggests, such statements tend to reflect the fact that Marx and Engels hold a rather passive conception of women as slaves in need of liberation (Vogel 1983: 61).

During the period of the Second International, August Bebel's book *Woman Under Socialism* developed a strong reputation. Much more Utopian than the work of Marx and Engels, it presents a clear view of a future socialist society based on the socialisation of education, health care and domestic labour. However, such plans for the reorganisation of society were not simply a matter for the future, but were bound up with the emerging debates around reform or revolution. As the reformist trend in social democracy was developing, so questions about women's rights were being posed. Interestingly, the leading women within the movement tend to be on the revolutionary wing. Some, like Rosa Luxemburg were not especially interested in the women's question, taking the rather economistic view that the struggle for socialism would resolve this. Others like Clara Zetkin and Alexandra Kollontai were concerned with the class basis of the 'woman question'. Zetkin follows Engels in arguing the class basis of women's oppression, but she is more specific in examining the form this takes under capitalism and how different classes and social groups are affected. Generally, bourgeois women want equality with bourgeois men and for the right to earn her own living and have her independence. By contrast, the working class woman is already a member of the workforce, but she suffers the double burden of being a wage-labourer and a domestic worker:

> Therefore the liberation struggle of the proletarian woman cannot be similar to the struggle that the bourgeois woman wages against the male of her class. On the contrary, it must be a joint struggle with the male of her class against the entire class of capitalists. She does not need to fight against the men of her class in order to tear down the barriers which have been raised against her participation in the free competition of the market place . . . Her final aim is not the free competition with the man, but the achievement of the political rule of the proletariat. (Zetkin 1984)

Like Lenin, Zetkin emphasised the importance of carrying out work among women on the basis that: 'We must not conduct special women's propaganda, but Socialist agitation among women' (Zetkin 1984). What Zetkin and Lenin are arguing for is not so much a feminist movement as a communist women's movement.

In Russia Lenin wrote a number of articles on the emancipation of women (Lenin 1965) but the more creative contribution comes from Kollontai. She argues the need to consider the social conditions of the day when considering the role and status of women. Any natural qualities are secondary to this. For women to be free, a new organisation of social and productive lives is necessary. However, this need for fundamental change does not mean that the struggle for reforms in the here and now is not important (Kollontai 1977: 58). In the debates over reform or revolution, Kollontai, like Zetkin, is clearly on the side of revolution, but both recognise that the struggle for reforms cannot wait for some future socialist society. This consideration influences Kollontai's position on bourgeois feminism where she draws a distinction between the demands of feminists and the demands of working class women. She argues that feminists seek equality within the framework of existing society (Kollontai 1977: 59). Therefore Kollontai is sceptical of alliances between the woman worker and the bourgeois feminist. But at the same time, she admits that: 'Customs and traditions persecute the young mother whatever the stratum of the population to which she belongs' (Kollontai 1977: 65). Kollontai's position on feminism might be summarised as distrust but not necessarily opposition.

Kollontai argues that 'the form of marriage and of the family is thus determined by the economic system of the given epoch, and it changes as the economic base of society changes' (Kollontai 1977: 223). If this sounds familiar to the claims of Engels, then she also goes on to suggest something akin to the withering away of the state so that if

> the family loses its significance as an economic unit . . . the material and economic considerations in which the family was grounded cease to exist . . . Once the family has been stripped of its economic functions and its responsibilities towards the younger generation and is no longer central to the existence of the woman, it has ceased to be a family. The family unit shrinks to a union of two people based on mutual agreement. (Kollontai 1977: 226)

She goes on to specify how such relationships must be based on complete freedom, equality and genuine friendship. Many of Kollontai's views were considered too radical even by the Bolsheviks. Despite criticising the bourgeoisie for its individualistic code of sexual morality and propriety, Kollontai herself was condemned for representing bourgeois decadence. Nevertheless, the Bolsheviks did initially establish political and legal rights for women including divorce rights, secular marriage, free abortion, property rights and the abolition of illegitimacy. But the material conditions to support these reforms were not present in Russia and these rights were withdrawn by the Stalinist bureaucracy who needed the family unit to reinforce the state.

Marxist Feminism

We can see from these various issues that the family and household are central to understanding the gender division of social production. The family is regarded as the main site of women's oppression and the subordination of women is essential to its maintenance. The family must be conceived of as an economic institution that in effect represents the privatisation of the domestic sphere. Debates between Marxist feminists started to examine how capitalism defines the spheres of public and private, or of wage-labour and domestic forms of work. What became known as the domestic labour debate sought to understand women's work in the home while relating this to women's oppression under capitalism. Previous writings such as Engels' tended to deal with the exploitation of women in relation to their position in the labour market. Indeed there is much to say here in terms of forms of discrimination against women in the workplace, the restrictions of part time, temporary or low paid work, women's lack of union rights and so on. However, the domestic labour debate sought to extend the concept of labour to deal with domestic work.

According to Heidi Hartmann (1981), domestic labour is that portion of necessary labour performed outside the sphere of capitalist production.

Because of high costs the domestic burden falls on the private sphere of unpaid labour within the household. The domestic labour position stresses the importance of unpaid work in supporting the wage-labour economy. This raises the Marxist question of the value of domestic labour. It is argued that domestic labour does not directly produce surplus value, but it does produce use values within the home. This in turn contributes to the reproduction of labour power, which in turn is the source of surplus value under capitalism.

This position has been described as a dual systems theory insofar as women's oppression is regarded as an effect of both capitalism and patriarchy. Other feminists like Iris Young have challenged this by arguing that the two should be combined into a 'gender division of labour' to show that capitalism itself is *essentially* patriarchal. In other words, women's oppression is based, not on patriarchy *and* capitalism, but on patriarchal capitalism. This avoids the danger of regarding women's oppression as something somehow separate or distinct from capitalism, a view which may lead to a segregation of women's issues (Young 1981: 64).

Alternatively, other feminists like Shulamith Firestone and Kate Millet emphasise the specificity of women's oppression in more radical feminist terms. Millett gives primacy to male domination as a form of explanation while Firestone credits Engels with having realised that the fundamental division between men and women goes back in history and is based on fundamental biological differences. She argues that women form a class for biological reasons (Firestone 1970: 4–5). By contrast, Juliet Mitchell in *Woman's Estate* argues against focussing on women's physical weakness complaining that the problem is often reduced to the question of women's capacity to work. The traditional view is that because women are excluded from socially productive work, emancipation requires woman's reintroduction into the public sphere of work. Mitchell complains that even in Simone de Beauvoir there is a primary emphasis on economic subordination, particularly in relation to private property. Rather than reducing oppression to a particular structure, Mitchell argues that we have to see the various elements within this process – in particular, the combination of production, reproduction, sexuality and socialisation (Mitchell 1971: 100–01).

These issues are also explored by Michele Barrett in arguing that Marxist feminism should look at the connections between gender relations and processes of production and reproduction 'to explore the relations between the organization of sexuality, domestic production, the household and so on, and historical changes in the mode of production and systems of appropriation and exploitation' (Barrett 1988: 9). She argues that we cannot just understand women's oppression from the point of view of its functionality for capitalism – that is, the reproduction of labour power through domestic labour and the provision of a cheap and flexible reserve army of labour (Barrett 1988: 248). Gender divisions precede the development of capitalism, however, it is also true that gender is a social and historical construct. Barrett looks at the work of Althusser as a way of placing emphasis on the production of ideology in the family sphere. As capitalism has developed, the issue is how the family has been perpetuated. The family produces an ideology that naturalises domestic relations and identities. Women are defined as mothers and housewives. The family also acts to legitimate hierarchy and authority relations. More recent work, influenced by post-structuralism (e.g. Butler 1990), looks at the construction of female subjectivity and replaces the concept of ideology with that of discourse.

Conclusion

What do these debates reveal? Maybe that Marxism can help in showing the relation between ideas, identities and real material conditions and in linking oppression to class society. Problems with the Marxist approach stem from reductionism and economism. The question that inevitably follows is therefore, how necessary is women's oppression to capitalism? It might be argued that capitalism need not be intrinsically racist. Need it be intrinsically sexist? It might be argued that the problem of women's oppression is more fundamental insofar as it is related to the division of labour. Given this division of labour, we have to ask, to what extent do *all* men benefit from the oppression of women? This raises questions about how to organise against oppression. Does it require an autonomous women's movement? At the same time, there is a danger of putting all women together into one movement. Just as Marxism may make the economistic error of seeing a homogeneous working class, so it would be wrong to see gender in these terms. What should women do? Clearly they should not wait for the revolution, but should fight for reforms that benefit women in the here and now – childcare, abortion rights, employment rights and so on. All women, not just working class women, are affected by such basic issues. But then again, we are back at the issue of whether struggles against women's oppression are related to struggles against capitalism.

Marxism, Nationalism and the National Question

Marxism does not have any clear theory of nationalism, yet the many pages of arguments testify to the fact that the national question is a particularly important issue for Marxism. This is especially so insofar as Marxism is a political movement and needs to intervene into struggles and deal with the most important issues facing the working class and oppressed peoples. Because of this, and the fact that there is little by way of an established theory, writings on the national question are often contradictory, dictated by particular historical or political circumstances. They are also, in the classical Marxist period, rather polemical, indicating how a particular position on the national question is related to the need to take a line or to pass a resolution or thesis. These writings on the national question – by the likes of Marx, Engels, Lenin, Luxemburg and Stalin – are very interesting. However, they have to be seen in the context of particular debates. Since the triumph of Stalin, what was written in the classics has been turned into orthodoxy to be applied in all circumstances. After examining classical Marxism, this section looks at how the contemporary writers Tom Nairn and Benedict Anderson have sought to reinterpret the issue of nationalism.

Marx and Engels

For Marx and Engels, the national question is inextricably linked to the issue of social and economic development. Reading the *Communist Manifesto* it would seem that the workers have no country and hence no national question. Yet, it is also suggested that the workers must help the bourgeoisie overthrow feudalism. Therefore workers should support national movements insofar as this helps further bourgeois revolution. The working class should put itself at the head of this struggle without, however, adopting *bourgeois* nationalism. As the *Manifesto* says:

> The working men have no country. We cannot take from them what they have not got. Since the proletariat must first of all acquire political supremacy, must rise to be the leading class of the nation, must constitute itself as the nation, it is, so far, itself national, though not in the bourgeois sense of the word. (Marx and Engels 1973: 84)

For Marx and Engels the working class must first unite and consolidate its forces at the national level, moving beyond localised struggles in order to become the leading political class. However, if this means that the working class must form itself into a national class, it does not mean that the working class should become nationalists for victory for the working class at the national level will put an end to national conflict at the international level and end all national divisions: 'In proportion as the antagonism between classes within the nation vanishes, the hostility of one nation to another will come to an end' (Marx and Engels 1973: 85). National oppression has to be got rid of before internationalism is possible, but the *Manifesto* claims that already:

> National differences, and antagonisms between peoples, are daily more and more vanishing, owing to the development of the bourgeoisie, to freedom of commerce, to the world market, to uniformity in the mode of production and the conditions of life corresponding thereto. (Marx and Engels 1973: 85)

Ironically then, supporting national movements furthers this progress and strengthens those factors that will do away with national differences. More problematic is that in one place Marx and Engels are suggesting that the class struggle will overcome national divisions, while the latter, more economically deterministic quotation suggests that the development of capitalism and the growth of the bourgeoisie is already doing this.

Marx and Engels might be accused of displaying too much faith in historical development and the civilising, progressive role of capitalist development. The quote from the *Manifesto* also shows the danger of an evolutionary paradigm that renders the national question of secondary importance. Economic development is seen as primary with the national question, like politics and ideology, confined to secondary, superstructural status. National movements are then assessed, not in their own right, but in relation to their contribution to capitalist development. The national question is reduced to the matter of whether the national bourgeoisie can play a progressive role with the development of capitalism taking precedence over national considerations.

Rather than looking at issues like language and common culture, it is economic development and homogeneity that constitutes a nation for Marx and Engels. For this reason we find them strongly supporting German unification as the continuation of a progressive bourgeois revolution. Critics might suggest that in doing so they accommodate to German nationalism. More worrying is that Marx and Engels take up Hegel's derogatory concept of non-historic peoples to describe smaller nations. In contrast to the Germans, smaller nations like the Czechs and South Slavs (Serbs and Croats) are 'peoples which never had a history of their own . . . [they are] not viable and will never be able to achieve any kind of independence' (Marx and Engels 1975: 367). Engels declares them to be 'non-historic', non-progressive, and unsupportable. According to Marx and Engels' earlier work, the national movements of the Czechs and South Slavs lacked any liberatory or revolutionary significance. These were the struggles of non-historic peoples who had never formed a state and cannot be expected to do so in the future. But the position of Marx and Engels on national self-determination was affected by the big power politics of the time. National movements are seen as a progressive force when advancing the bourgeois revolution against feudalism and patriarchalism. The South Slavs were not supported in 1848 against the Hapsburgs but were later supported against the Russians and Ottomans. The issue for Marx and Engels is whether a national movement can play a progressive role in advancing the condition of society.

In fact we can find a more positive view of national struggles in the later writings on Poland and Ireland. Ireland's forced union with England perhaps provides the clearest sense of the interaction between the national and social question. Ireland's domination by England provided a reserve army of labour for the industrial revolution. Marx and Engels write that the Irish need self-governance and independence, protective tariffs against England and an agrarian revolution. It is also claimed that as soon as the agrarian bourgeois-democratic revolution breaks, a social revolution will break out in Ireland

(Marx and Engels 1971: 162). It is also suggested that Ireland's connection with England has a negative effect in acting as England's weak spot. The Irish struggle disrupts the British workers' movement and it is in the interests of the English working class to get rid of the connection with Ireland. Otherwise, the repression of that nation will itself be transplanted to the dominant nation. This helps explain the statement that: 'Any nation that oppresses another forges its own chains' (Marx and Engels 1971: 163).

To summarise the position of Marx and Engels, the national question is linked to the bourgeois revolution. These bourgeois–national revolutions are seen as the stage preceding that of socialist transformation. Such struggles are progressive insofar as they advance this cause, but are not progressive in themselves. However, because Marx and Engels maintain a preference for larger states as representing a more advanced and viable economic entity, it is possible to suggest that workers have an interest in nationalist projects for unity, something that would be taken up by the revisionists in the Second International.

The National Question in Classical Marxism

Marx and Engels claimed that the workers had no country, yet they supported the national struggle for German unity. The German Social Democrats claimed to be internationalists yet by the time of the First World War they were supporting expansionist German imperialism. The unification of Germany and development of the German nation-state led to the belief among the social democrats and the German trade unions in particular, that they had an interest in the national cause if it meant improving the conditions of the German working class. The *Manifesto* had claimed that workers do not have a stake in the bourgeois nation-state, but clearly they did. The German workers had a real material interest in supporting the German nation. Nationalism had become a way of life.

Karl Kautsky, the main theorist of the Second International and a collaborator with Engels, took a pragmatic line on the national question. The question had to be considered in relation to the configuration of the large multi-ethnic empires. But as long as the question was treated pragmatically, Marxists were unable to come up with a theory. As Munck says 'Nationalism as a concept was not an issue for Marxism; the issue was a multitude of individual national struggles' (Munck 1986: 33). The Austrian Marxist Otto Bauer made a stronger contribution to theorising the national question. For him the nation is a totality of people bound by a common destiny. The character of a nation derives from its history and he describes this nation as a 'community of fate' (Munck 1986: 39). This is a more ideological conception of the national question, however, for most writers of this period an economistic focus remains the dominant feature. Rosa Luxemburg's stance, for example, is usually singled out as a case of economistic thinking. Within Poland a fierce dispute broke out between the Polish Socialist Party which supported Polish independence as the most pressing issue and Luxemburg's Social Democratic Party of Poland which saw the national question as a distraction from the class struggle. Luxemburg was opposed to the self-determination of Poland which she believed would only lead to the domination of the reactionary bourgeoisie and landowners. Poland was for her an unviable state and such states should be opposed in favour of larger economic units.

Luxemburg tended to see the national struggle as weakening the struggle of the working class. Of course national rights might be supported but only as one might support any liberal right. Since only socialist revolution can guarantee such rights the working class and oppressed minorities should make common cause in overthrowing capitalism. Only socialism can resolve these questions, consequently the national question is a secondary historical issue. Luxemburg argued that with the development of imperialism, the era of the nation-state was in fact being left behind and any talk of national unity was dangerous.

Lenin took a rather different line. For him, national struggles could be aimed against imperialism and this issue led him to make the important distinction between oppressor and oppressed nations and consequently to distinguish between the nationalism of the oppressor and that of the oppressed (Lenin 1964b: 409).

Like Marx, Engels and Luxemburg, Lenin was generally in favour of the larger state entity since this provides the best conditions for economic development. However, Lenin's analysis of capitalist development had led him to conclude that imperialism was its 'highest stage' and that consequently the task was not so much to help capitalism develop further as to overthrow it. In the age of imperialism, the struggle of nations against their oppression by others can be used to attack the position of the national bourgeoisie. The national struggle offers opportunities for social struggle, particularly in a country like Russia which is a 'prison of peoples'. In such multi-national states and empires, the class struggle and the tasks of national democratic revolution are combined in that only the revolutionary working class can see such demands through (Lenin 1964b: 151).

Consequently the Russian Social Democratic and Labour Party passed a resolution at its 1903 Congress recognising the right of nations to self-determination. The right to self-determination means right to free-secession, but although Lenin's Bolsheviks supported the right to secession, this was not necessarily what they would advocate. Rather, the stress would be on consensual union and voluntary association with the right to secede if necessary. If these democratic conditions are in place, then there should be no need to secede for, in Lenin's view, the 'closer a democratic state system is to complete freedom to secede the less frequent and less ardent will the desire for separation be in practice, because big states afford indisputable advantages . . . from the standpoint of economic progress' (Lenin 1964c: 146). Despite supporting the right to self-determination, the aim of socialism is not to divide the world into lots of smaller states, but to bring them together and integrate them. In large states socialists should support the rights of smaller national minorities, while those in small nations should argue for voluntary integration (Lenin 1964c: 347). Lenin's position on self-determination, then, was that:

> We demand freedom of self-determination, i.e., independence, i.e., freedom of secession for the oppressed nations, not because we have dreamt of splitting up the country economically, or of the ideal of small states, but, on the contrary, because we want large states and the closer unity and the even fusion of nations, only on a truly democratic, truly internationalist basis, which is *inconceivable* without the freedom to secede. (1964b: 413–14)

Lenin's position on the national question also has radical consequences for anti-colonial struggles. His theory of imperialism divides the world into the advanced capitalist countries of Western Europe and the United States, the countries of Eastern Europe and Russia, and the semi-colonial and colonial world. The position of Marx and Engels on the colonial question is that it is primarily an economic issue. They did not think of colonies as nations with a historical role. Therefore colonialism was regarded as an objectively progressive process in shaking-up the socio-economic foundations of these countries, although it may be objectionable at a moral level. By contrast, Lenin's position is that in the advanced Western countries the progressive element of the national struggle had been completed, but that the anti-colonial struggle is a progressive liberation movement against imperialism.

Thus with Lenin and the Third International, debates on the national question went beyond Europe to the colonial and semi-colonial world and the struggle for national liberation. The emergence of Stalinism and the beginning of the Cold War can actually be said to have furthered this development. After all, the national question became the main area where Stalin was taken seriously even by his political opponents. A nation, he declared, 'is an historically evolved, stable community of language, territory, economic life, and psychological make-up manifested in a community of culture' (Stalin 1954: 349). This formulation is rigid and imprecise, but it is remarkable how many non-Stalinists take it seriously. With the world divided into spheres of influence, Stalinist Communism could take a Third World orientation. This led to attempts to marry Marxist discourse with nationalist projects in Africa, Asia and Latin America. Some movements such the Cuban struggle had an independent basis. Others used Marxist or Communist rhetoric in an opportunistic way. There may be many doubts about how Marxist these movements were, but certainly they had a progressive element in carrying forward national and agrarian reforms.

More Recent Arguments

More recently the work of Tom Nairn has made a big impact on Marxist theorisation of nationalism. But to understand his position it is necessary to go back to the period of classical Marxism and look at Gramsci. Gramsci can be said to stress the national–popular component of political struggle. He links his understanding of nationalism to the concept of hegemony so that the construction of an historical bloc is expressed through and draws upon national and popular aspirations. Gramsci's stress on the importance of developing a national–popular will is clearly influenced by Machiavelli and other Italian writers, but it is also a recognition that Communists must forge a similar kind of project. This should not be regarded as an accommodation to nationalism, but is a recognition of the nation component of a struggle and the particular national–social conditions under which it takes place.

The Scottish socialist Tom Nairn applies some of Gramsci's analysis in terms of the particular historical bloc making up the British state. We later look at how, with Perry Anderson, Nairn applies this to history and politics. Here, we concentrate on the national component. As the title of Nairn's book *The Break-up of Britain* indicates, the British nation-state or historical bloc is an uneasy compromise. He looks at this in terms of the decline of the old empire and the emergence of new tensions and centres of disruptive development. It is argued that the British nation-state is unable to deal with these problems due to its archaic nature. In particular, Nairn looks at Britain's archaic national ideology, a 'great power' nationalism of a particularly conservative nature. Promoting a conservative form of national unity, this ideology of the British state is a politically inert form of nationalism (Nairn 1981: 42). It places its faith in the mystique of the system and an arcane sovereignty. It is moderate, orderly and tolerant, but is backward-looking, complacent and insular (Nairn 1981: 44). In short, it is unable to deal with the problems posed by new forms of national-hegemonic crisis generated by the transformation of Britain's imperial role.

Nairn writes that the theory of nationalism is Marxism's great historical failure (Nairn: 329). But just as he tries to explain the failure of British national ideology, so he also tries to explain the failure of Marxist theory in historical terms. Such a failure was inevitable for Marxists before Stalin were struggling to understand a process of capitalist development that had not gone far enough. This period was one of uneven development. Yet the classical Marxists believed that the world would somehow straighten out with the aid of a socialist revolution in the developed countries (1981: 355).

The key issue for Nairn is unevenness of development and it is this context that makes nationalism an interesting issue and a potential force for social change. Drawing somewhat on Ernest Gellner's idea that nationalism is linked to unevenness of modernisation and industrialisation, Nairn looks at areas that have emerged from backwardness that are on the fringe of metropolitan growth zones. He explores how they suffer from relative deprivation and are drawn into action against this. Nairn calls this a neo-nationalism and applies it to nations like Scotland (1981: 128). He sees hope in the emergence of Scottish and Welsh nationalism in the 1960s. The uneven development of the British state amplifies its problems and provides a shaky foundation for maintaining the historical bloc. Neo-nationalism, he argues, will prove to be the grave-digger of the British state and will be the principal factor in making a socially progressive revolution of some sort.

Nairn discusses cultural sub-nationalism through Gramsci's distinguish between state and civil society. In doing so, Nairn breaks from an economistic understanding of nations and gives more weight to cultural factors. This is interesting when applied to small nations like Scotland and Wales. These are not colonial or semi-colonial countries but are in fact part of an imperialist British state. Their people have benefited economically from imperialism. Yet they suffer culturally and politically. Therefore Marxism should address itself to the issue of cultural oppression even in areas, like Catalunya for example, which are economically prosperous. The issue of national and cultural rights is one that should be looked at on its own merits, not simply as part of some broader socio-economic project.

This greater cultural sensitivity leads finally to Benedict Anderson whose work fits more loosely into the Marxist category. Anderson claims that the tran-sition from religious and dynastic communities to the modern nation ushers in a fundamentally different way of apprehending the world. His work looks at the development of capitalism but also specific things like the development of print media, vernacular language and cultural institutions, creating unified fields of communication and breaking down the old elite culture. These devel-opments can be seen as a combination of cultural system and political leader-ship. The construction of national myths about the nation's past serve to legitimise the present. Ideologies are rooted in cultural practices. This leads to the description of the nation as an imagined community: 'It is *imagined* because the members of even the smallest nation will never know most of their fellow-members, meet them, or even hear of them, yet in the minds of each lives the image of their communion' (Anderson 1991: 6). This personal and cultural feel-ing of belonging is something that Marxists need to recognise and defend.

Conclusion

Marx and Engels argue that the actions of the working class will put an end to national issues. However, it might be argued that the 'internationalism' of Marxists is often based on the advanced Western countries and Eurocentric ideas of freedom, democracy, justice and equality. The early writers did sup-port the national projects of big nations. However, they were generally unsym-pathetic to the national aspirations of small nations and colonies. By contrast, Lenin believed that bourgeois nationalism has a democratic content, but he only applies this to oppressed nations struggling against an oppressor nation.

Lenin's distinction between oppressor and oppressed nations is an important development. However, it is still limited by a certain amount of economism as well as what Nairn describes as the archaic state forms of that time. In today's world it is not so straightforward to divide the world into oppressor and oppressed nations or into imperialist and semi-colonial states. More recent Marxists such as Nairn have started to recognise that nations have certain cultural and political rights irrespective of their stage of capitalist development. Tom Nairn's Scotland, for example, simply does not fit into the oppressor / oppressed schema. Rather, socialists should defend national rights and be prepared to support national movements as a matter of principle, without that necessarily meaning that in doing so they become nationalists.

Historical Debates

The last section looked at Tom Nairn's analysis of nationalism and the British state. This section examines the theory of British history developed by Nairn and Perry Anderson and the alternative approach offered by E.P. Thompson. The Nairn–Anderson / Thompson debate might be seen as a clash between structural and praxis theories of history but it is worth emphasising that both standpoints take the view that history is made by different social groups rather than abstract structures. We begin this section, however, by looking at the theory of history advanced by G.A. Cohen which does not base itself on social groups, but advocates a theory of history based on the development of the productive forces. We also examine the various attempts by Marxist historians to understand the transition from feudalism to capitalism.

Productive Forces and Class Struggle

Is history driven by the economic base and the development of the forces of production? Or is it driven by social relations and class struggle? According to one interpretation, history is about the progression of different modes of production and the different ways in which the basic economic relations of society are organised. There is good cause to link history so firmly to modes of production. Marx and Engels write in the *German Ideology* that: 'The first *historical* act of these individuals distinguishing them from animals is not that they think, but that they begin to *produce their means of subsistence*' (Marx and Engels 1965: 31n.). The first historical act is therefore the production of the means to satisfy our needs. The process of production is a necessary feature of all societies, but the way in which this productive process is organised assumes a particular historical form. But the extent to which production determines other aspects of social life is controversial and this section is concerned with Marx's claim in the 1859 Preface that: 'The mode of production in material life determines the general character of the social, political and spiritual processes of life' (Marx 1975a: 425). A counterview is that it is not so much the productive process that determines social and historical forms, but rather, that history and society are a product of class struggle. As Marx and Engels write in the *Communist Manifesto*: 'The history of all hitherto existing society is the history of class struggles' (Marx and Engels 1973: 67). History, therefore, is not about the development of the productive forces, but about real, living processes. History is not a thing in itself or a hidden hand: 'History does nothing, it possesses no immense wealth, it wages no battles. It is man, real living man who does all that' (Marx and Engels 1956: 125).

G.A. Cohen is part of what has been termed analytical Marxism, a school that attempts to use contemporary (mainly Anglo-American) philosophical methods to assess Marxist claims about society. In applying himself to Marx's theory of history, Cohen is concerned to establish a consistent basis by which Marx's theories can be applied. The basis he finds is a strong form of productive forces determinism. Therefore Cohen agrees with the 1859 Preface that it is the level of development of the productive forces that explains that society's relations of production. This in turn explains the nature of the political and ideological superstructure that arises. A particular stage in the development of the productive forces gives a particular form of commerce and consumption, family or class. Therefore, as Marx writes in the *Poverty of Philosophy*, 'the hand-mill gives you society with the feudal-lord; the steam-mill society with the industrial capitalist' (Marx 1963: 109).

Cohen advances two arguments. The first is the development thesis – that the productive forces tend to develop throughout history. The second is the primacy thesis – that the nature of the productive relations in a society is explained by the level of development of its productive forces (Cohen 1978: 134). The first is a teleological view of history that gives it a purpose or design based on the continued development of the productive forces. The second thesis leads to a functional explanation of the relations of production as existing to facilitate the development of the productive forces. Crisis emerges when productive relations act as fetters on the further development of the productive forces. But first history must run its course for, according to Marx the determinist: 'No social order is ever destroyed before all the productive forces for which it is sufficient have been developed' (Marx 1975a: 426).

Cohen maintains that it is change in the productive forces that brings about change in production relations so that 'forms of society rise and fall according as they advance and retard the development of the productive forces' (Cohen 1978: 285). He does admit that class struggle is a part of this process (ibid). But the productive forces are the real historical actors. As they outgrow the existing relations of production these relations become fetters on further development and so begins a revolutionary crisis.

A critique of this position is outlined by S.H. Rigby. Cohen assumes that productive forces develop and that this leads to social change, but historically this has not necessarily been the case. The fall of the Roman Empire saw the productive forces destroyed by the barbarians, but the subsequent decline in agriculture and industry paved the way for feudalism. As Rigby notes, the emergence of a new mode of production was based, not on the development of the productive forces, but on their regression (Rigby 1998: 152). Likewise, with the rise of capitalism, Rigby argues that rather than explaining this in terms of the development of the productive forces, it is possible to explain this through developments in class relations. Marx looks at the emergence of a free proletariat and the new opportunities given to capitalist landowners by the Reformation. He looks at the role of the state and the functioning of class and political power (Rigby 1998: 159). Again we are back to the issue of which Marx to read. We have also come to what has been called the transition debate.

The Transition to Capitalism

The transition debates constitute an attempt by Marxist historians to identify the 'prime mover' in the transition from feudalism to capitalism. Maurice Dobb argues that the transition from feudalism to capitalism was the result of a problem inherent in feudalism itself rather than the development of external factors like merchant commerce. He argues that the inefficiency of feudal production meant that the rising population could not be satisfied. In addition, the increasing demands of the ruling class for revenue led to a dramatic fall in living standards. The problem with Dobb's account, according to Rigby, is that even if we accept this, it does not explain why capitalism should emerge from this crisis (Rigby 1998: 161). Paul Sweezy, by contrast, stresses external factors, in particular the growth in trade that led to a new system of commodity production and the growth of the market economy and the urban bourgeoisie. Again Rigby has problems with this. He believes such a theory shows no reason why a system of free tenants paying money rents should give way to a capitalist system based on wage-labour (Rigby 1998: 163). It seems that Rigby is rather bored by debates over internal versus external causes of transition. He writes that: 'The key question of the transition debate is not "why did capitalism replace feudalism?" but (for instance) "why did capitalism emerge in England in a particular period and in a specific form?" ' (Rigby 1998: 163–64).

Rodney Hilton and later Robert Brenner (1985) offer an alternative approach to historical analysis. Rather than looking at factors such as population growth or trade, they argue it is necessary to focus on concrete forms of class struggle. The effects of these struggles lead to quite different forms of social development in different countries. Brenner's work incorporates the political and economic struggle of peasants into an explanation of the emergence of European states. In Eastern Europe the landlords were able to maintain a strict form of serfdom because of the weakness of the peasant communities and their common institutions. The varying strengths of the peasants and lords also determined the political and economic settlement that resulted in the west: in France the peasants won security of tenure and fixed rents while the weakened lords were forced to turn to the state for revenue. This contributed to the centralisation of power around the monarchy and the rise of the absolutist state. Because of the weakness of the landlords, the absolutist state was able to appropriate the peasant produce. The situation in England was that landlords were unable to maintain their feudal position, but did manage to maintain large farms through employing wage-labour and it was this that allowed for capitalist development and the industrialisation process. These different countries have the same starting point in terms of productive forces, but enjoy very different historical development due to particular forms of class relations.

Perry Anderson also takes a political and class-based position on the transition from feudalism to capitalism where he argues that Absolutism takes on a significance due to it being a redeployed apparatus of feudal domination. However, we examine the peculiarities of feudal resistance, not through his work *Lineages of the Absolutist State*, but through the debates that developed over the nature of the English revolution.

English History

The analysis of the English revolution by Perry Anderson and Tom Nairn looks at history not in terms of linear development or smooth transition, but in terms of a radical disjuncture between the economically dominant class and the peculiarities of the political bloc. Anderson and Nairn's thesis is that because the English revolution was the first bourgeois revolution, the bourgeois class in England was weak and underdeveloped and that rather than carrying through a fully fledged bourgeois revolution, it 'won two modest victories, lost its nerve and ended up by losing its identity' (Anderson 1992: 29). In fact, Anderson and Nairn argue, the revolution was primarily a fight between sections of the aristocracy which overshot its political intentions, creating a vacuum into which the emerging bourgeoisie stepped. Being too weak to carry through the revolution on its own terms, the emerging bourgeoisie made a compromise with the old aristocracy and a new ruling bloc emerged within which the aristocracy remained hegemonic. It was a bourgeois revolution, but only by proxy (Anderson 1992: 17).

While this paved the way for the momentous development of capitalism, it also produced a new ruling class that was heavily influenced by aristocratic residues. Rather than the economic structure determining the political and cultural superstructure, Anderson argues that a bitter, cathartic revolution 'transformed the structure but not the superstructures of English society' and that 'a landed aristocracy, underpinned by a powerful mercantile group, became the first dominant capitalist class in Britain' (Anderson 1992: 29). This meant that although there was initially a rapid development of capitalism, ultimately the historical bloc began to restrict further development. The archaic state form with its feudal relics was not helped by the development of Britain's imperial role which reinforced the more traditional institutions and led to political complacency. The influence of imperialism meant that domestic interests were tied to foreign interventions. That Britain remained unoccupied and undefeated after two world wars meant that the old social structure was preserved. When economic problems did develop, the state apparatus was therefore ill-equipped to deal with them. Britain's historical bloc was feudalistic and 'gentlemanly' in its outlook, imbued with a set of beliefs, values and traditions that were inappropriate for the development of modern capitalism. British capitalism was ultimately undermined by British culture, politics, state and civil society, by Eton, Oxbridge and the House of Lords, and by its amateurish personnel who failed to develop a modern, progressive world-view.

Anderson and Nairn argue that the British social formation is now in a state of political crisis. The ruling bloc, for many years untroubled by social conflict, is now totally inadequate at dealing with political and economic change. Its continued existence is owed to the half-heartedness of the industrial bourgeoisie, and the defensive, subordinate character of the working class. It is argued that because the political revolution came long before the process of industrialisation, the bourgeoisie was unable to develop a political ideology to reflect changing material conditions. Likewise, the English working class grew up without clear ideas so that, in contrast to the rest of Europe, it had neither bourgeois nor socialist ideology to turn to or interact with. The British working class developed into what Gramsci terms a corporate class that accepts its position within the system and is unable to transform itself into a hegemonic group. It has a limited consciousness of its role which is restricted to the ideas of gradual reform and piecemeal change enshrined in the structures of British labourism. It has no vision beyond this. As Anderson puts it: 'In England, a supine bourgeoisie produced a subordinate proletariat. It handed on no impulse of liberation, no revolutionary values, no universal language' (Anderson 1992: 17).

Anderson's strong views are contested by a number of British historians, in particular E.P. Thompson who argues that the model of a hegemonic (and aristocratic) ruling class and a subordinate, corporatist working class is too schematic, leaving one class as ruled and one class fraction as ruling, with little in between. Thomson also objects to a model that concentrates attention upon one dramatic episode – *the* Revolution – to which all that goes before and after must be related; and which insists upon an ideal type of this Revolution against which all others may be judged (Thompson 1978: 257).

Thompson's alternative is more subjective and cultural and less structural than that of Anderson and Nairn. Thompson's emphasis is on agency and the role of the masses and his is a history from below, unearthed by an archaeologist intent on re-examining history from the point of view of those who have been forgotten. He is concerned with developing a history of popular movements, customs and traditions, common experiences, quiet dissatisfaction and open revolt. History, for Thompson, is the embodiment of class struggle.

Thompson's book *The Making of the English Working Class* emphasises 'making' because it is a study of an active process, which owes as much to agency as to conditioning.

> By class I understand a historical phenomenon, unifying a number of disparate and seemingly unconnected events, both in the raw material of experience and in consciousness. I emphasise that it is a *historical* phenomenon. I do not see class as a 'structure', nor even as a 'category', but as something which in fact happens (and can be shown to have happened) in human relationships. (Thompson 1968: 9)

Thompson's approach fits into the category of praxis Marxism. Class is not something generated by objective conditions alone, but is a self-conscious product. As Thompson puts it: 'The working class did not rise like the sun at an appointed time. It was present at its own making' (1968: 9).

Conclusion

We find that in history, as with other areas, Marx leaves a disputed legacy. There is no clear answer to be found in Marx as to whether history is a product of the development of the productive forces or if it is primarily as result of class struggle. We may want to object to Cohen's functionalist account of historical development, but he is only following through with what is already there in Marx's 1859 Preface. Of course, there are many other places – the political writings in particular – where there is more emphasis on class struggle. But then again, we have to understand that this class struggle takes place within some sort of set of social conditions.

One may compromise along the lines of combining class struggle with social structure so that 'men make their own history, but they do not make it just as they please; they do not make it under circumstances chosen by themselves, but under circumstances directly encountered, given and transmitted from the past' (Marx 1973b: 146). This still, however, leaves open the question of emphasis. In the historical debates between Anderson and Thompson, Thompson is charged with giving too much weight to human agency to the point of working class romanticism more in the mould of William Morris rather than Karl Marx. In return, Thompson accuses Anderson of being too structuralist, but is this really the case? It could be, as Nicos Poulantzas (1976) is keen to point out, that both approaches are overly culturalist and place too much emphasis on shared experiences, meanings and values at the expense of objective social relations. If Thompson overemphasises the consciousness of the working class, Anderson and Nairn overemphasise the peculiarities of the English ruling class, in particular, its influences and outlook. Poulantzas believes this yields too much to class consciousness and proposes a more structural explanation – that the peculiarities of the English social formation are a product of the overlapping of different modes of production.

Gramsci adds a degree of complexity to the Marxist understanding of bourgeois society and its historical development. Rulership comes not simply from the dominant economic position of the ruling class, nor from the simple exercise of coercive force, but must be based on the construction of an historical bloc opening up the possibility, explored by Anderson, Nairn and Poulantzas, that there may be a radical disjuncture between the economically dominant class and the peculiarities of the political bloc. The danger of these approaches is that they may over-emphasise the historico-cultural aspect of the hegemonic process at the expense of the economic which, after all, is the distinctive element in Marxist social theory. The next section therefore goes on to look at an alternative application of Gramsci's ideas to modern society which draws on Gramsci's writings on the organisation of the production process and its effects on wider society.

Economy and Society

If there exist dangers of historicism and culturalism in the application of Marxist theory, how can a focus on economic factors be maintained without becoming economistic and reverting to productive forces determinism? We have already mentioned how Gramsci tries to counter Marxist economic determinism. He correctly sees the falling rate of profit as a *tendency* rather than as an iron-law, a theory of which is 'obtained by isolating a certain number of elements and thus by neglecting the counteracting forces' (Gramsci 1995: 429). The point is that in complex social formations, there are various counteracting forces that intervene into the economic process and affect it in various ways. This section looks at Fordist methods of production as just such an attempt to affect the economic process. It argues that economic developments cannot be understood according to the simple autonomous logic of the economic base or forces of production, but have to be examined in the wider socio-political context, including the wider relations of production, social organisation, production methods, state intervention and international relations. This section will introduce the approach of the regulation theorists before debating the issue of post-Fordism.

Fordism

Fordism refers to an intensive organisation of the production process and the associated social and political consequences of this. Gramsci uses the terms Fordism and Taylorism to describe the reorganisation and modernisation of the production process in line with new developments in technology and management. Henry Ford's motor company exemplifies the mass production of a standardised product enabling the generation of mass consumption. Mass production is achieved through new techniques of conveyor belt assembly, capital-intensive large-scale factories, highly regulated work practices, hierarchical and bureaucratic systems of management, and new wage structures often based on trade union involvement. The specialisation of the production line leads to an increasingly complex division of labour which requires a type of social education and training. These help enforce political and ideological control over the workforce while higher wages, social benefits and consumer goods secure social consent to these new methods.

For Gramsci these developments have a wider social character which he describes as Americanism in response to the growing world hegemony of the United States. This is not simply an issue of international politics, but of socio-economic hegemony just as today we might say that Americanism is experienced through the promotion of the neo-liberal agenda. With emphasis placed on the rationalising drive of capitalist production methods, Gramsci's claim is that hegemony is born in the factory (Gramsci 1971: 285) but that it goes on to infiltrate all aspects of social life. Americanism and Fordism reflect a growing rationalisation of society that permeates all aspects of popular life. It develops a tendency towards standardisation and conformity, including ways of thinking and acting. This is encouraged by the development of a mass media, a bureaucratic political apparatus, and a popular culture industry. Gramsci writes that Americanisation requires a particular environment, social structure and type of state (Gramsci 1971: 293). The 'Fordist' state plays an active role in developing the economy and civil society. The interventionist or regulatory role of the state is backed up with underlying changes in economic production and the co-option of the organisations of the working class as witnessed by the role of social democracy in post-war Western Europe. Despite political organisations and trade unions being given a more active role in the historical bloc, corporatism prevails so that the majority of workers are not in a position to advance their own demands. Fordism, therefore, might be seen as a particular example of Gramsci's passive revolution. Gramsci argues that passive revolution is based on the development of the superstructure in accordance with the economic structure where 'what is involved is the reorganisation of the structure and the real relations between men on the one hand and the world of the economy or of production on the other' (Gramsci 1971: 263).

Approaches to Fordism argue that it has created the conditions for, and vice versa, been facilitated by, state involvement and intervention. Mass production is the basis on which state interventionist Keynesian theories rest. The state injects large amounts of capital into the economy while growth is facilitated by large expenditure and use of credit which in turn provides the economic conditions for a consumer society. Mass production and mass consumption have been key factors in the maintenance of the post-war order. However, post-war social consensus also required various welfare policies and a new set of ideas and values appropriate to such projects. Thus the post-war economic project is inseparable from the post-war set of social alliances and to talk of economic development necessitates an examination of the social and political conditions through which this is expressed.

Regulation Theory

There are several different strands of the regulation approach. However, all challenge the economistic assumption that we can explain economic development simply in terms of inherent laws of capital – whether this be the tendency of the productive forces to develop or the tendency of the rate of profit to fall. Instead, attention shifts from inherent laws of capital to the social conditions necessary to try and overcome any inherent tendency towards crisis. Bob Jessop explains that this is done by introducing the idea of an *industrial paradigm* as a model governing the technical and social division of labour. The *regime of accumulation* is a complementary pattern of production and consumption that is reproduced over a long period. The *mode of regulation* is 'an emergent ensemble of norms, institutions, organisational forms, and patterns of conduct that can stabilise an accumulation regime' (Jessop 2002a: 93).

Starting from the driving force of capital accumulation, regulation analysis tries to show how this is organised and regulated. Economic reproduction is not an automatic process but requires social and political intervention. In particular this gives a prominent role to the state and what Jessop calls state strategies along with the workings of other social institutions, structures and international bodies.

The Parisian regulationists take their starting point from the work of Aglietta and his study of monopoly capitalism in the United States. Modes of regulation are dominated by the wage relation. Intensive regimes have a monopolistic form of regulation. The Parisian school, which also includes Lipietz, looks at various societal forms and norms and is more influenced by Althusser, Poulantzas and the structuralist tradition. The Amsterdam school, most notably van der Pijl, is more influenced by Gramsci and his idea of different class fractions. So too is the German school of Joachim Hirsch with its emphasis on the process of 'societalisation' or the society effect that explains modes of mass integration and their relation to the historical bloc. There are also those like Bob Jessop who draw heavily on the work of Gramsci and the idea of hegemonic strategy.

Regulation theorists argue that the post-war period is characterised by a new regime of accumulation which is to say that a number of deep social changes have occurred which are organised into a regime that helps facilitate the accumulation of capital. In particular, this period is characterised by a new form of state regulation based on the interventionist policies of Keynesianism, corporatism, nationalisation and welfarism. The era of Fordism is based on the state playing an active role in the economy and civil society in the belief that this is the best way both to advance the accumulation of capital and to secure consensus in civil society. This leading and directing role of the state is articulated through the projects of the leading or dominant social groups or class fractions. Through various state strategies, these groups must ensure both the conditions necessary for capital accumulation and the consent necessary for class rule. This relationship between class interests and the interests of capital is vital. Unfortunately, many attempts at analysis have lost this balance becoming either 'capital theoretical' or 'class theoretical'. The important issue is therefore whether a particular hegemonic project can reconcile the needs of capital with the needs of its own class leadership (Jessop 1990: 40). There is an inherent connection between forms of regulation and particular hegemonic orders and therefore crisis – such as the crisis of the post-war order – must be analysed in relation to both forms of regulation and the hegemonic bloc.

The different theorists of the regulation school develop impressive analyses of the post-war order, but occasionally writers like Aglietta and Lipetz are overly formalistic in outlining the functions of regulation. The mode of regulation is responsible for the reproduction of the regime of accumulation and this involves an ensemble of institutions and norms centred around state intervention. The danger in this analysis is the tendency to regard external and contingent factors as internal and necessary so that the conditions for capital accumulation are secured through the existence of inclusive, self-reproducing and self-regulating 'modes' or 'regimes'. This is sometimes apparent in various regulationist attempts to analyse the crisis of Fordism. For if capital accumulation is too strongly liked to an accumulation regime and form of regulation, then we end up with an 'institutional fix' whereby the problems of capitalism are shifted to the institutional level rather than representing something more intrinsic. And if the importance of modes and regimes is over-stated, then we can end up with a paradigmatic view of Fordism whereby the crisis of one regime of accumulation must be resolved by replacing it with another (post-Fordist) one. This idea that capitalism simply passes from one regime of accumulation to another concedes far too much to the view that capitalism is a relatively stable, self-regulating system with social forms that neatly correspond to the needs of accumulation. If Fordism is considered to be a regime of accumulation then its crisis lies in precisely the fact that such regimes ultimately cannot go on regulating capital accumulation. In this case Fordist methods proved too regimented and inflexible, too committed to large-scale production, consumption and investment – something we now consider.

Post-Fordism

The Fordist–Keynesian model of state intervention has given way to neo-liberal economic and social policy. For many regulation theorists there has been a shift towards a post-Fordist regime of accumulation based on the deregulation of markets and the flexibilisation of production methods. For other analysts of post-war politics, the notion of periods of Fordism and post-Fordism is problematic in that it lays too much stress on the ability to regulate capitalism and wider society. It suggests that the contradictions of the capitalist mode of production and the dynamic of class conflict can both be resolved by some sort of institutional fix. But this is to give regimes of accumulation too much power. It is to forget that Gramsci's notions of the integral state and the passive revolution are founded on the weakness of the bourgeoisie rather than on some inherent ability of capitalism to reorganise itself.

In the 1970s Fordist methods were exposed as being too rigid and cumbersome. As a process of flexibilisation occurred, the term post-Fordism was used to describe new production methods and management techniques. The manufacturing process has been made more flexible, accompanied by state strategies of economic de-regulation and liberalisation. The consequence of these processes is a new, more uncertain and diverse society with a flexibilised workforce and social and spatial fragmentation and dispersal. Post-Fordism is strongly linked to developments in technology, notably electronics, computing and communication. These all allow a more flexible system of production and decentralised forms of organisation. This in turn encourages a move away from mass consumption towards more individuality in lifestyle.

These changes have led to fashionable new mainstream social theories starting with Bell's post-industrial society, Lash and Urry's end of organised capitalism and economy of signs and space, Beck's risk society, Giddens' reflexive modernisation and Castells' network society. All seem to celebrate the fact that changes in the role of work and the labour process have weakened the power of skilled industrial workers. Within Marxism, the apparent decline in the traditional working class has led Andre Gorz to bid 'farewell to the working class' and to argue that struggles of new social movements like environmentalism and the women's movement will take over. The British *Marxism Today* current linked post-Fordism to the idea of 'new times'. Some of this theorising is considered in Chapter 8 when we look at the post-Marxist project.

But does post-Fordism really exist as *the* dominant economic system or mode of regulation? At best such theories might indicate the deficiencies of Fordism and it is certainly profitable to investigate the crisis of Fordism and the growth of flexibilisation or neo-Fordism. But the 'farewell to the working class' thesis is deficient in two major ways. First the thesis is Euro-centric insofar as it concentrates on developments in the advanced capitalist countries while ignoring the massive expansion of the working class around the world. Second, the working class is defined sociologically rather than according to Marx's description of those who are forced to sell their labour-power. Post-Fordist approaches may contain a number of insights into the production process, but it is necessary to consider how the flexibilisation of production is bringing about changes *within* the working class – such as the feminisation of the workforce or the exploitation of migrant labour – rather than suggesting that the working class no longer exists or that class struggle is a thing of the past.

Conclusion

Capital accumulation does not stand alone, nor does it stand within an exclusive regime like Fordism or post-Fordism. It is affected by a range of external, contingent, historical and political factors, not least the class struggle. Aglietta emphasises struggle when he writes that he rejects 'the idea of a superstructure that acts from the outside on a similarly autonomous infrastructure . . . rather . . . the institutionalisation of social relations under the effect of class struggles is the central process of their production' (Aglietta 1987: 29). However, the 'superstructure' must not be entirely internalised or else we are back with an institutional paradigm rather than a contradictory social ensemble.

Regulation theory places a great emphasis on regimes of accumulation, but capitalism's greatest contradiction lies in the fact that its anarchic nature both demands regulation and frustrates it. Attempts at regulation are affected by other factors such as different forms of capital as well as wider social and political factors like different class fractions and hegemonic projects. Regulation is in the hands of different social groups and institutions ensuring that there is no necessary link between capital and class interests. Rather, we are back to the issue discussed by Marxist historians – the contradiction between economic processes and political blocs.

Analysing Thatcherism

Having introduced the work of the regulation school, we conclude this chapter on applications by looking at a debate that took place over the nature of Thatcherism in Britain. It is useful to briefly cover this debate at this point because we have, on the one hand, the arguments of Jessop *et al.*, who apply their concepts of regulation to the Thatcherite project. On the other hand we have the work of Stuart Hall and his concept of authoritarian populism. Hall draws on Gramsci's theory of hegemony – particularly its moral and ideological aspects – while also being influenced by the sort of discourse theory that we shall cover in Chapter 8. Jessop *et al.*, also draw on Gramsci, but emphasise a more structural approach that is influenced by the work of Poulantzas and also the critical realist approach. By examining this debate here, we can therefore summarise the debates on regulation, while also moving on to the critical realism – discourse theory debate of Chapter 8.

Stuart Hall uses Gramsci and concepts like hegemony, passive revolution and historical bloc to show that Thatcherism is not just the same old from of class domination. Rather, it constitutes as radically new political project and articulation of social forces. The concept of historical bloc indicates that social composition is a complex and heterogenous process that cannot be straightforwardly reduced to an economic or class basis. Thatcherism represents a struggle to contest and disorganise an existing political formation – the social democratic consensus of the post-war period – by intervention into different social spheres – economic, civil society, intellectual and moral life (Hall 1988: 7). Thatcherism as a political ideology articulates and condenses often contradictory discourses, blending traditional conservative values with radically different neo-liberal ideas. Its success is based on its ability to break-up the existing consensus and develop its own. This is not an easy task as it strives to articulate the interests of different groups into a coherent position, combining traditional Tory values of nation, family, duty, authority and tradition with new neo-liberal values of aggressive competition, self-interest and anti-statism (Hall 1988: 48).

Hall is well known as a theorist of culture and discourse going back to his time as Director of the Centre for Contemporary Cultural Studies at Birmingham University. This work, drawing on Althusser, among others, looked at how ideology works to articulate subjects. Hall's work on Thatcherism therefore concentrates on the way that it functions as an ideology and the way that it articulates various social forces. The 'cultural turn' of the 1970s is concerned with moving away from Marxist notions of base and superstructure to focus on culture as a key contested space. By drawing on Gramsci these theorists argue that culture is the terrain where different social forces wage a war of position to try and capture a base of support. As Hall says of Thatcherism:

> Its reworking of these different repertoires of 'Englishness' constantly repositions both individual subjects and 'the people' as a whole – their needs, experiences, aspirations, pleasures and desires – contesting space in terms of shifting social, sexual and ethnic identities, against the background of a crisis of national identity and culture precipitated by the unresolved psychic trauma of the 'end of empire.' (Hall 1998: 2)

Hall is influenced by Nicos Poulantzas's idea of the rise of authoritarian statism. He also draws on Ernesto Laclau, another writer influenced by Althusser's conception of ideology, to develop his notion of authoritarian populism. Hall takes from Laclau the idea that ideological elements have no necessary class belonging. We have to look at the ways these elements are articulated by discourse into class practices. Laclau argues that popular-democratic discourses are constructed around the contradiction between the people and the power-bloc. For Hall, one reason for Thatcherism's success is its ability to step into an ideological vacuum and exploit the space in traditional ideologies like law and order or popular morality, relating to the immediate experiences of the masses (Hall 1998: 143). Thatcherism has 'worked the more traditionalist elements systematically in an authoritarian direction' (Hall 1998: 144). However, because of the contradictions involved between power bloc and people, the issue of democracy now becomes a major terrain of contestation. The left has to challenge the right for popular support, exposing the contradiction between the populist ideology of Thatcherism and its strong-state authoritarianism.

Hall does locate his cultural and ideological approach in the context of the structural crisis facing 1960s Britain, in particular, its industrial and economic decline. However, as well as looking at the organic basis of this crisis, Hall argues that we need to follow Gramsci in looking at its conjunctural aspect. The conjunctural is defined not simply by economic conditions, but by the effects made to defend the status quo. It may be defensive or formative, attempting to construct a new historical bloc, encourage new political config-urations and philosophies, and articulate new ideological discourses. These elements do not emerge easily but have to be constructed through patient polit-ical and ideological work (Hall 1988: 43). Hall's focus on Thatcherism's authoritarian populist appeal is therefore directed against reductionist read-ings of Thatcherism that see it simply as a product of economic circumstances. Authoritarian populism is a form of passive revolution to mobilise a base of support. It refers to the modalities of political and ideological relationships between the ruling bloc and dominated groups (Hall 1988: 43). Hall's approach emphasises Gramscian themes like the crisis of party political repre-sentation and the role of common sense and popular politics. Thatcherite dis-course plays upon people's everyday experiences and existing beliefs, something the left needs to recognise if it is to construct an alternative strategy.

The response from Jessop *et al.*, argues that Hall's approach is overly concerned with the Gramscian focus on balance of forces without looking at structural sources of power (Jessop *et al.* 1988: 16). They argue the need to look at Thatcherism in the context of the long-term decline of the British economy which,

> requires us to move beneath the surface of political life to examine the dynamics of different forms of political representation, modes of policy making, forms of inter-vention, and even more importantly, the changing social bases of the state and the general projects which endow the state with some internal coherence and broader social significance. (Jessop *et al.* 1998: 28)

Their critique shifts the analysis of Thatcherism to a general account of the con-temporary state and its management of different class interests while also emphasising the neo-liberal element of Thatcherism in relation to accumulation strategies. The development of Thatcherite policy is less a question of popular mobilisation than of how to manage the complex relations between different class fractions in the context of the structural crisis of the state and associated power bloc. Jessop *et al.*, argue that it is necessary to examine the political programme of Thatcherism in relation to accumulation strategy. Many of Thatcherism's economic strategies do not derive from authoritarian populism (Jessop *et al.* 1998: 84). Although authoritarian populism is an interesting and useful concept, by making it so central, Hall's approach generates inadequate strategic conclusions, focussing too much on the politics of electoral support and mobilisation, without giving enough attention to wider questions of govern-mental power and the recomposition of the power-bloc (Jessop *et al.* 1998: 97).

Hall's reply is to argue that he is deliberately foregrounding the political–ideological dimension and forms of hegemonic politics (Hall 1988: 150) concentrating on the change in the balance of forces, and the modalities of political and ideological relations between different classes and the state (154). He says that he agrees with Gramsci's claim that hegemony has to be grounded on the 'decisive nucleus of economic activity', but that in his own work he is determined to focus on the ideological terrain (156). This immediately raises the question of whether it is possible to concentrate on the political–ideological without going into the question of its relationship to production and accumulation.

Jessop *et al.*, reply by stating that it is not possible simply to focus on the cultural or ideological element. We have to look at the interactions of ideology, politics and economy as functions of the modern state (Jessop *et al.* 1998: 117). Hall's approach typifies a general weaknesses in Gramscian analysis, tending to neglect the structural determinations of hegemony by focussing on the politics and ideology of class leadership (Jessop *et al.* 1998: 113). For Jessop *et al.*, the long-term stability of hegemony is rooted in specific forms of state – structural or strategic selectivity – and specific ways of organising production (Jessop *et al.* 1998: 115). They argue that Hall focusses on modalities of politics and ideology while ignoring relations within the ruling bloc, the state and production (Jessop *et al.* 1998: 116).

We can see, then, how Jessop *et al.*, employ a broader approach, drawing on regulation theory to look at the structural basis of Thatcherism. For them, Thatcherism has to be seen as an economic strategy, a way of structuring the British economy, a neo-liberal accumulation strategy based on privatisation and deregulation (Jessop *et al.* 1998: 120). They also place more emphasis on the social basis of the state and institutionalised modes of mass social and political integration (Jessop *et al.* 1998: 156). The notion of accumulation strategy sheds light on models of economic growth and their associated institutions and range of government policies. The concept of state strategy refers to patterns of intervention into the economy that favour the course of an accumulation strategy. They then move on to discuss hegemonic projects in this context – as national–popular programmes of political, intellectual and moral leadership that advance the long-term accumulation strategy while granting concessions to the masses in return for their support (Jessop *et al.* 1998: 162). This type of structural grounding and stratified notion of different structures, strategies and institutions has two major influences. The first is the analysis of the state provided by Poulantzas – which Jessop *et al.*, draw upon heavily. The second influence is the emerging school of critical realism, something that will be outlined in detail in Chapter 8.

Conclusion: The Social and the Economic

All these sections reveal one thing, that the application of Marxist theory to social issues raises the question of the relative weight given to economic factors. Of course what is distinctive about Marxist social theory is its recognition of the centrality of production. However, as all these debates indicate, production need not be interpreted in a narrow economic sense. The role of production in society is the very basis of historical materialism, however, while production entails an economic process it is much more than that. The conditions of production are social conditions of production and economic processes such as the development of the productive forces or the tendency of the rate of profit to fall have to be considered in relation to a range of social factors.

On feminism and nationalism we can say that each are movements with their own specificity that cannot be reduced to a prior economic level. We could say, in line with the critical realist approach of Chapter 8, that these issues have their own emergent characteristics and that they cannot simply be explained in terms of some prior level of analysis. What is required is a causal pluralism that regards the social as a complex of many different processes of which some (economic) ones have greater significance, but not absolute determining power. In historical debates we see how some approaches adopt a mono-linear approach that places emphasis on the determining force of one aspect of the social system (the economic base or the forces of production) while other approaches see history in terms of an interaction between various economic, political and cultural forces and the conflict between social systems and social agents.

The section on economics introduced the regulation approach which, in the words of Bob Jessop 'treats economic activities and institutions as socially embedded and emphasises that it is impossible to secure continued accumulation purely through economic mechanisms' (Jessop 2002a: 89). Jessop's approach breaks with crude base-superstructure or forces-relations dichotomies and introduces a complexly structured social system whose economic mode of production is reproduced through an array of social structures and institutions. Jessop calls his approach strategic-relational in that it sees social systems as reproduced through the interactions of different social groups and institutions or through different hegemonic projects and state strategies that become institutionalised over time. This approach is an exemplification of the critical realist approach that is outlined in Chapter 8. Such an approach will be contrasted with the post-Marxist approach which also informs debates over post-Fordism, but tends to take a cultural turn away from modes of economic production, towards systems of cultural consumption and discursive articulation.

Further Reading

On Marxism and Feminism Engels' *The Origin of the Family, Private Property and the State* is a must read. Kollontai's work is also worth reading. On more recent debates, Sargent (ed.) *The Unhappy Marriage of Marxism and Feminism* (1981) contains interesting debates. Barrett's *Women's Oppression Today* (1988) is also interesting. Hennessy's *Materialist Feminism and the Politics of Discourse* (1992) brings together debates on Marxism and post-Marxism.

The best introduction to Marxist debates on nationalism is Munck's *The Difficult Dialogue: Marxism and Nationalism* (1986). Marx and Engels's views on national movements are quite scattered, but their writings on the Irish national question have been collected together (1971). Nairn's *The Break-up of Britain* (1981) gives his account of the national question and the future of the British state. Erica Benner's book *Really Existing Nationalisms* (1996) is a very good new addition to the literature.

On history, Rigby (1988) provides an excellent and critical overview. Cohen's *Karl Max's Theory of History: A Defence* (1978) sets out his functionalist account. Aston and Philipin (eds), *The Brenner Debate* examines the class struggle view. Thompson's *The Making of the English Working Class* (1968) is justly famous. Anderson's arguments are collected together in *English Questions* (1992).

Gramsci's *Prison Notebooks* has a section on Fordism. Aglietta's *A Theory of Capitalist Regulation* (1987) has been very influential. Jessop's work continues to apply a regulationist and strategic-relational approach to the state, his latest book being *The Future of the Capitalist State*. Amin (ed.) (1994) introduces Post-Fordist debates.

For the debates on Thatcherism see Stuart Hall's *The Hard Road to Renewal: Thatcherism and the Crisis of the Left* (1988). Hall's reply to Jessop *et al.*, 'Authoritarian Populism: A Reply to Jessop *et al.*' is also reprinted in Jessop *et al.*, *Thatcherism: A Tale of Two Nations* (1988) The articles can also be found in *New Left Review* numbers 147, 151, 153, 165 and 179 (all online at www.newleftreview.co.uk).

8

Beyond Marxism?

Introduction

Having examined Marxist social theory according to its different schools and in its various applications, we are perhaps no clearer as to what exactly Marxist social theory is. This is a real historical problem as Marxism tries to come to terms with its disputed legacy in the light of the collapse of the USSR, the defeats of the workers' movement in Western Europe and the rise of neo-liberalism. This chapter is concerned with the perceived crisis of Marxist social theory by looking at how two very different schools have attempted to deal with the issue of Marxism's future. It should be stated here that both positions, post-Marxism and critical realism, are more philosophical than social theoretical insofar as philosophy is concerned here as a conceptual critique which analyses the claims that Marxism is making and criticises them – assessing such things as method, epistemology (claims about knowledge) and ontology (claims about reality). Neither position is Marxist as such, but both are keenly concerned with the status of Marxist theory and both, consequently can be used to consider what Marxist theory should be. At this late stage in the book, since we are now debating what Marxism is, I intend to abandon impartiality and adopt a critical realist form of structural Marxism.

Marxist Spectres

Structural Marxism and Gramscian Marxism became influential in Britain in the 1970s and the two often combined in the fields of cultural studies and literary criticism. The fallout from this was a turn to poststructuralism, particularly the work of Jacques Derrida and Michel Foucault, and to various forms of post-Marxism that reacted against the rigidities of structuralism and the determinism or reductionism of Marxism.

Derrida's project of deconstruction focuses on the production of meaning through the text. It argues that the dominant Western forms of knowledge have sought to impose meaning or identity by trying to stabilise meaning around a fixed point at the expense of different or alternative meanings. This process, by which, to give an example, a white, male, Eurocentric and rationalist discourse gains ascendancy, is described as logocentrism. Certain meanings have been elevated over others by means of imposing a certain discursive framework and excluding those identities that fall outside it. But if logocentrism is the imposition of a fixed identity or presence, it can be undermined by showing how this presupposes a set of power relations and how those relations might be other than they are. Deconstruction can therefore be seen as a political project insofar as it encourages us to challenge logocentric discourse by exploring the play of radical otherness or *différance*. This term implies both differing and deferring, raising the issue of both the context of meaning, and how it may change over time. An example of a deconstructive project would be the attempt to apply a feminist reading to certain classical texts in order to question or challenge dominant male discourse and its privileging of such terms as rationality, authority, and masculinity. This would raise both the question of how meaning is derived through the exclusion of other (feminine) terms, and also how a particular meaning may always be transcended over time.

Derrida continues his critique of fixed identity and presence in his book *Specters of Marx* whose very title attempts to undermine the certainty of appearance and identity. The elusive spectre rejects the assurance of presence for the subversiveness of an apparition. The bodiless and ungraspable character of the spectre might also be applied more widely to a whole domain that Derrida calls hauntology. This neologism is a subversion of ontology and throws the concept of being into doubt insofar as we cannot be sure what is 'real' and what is merely an 'appearance'. Such a domain, Derrida believes, is well described by certain Marxist concepts, in particular those that analyse the phantom-like commodification of the world and the way that social relations take a ghostly fetishised form (Derrida 1994: 166). Derrida explores the spectrality of Marx's account of the phenomenology of capitalism and wider society and the dominance within this society of spectral forms like commodity fetishism which have a mystifying effect in the way they bring social objects to life and in doing so give them the form of commodities and exchange values.

If capitalist society is spectral, it is nevertheless haunted by an alternative – the spectre that is haunting Europe, the spectre of Communism. When Marx and Engels wrote these words communism did not yet exist, but its spectre held Europe in fear. Now, after the fall of the so-called communist regimes, Derrida believes that Marxism can never exist as a system or constitute itself as a coherent movement. Indeed, any such attempt to do so would be undesirable as it would represent, once again, an attempt to impose meaning and identity. The consequences of such approaches have already been seen in the form of totalitarian states, authoritarian parties and rigid doctrines. However, while rejecting the bodily forms of Marxism, Derrida embraces its spirit, arguing the need to:

> Distinguish this *spirit* of the Marxist critique, which seems to be more indispensable than ever today, at once from Marxism as ontology, philosophical or metaphysical system, as 'dialectical materialism', from Marxism as historical materialism or

method, and from Marxism incorporated in the apparatuses of party, State, or workers' International. (Derrida 1994: 68)

It is this critical spirit of Marxism, rather than its distorted bodily forms, that Derrida believes should be embraced. Therefore, even if it is only in a 'spiritual' or critical sense, he is at least defending something in Marx and something of the Enlightenment while taking a stand against the anti-Marxist, 'end of history' sentiments of postmodernism and neo-liberal ideology. The critical spirit of Marxism must be 'conjured up' to inspire some new form of emancipatory politics:

> if there is a spirit of Marxism which I will never be ready to renounce, it is not only the critical idea or the questioning stance . . . It is even more a certain emancipatory and *messianic* affirmation, a certain experience of the promise that one can try to liberate from any dogmatics. (Derrida 1994: 89)

This conception of the messianic must be thought of as a promise that is made now even though what is promised is not here and will never be fully present. The trouble with Derrida's position is that if ever the promise was to be fulfilled we would be back to the imposition of some sort of identity or meaning or 'metaphysics of presence'.

Therefore, deconstruction tends to limit itself to epistemological questions concerned with the functioning of language or the text, and the status of meaning within it. This is very important in one respect for it teaches us to critically engage with various theories, including Marxist ones, and to question their assumptions and dogmatism, their status as 'sacred texts' and their imposed homogeneity. A deconstructive reading of Marxist social theory can be very useful in questioning various assertions and assumptions, so long as this does not simply become deconstruction for the sake of it. More problematic are the ontological implications of deconstruction in that to the extent that everything is mediated through the text, we are not allowed to go beyond it and develop an ontology or theory of being. This makes it impossible to locate any fundamental human needs or interests because we cannot ground these in the wider social world. We can only speculate on the promise of what might be to come and this leaves Derrida unable to make any kind of convincing case for a radical project. His messianic invokes a messiah who will never come and whose coming would in any case be undesirable. So despite the epistemological insights, Derrida's approach is politically problematic, something that carries over into the ideas of those post-Marxists who draw upon him.

Post-Marxism

Ernesto Laclau and Chantal Mouffe call themselves post-Marxists and discourse theorists. The two terms coincide in the sense that they believe

Marxism focuses too much on material reality and needs a discursive turn. We will later see how critical realism, as an alternative approach, argues that we need both a cultural turn and a renewed emphasis on material reality, not one or the other. Post-Marxism however, rejects any distinction between discursive and non-discursive practices. Every object is constituted as an object of discourse (Laclau and Mouffe 1985: 107). For example, a chess board might be described as lumps of polished wood moving around another piece of polished wood, but it acquires a certain meaning and a set of rules through discourse.

Post-Marxism can be described as an attempt to blend aspects of Marxism with other philosophical and cultural theories such as deconstruction, postmodernism and Foucault's politics of power. The main theme of Laclau and Mouffe's post-Marxism can be said to be a questioning of so-called reductionism in Marxism and an insistence on social contingency in opposition to determinism. In particular, they question the emphasis given to the economic or the mode of production and to the importance of class. Marxism is criticised for trying to grasp history through some underlying development of mode of production or class struggle. This reductionism prevents Marxism from grasping both the plural nature of society as an 'indeterminate space' with no fixed essence, and the radically contingent nature of social forces whose identity is never fixed, but is open and incomplete (something we can see as following from Derrida). Post-Marxism claims to maintain an emphasis on political processes, and indeed suggests that by rejecting class determinism it becomes more radical in its politics, rejecting the privileged agency of the working class and supporting a form of politics based on a plurality of potentially radical subject positions. New political agents can be found in various social movements that radically challenge the fixing of political identity.

The work of Laclau and Mouffe can therefore be seen as a radically contingent form of identity politics. From Derrida and deconstruction they take the idea that identity can never be fixed. The instability of signification forms the basis of antagonism and it is this essential antagonism that creates the basis for the openness of politics. There is no underlying basis to social antagonism, only the openness and indeterminacy of the social itself (Laclau and Mouffe 1985: 144–45). The main political issues are not essentialist struggles like class politics, but contingent issues around such things as environmentalism, feminism and multi-culturalism where agents are motivated by a struggle for radical autonomy. Laclau and Mouffe's emphasis on contingency and antagonism leads them to a concept of hegemony. They argue for this on the basis that:

> It is no longer possible to maintain the conception of subjectivity and classes elaborated by Marxism, nor its vision of the historical course of capitalist development, nor, of course, the conception of communism as a transparent society from which antagonisms have disappeared . . . we have constructed a concept of hegemony which, in our view, may be a useful instrument in the struggle for a radical, libertarian and plural democracy. (Laclau and Mouffe 1985: 4)

Laclau and Mouffe believe that the growing importance of the concept of hegemony indicates a recognition by certain Marxist theorists like Gramsci that the orthodox Marxist approach is untenable. They argue that: 'Faced with the rationalism of classical Marxism, which presented history and society as intelligible totalities constituted around conceptually explicable laws, the logic of hegemony presented itself from the outset as a *complementary* and *contingent* operation' (Laclau and Mouffe 1985: 3). Laclau and Mouffe's book *Hegemony and Socialist Strategy* gives hegemony a central role by tying it to the articulation of discourse and making it the main political moment in the creation of social identities. By freeing hegemony from the concept of class or any central articulating subject, it can express this radical contingency of politics. Indeed, all social objects are constituted according to their discursive articulation which indicates their purely contingent character. The focus is shifted to the process of articulation itself rather than to any particular articulator such as a particular social group. As with postmodernism, post-Marxism argues that social entities have no significance outside of discourse. Indeed, the social is exclusively a discursive space: insofar as the social has no single constituting principle underlying it, the social *is* discursive articulation (Laclau and Mouffe 1985: 114).

Laclau and Mouffe state that 'we will call *articulation* any practice establishing a relation among elements such that their identity is modified as a result of the articulatory practice. The structured totality resulting from the articulatory practice, we will call *discourse*' (Laclau and Mouffe 1985: 105). However, it is important to distinguish between the articulation process and that which is articulated. As a criticism of Laclau and Mouffe it might be suggested that the process of hegemonic articulation to which they attach such central importance is not the primary origin of interests but a particular mediation under particular conditions by certain groups. But since Laclau and Mouffe deny that the material world has any significance outside of discursive articulation, interests are deprived of any lasting significance. The result is that Laclau and Mouffe embrace a relativism that denies relatively enduring interests as well as the lasting significance of other social processes, relations, human needs and identities. A more orthodox Marxist response would be to argue that for a hegemonic project to articulate interests at all pre-supposes that there are real material interests that can be articulated. This response need not deny the importance of discursive articulation, but suggests that this has to be the discursive articulation of something that already exists, that already has something about it that is worth articulating. While interests may be discursively articulated, discursive articulation is not all there is to interests, for an interest is an interest *in* something that cannot simply be reduced to the process of discursive articulation. Interests have an extra-discursive basis that gives a relative fixity to discursive articulation.

The concept of hegemony, as normally understood, allows that particular groups or classes may articulate what they see as their (already existing) interests through a hegemonising project or historical bloc. However, Laclau and Mouffe totally change Gramsci's conception of historical bloc as a process that unifies material structure and political and cultural superstructure and instead they redefine it as entirely contingent:

> Every historical bloc – or hegemonic formation – is constructed through regularity in dispersion, and this dispersion includes a proliferation of very diverse elements: systems of differences which partially define relational identities. (Laclau and Mouffe 1985: 142)

Gramsci conceives of the historical bloc in relation to structures, Laclau and Mouffe define it in terms of the dispersal of discrete atomistic elements. In keeping with much of the 'New Times' and 'post-' society literature which suggests that Marxism is a product of an industrial society and a form of modernity long since gone, Laclau and Mouffe argue for the growing complexity of advanced industrial societies and a growing proliferation of differences. These cannot be fixed into a stable articulatory structure (Laclau and Mouffe 1985: 96). However, there seems to be a serious contradiction here which can be explored by posing the question: why are advanced industrial societies increasingly complex and contingent? Laclau and Mouffe thus usher back in the sort of periodisation of history that goes against their stress on contingency. They argue that the hegemonic dimension of politics expands as the open character of the social increases. They write that in a medieval peasant society the area open to differential articulations is minimal and that the hegemonic form of politics only becomes dominant in modern times when the area of articulatory practices is broadened (Laclau and Mouffe 1985: 138). This sort of periodisation is problematic for the argument Laclau and Mouffe are trying to put forward. If history can be periodised in this way, then we have to ask, how did we get to modernity and then again to advanced industrial society? If different periods are characterised by a proliferation of differences, then what causes this proliferation of differences? What causes the transition from one period to another? If this is something internal to discourse, no account is given of what this might be. If growing antagonism, contingency and difference has been caused by something else then it presupposes something external to the contingency of society; it is operationalised by an historical logic which must be logically prior to discourse. This then undermines their argument. In sum, Post-Marxism and deconstruction develop a philosophical critique of Marxist 'foundationalism', however they struggle to offer a coherent alternative *social theory*.

Marxism and Philosophy

Critical realism is another philosophical approach that can be applied to the problems of Marxism. Unlike post-Marxism and deconstruction, critical realism (at least in the earlier work) does offer a philosophical critique of aspects of Marxism that may allow a more convincing social theory to emerge, whilst taking into account some of the critiques and concerns raised by post-Marxism and deconstruction. The focus here is on the earlier works of critical realism as the later work is more problematic in this respect.

Critical realism is conscious of its own role and the fact that it is distinct from Marxism insofar as Marxism is a theory of society, while critical realism, as a philosophy, is a theory of social (and natural) science. While Marxism produces first-order knowledge of society, philosophy is second-order knowledge in that it is knowledge of this knowledge of society although inevitably this philosophy and social theory get mixed up.

In fact critical realism can begin its task of analysing Marxist approaches by criticising those forms of Marxism where social theory and philosophy do get mixed up. For example, in the praxis Marxism of Lukács, Korsch and Gramsci, we find a rejection of the mechanical schema of orthodox Marxism, but still a philosophical schema whereby history becomes the process of confirmation of subjective class-consciousness. It is understandable why, in opposing deterministic or 'vulgar' materialism, Marxists like Lukács, Gramsci, Korsch and Sartre should emphasise the concept of praxis. But following Roy Bhaskar, we can say that these theorists embrace a historicism that reduces Marxism to the theoretical expression of the working class, that dismisses other forms of knowledge (including, often natural science) as bourgeois ideology, and that sees Marxism as a self-sufficient, comprehensive and totalising standpoint (Bhaskar 1991: 172). Such an approach is indicated by Lukács's belief that 'self-knowledge coincides with knowledge of the whole so that the proletariat is at one and the same time the subject and object of its knowledge' (Lukács 1971: 20). Marxism, instead of being a social scientific analysis, becomes a perspective, or world-view that will be confirmed by history. The common problem with both mechanical Marxism and its praxis-based alternative is that they both impose a philosophical framework (a teleology of inevitable development) onto historical materialism thereby pre-judging and undermining any social theoretical analysis of the actual social situation.

Critical realism (in its earlier form) does not seek to provide Marxism with a philosophical overview, but instead sets itself the more humble 'under-labouring' task of clarifying social theory. By standing 'outside' Marxism, it can offer itself as a critical tool that is intimately connected, but not reducible, to the theoretical practice of Marxism. Meanwhile Marxist social theory is advised to draw on an explicitly critical realist philosophy capable of sustaining an ontological account of the world. By this, critical realists mean a firm distinction between the knowledge that we have of the world and the knowledge-independent world itself. This means a focus on the independently existing reality that knowledge and action try to comprehend or change, a reality described by Bhaskar as the *intransitive* domain. It is contrasted with the *transitive* knowledge that tries to comprehend or explain it. This transitive knowledge of the world has many forms including the various theories that form a kind of raw material for scientific practice. Transitive knowledge is antecedently established knowledge which is used to generate new knowledge. This includes established theories, models, methods, facts and so on (Bhaskar 1978: 21). By contrast the intransitive is that which science seeks to study. Intransitive objects of knowledge are those structures, relations, processes and generative mechanisms which exist independently of us in a relatively enduring state. Therefore, while science is a transitive process with antecedent knowledge that is dependent on human activity, its objects are intransitive objects which do not depend on either (Bhaskar 1978: 22).

Critical realism makes what it claims is a transcendental realist argument in that transitive knowledge (and the practice of social theory) depends on this independently existing reality to which it refers. Therefore, the intransitive is a condition for the intelligibility of the transitive. Reality must exist independently of our knowledge of it if scientific development and debate are to have any relevance. However, the social world differs from the natural world in a number of important ways, in particular that social structures are bound up with the activities of the agents that they govern and that, therefore, society has a conceptual aspect. But against the praxis Marxists and those, like Habermas, who are influenced by the hermeneutic tradition, critical realism maintains that society is not exhausted by its conceptual or praxis aspects and that we should discuss and study objective social structures.

While Bhaskar insists on the irreducibility of the intransitive, his transitive is necessarily flexible. Philosophy must recognise knowledge to be transient and influenced by social, historical and ideological factors. Consequently, critical realism advocates *epistemic relativity*. This is to recognise that we have no guaranteed access to truth, that knowledge is socially constructed and that there is no direct correspondence between knowledge and its object. However, critical realism is opposed to judgmental relativism or the view, as is advocated by postmodernist and post-Marxist forms of relativism, that there are no rational grounds for preferring one belief to another and that essentially all beliefs are equally valid. Although it is correct to assert that there is no direct correspondence between knowledge and the independently existing objects of knowledge (epistemic relativism) it is necessary to assert that all theories are not equally valid, and that we should make judgements as to which theories and explanations are better than others on the grounds of explanatory adequacy (judgemental rationality) in relation to something that is real and which exists independently of our attempts to explain it.

Social Structure and Social Transformation

Critical realism moves from the structure and order of knowledge to the structure and order of that which knowledge is about. It is argued that the intelligibility of knowledge presupposes that the world is structured in a certain way with an enduring nature that is open to investigation. It argues that the world is stratified in the sense that these structures are ordered in a particular way. Science itself reflects this stratification; for example, biology is rooted in and emergent from physics. We can also see this sort of layering or stratification in society. However, the temptation for reductionism – that is, reducing explanation to the lower level – must be avoided. It is not possible to explain a biological process simply in terms of physical ones, nor should we explain political events (like elections) by reducing them to the mode of production (the needs of capital). Critical realism therefore advocates a theory of emergence, suggesting that higher strata may presuppose lower, more fundamental levels, but that these higher layers have their own irreducible properties and dynamics. Society is an open system where a variety of these structures and mechanisms operate together in various combinations giving the world a multi-faceted nature.

We can see therefore how critical realism can offer an alternative to reductionist Marxism and its base-superstructure or economic determinist models, without abandoning the idea of structure or ordering to the contingency of post-Marxism. Society is seen as comprised of a multitude of strata with structures that inter-relate and co-determine one another. Within this economic structures may still be regarded as the most important or dominant ones, but they are not exclusively determinant and the different strata of the social formation each have their own emergent (irreducible) properties, laws and powers.

What is distinctive about the social world, as opposed to the natural world, is that its structures do not exist independently of the activities they govern and they depend upon practical activity and human conceptions (although they are not reducible to these as praxis Marxists are prone to suggest). Critical realism attempts to show how intentional human activity takes place within a pre-existing structural context. It is through its transformational model of social activity (TMSA) that social structure and human praxis are combined. Putting structure and praxis together, Bhaskar argues that:

> Society is both the ever-present *condition* (material cause) and the continually reproduced *outcome* of human agency. And praxis is both work, that is conscious *production*, and (normally unconscious) *reproduction* of the conditions of production, that is society. (Bhaskar 1989a: 34–45)

In trying to grapple with the relation between structure and agent, the TMSA argues that social structures exist by virtue of human activity, but they also determine that activity. Human action is necessarily dependent on the existence of these social structures, however, the structures themselves depend upon being reproduced through such activity. Agents have some conception of this activity although by and large reproduction of the wider structure is unconscious or non-conscious. For example, most workers do not consciously set out to reproduce the capital–wage-labour relation, however, this is the consequence of large numbers of them acting upon an intention to earn a living.

Such a position clearly contrasts with the praxis approach that gives human action primacy over social structure (if indeed the latter is said to exist at all). However, critical realist structuralism is different from Althusserian structuralism in rejecting the idea that agents are passive 'bearers' of these structures. Structures definitely have causal primacy over agents so that people, although engaging in conscious activity, mostly unconsciously reproduce these structures. Structures pre-exist social agents while their functioning and effects are beyond the full comprehension or control of agents in their day-to-day activity. However, this does not mean that agents passively occupy structural locations. In fact, it is because of their structural location that agents have the *potential* to engage in transformative practice, albeit within definite limits. Because structures enable human action, agents can never step outside them. Therefore it is necessary to state that agents reproduce or transform structures rather than create them. This process of transformation assumes a strategic character in that social agents have to decide upon a strategy by which they can enact social change. These activities occur within definite structural limits and critical realism locates these strategies within the potentialities allowed by the social conditions. Elsewhere, I have argued how this necessitates a theory of hegemony that is structurally grounded in processes of social reproduction but is agentially enacted through hegemonic projects (Joseph 2002).

Emancipatory Critiques

Critical realism is a broad philosophical position that applies across the various scientific (and non-scientific) disciplines. In relation to social theory, this philosophical position becomes more critical. Good social science represents an explanatory critique in that it goes beyond a criticism of other ideas or theories by offering an explanation not only of why these theories get things wrong, but also why they occur and what it is that produces them. In this way, an explanatory critique connects wrong ideas to the social conditions that produce such ways of thinking. It examines whether there is a connection between particular social objects and false descriptions of them. If certain views of the world predominate, it is necessary to explain why this should be the case. And if these ideas are false or inadequate, it is necessary to produce a better explanation. If a connection can be established between false ideas about social objects and the social objects themselves, then a critique of these social objects follows. An alternative is posed, not just at the level of theory but also in terms of how the world could or should be.

A most obvious example drawn from Marxist social theory would be that of the commodity fetishism emanating from exchange relations. An explanatory critique would move from commodity fetishism itself to the reflection of this in social explanation. Such a stance can be found in some critical theory such as Adorno and Horkheimer's characterisation of positivist social theory as an example of how alienation in social life is reflected in the alienated form of social theory (positivism) and how the fetishism of exchange relations in social life produces 'identity thinking' in social theory and philosophy. Consequently, a critique of positivist social science requires an analysis of the atomised and commodified social conditions that these theories 'reflect'. This condition can also clearly be seen in Marx's critique of classical economic theory (or these days, neo-liberal economic theory) where he argues that the theory reflects the very conditions it tries to explain – and consequently cannot explain. Classical or neo-liberal economic theory is too closely tied to the structure of the capitalist economy while bourgeois theories of government and the state might be criticised for being too close to the actual bodies themselves. Once the origins of the inadequacies of these ideas are sought in the inadequacies of social structures and institutions, the question is immediately posed as to whether alternative structures or bodies might be envisaged. Just as Marx urged us to change the world, so the answer to many false ideas is to change the social relations behind them.

This leads us from the idea of explanatory critique to that of emancipatory critique. Critical realism supports not just a social scientific analysis of structures, but also a critique of these structures and their effects. It argues that a critique of inadequate theories and ideologies necessarily entails an analysis of the nature of the social structures that produce them. And in doing so it suggests that to rid ourselves of these false conceptions we need to rid ourselves of those things that produce them. The emancipatory critique moves from a critique of wrong social ideas to the origin of those ideas to a suggestion that things need not be what they are.

Critical realism questions not only social ideas, but also the social processes that generate such ideas. Historically, the social analysis of bourgeois theories is marked by an ahistorical, fetishised world view. By contrast, the exploited and oppressed have an interest in knowledge which the exploiters not only lack, but may have an interest in suppressing. Developing a critique both of the wrong ideas and the practices producing them is part of what Bhaskar calls hegemonic/hermeneutic struggles, isolating, for example, theory/practice inconsistencies (Bhaskar 1994: 94). But these scientific positions must be developed through a careful study of society. Just because the working class has an interest in explanatory knowledge, this does not mean that it flows naturally from their class consciousness.

If we accept that social theory and social reality are causally interdependent – that is, that social theory is practically conditioned by and has potentially practical consequences in society (Bhaskar 1989b: 5) – then neutrality in social theory, however desirable, is impossible. In this context, the practice of philosophy, in assessing social scientific theory, is also inescapably political. To deny this is, in fact to take a political stance – a conservative stance that defends the status quo, either of social reality, or of the methods used to study it, or more probably, both. Critical realism does not shy away from this problem, but embraces the political role it must play. It does this through emphasising such things as openness, diversity and historicity and exposing those theories that deny them.

Critical realism's stance, in relation to a study of the social world, is to emphasise its structure and complexity. To examine structure poses the question of whether this structure, or ensemble of structures, is hierarchical. If this is so, it is necessary to investigate which structures are dominant or have causal primacy. Recognition of the historicity of social relations also requires an investigation of the necessary conditions for the reproduction of the social formation. Critical realism argues that social structures have a relatively enduring character. However, the requirements for reproducing this enduring character need to be assessed. Thus it seems legitimate for critical realism to move from the question of the structure of society to the question of its maintenance. By pointing to unconscious reproduction, and possible exploitation as a consequence – as in the case of the extraction of surplus value – critical realism points to the need for an explanatory critique which can assess the *real* nature of such processes and explain the gap between individual intentions and the actual reproduced outcome of human practices.

Critical realism also argues that social structures generate and distribute upon agents certain causal powers, social identities and interests. It points to the need to examine these interests in their structural context and to assess the possibilities and limitations that these structures present for human action. In posing the question of their reproduction, critical realism highlights the *possibility* of their transformation. The next step is to examine the location of the various collectives of social agents and the transformative capacities that they might have. The act of transformation is the job of the agents themselves, while the description of social transformation is the job of the political analyst and requires an examination of the specific historical circumstances of such action. The radicality of critical realism flows, not from what it prescribes as a political solution to social ills, but through raising questions about society and scientific practice. Critical realism does not (or should not) provide the political solutions itself, but helps provide the basis for assessing such solutions. Various political conclusions flow from a critical realist analysis just as surely as critical realism can show that political conclusions flow from rival social theories. In assessing social science, critical realism takes a partisan stance. But this is done through criticising the assumptions of social theories and highlighting the connection between the errors of social theory and the contradictions at the level of social reality that these ideas in some way reflect. Critical realism should therefore be content with showing the importance of explanatory critique by posing the question of the possibility of transformation and in highlighting the need to study the specific structural and historical conditions. It should then let Marxist social theory get on with the job of doing this.

Conclusion

It has been fashionable since the 1960s and the rise of the new social movements to claim that Marxism is in something of a crisis. This was of course re-emphasised in the late 1980s by the fall of the Berlin Wall and the collapse of 'actually existing socialism'. It can be said that Marxism faces a dual crisis – both as a theory and as a movement. We can see how the post-Marxists and critical realists have responded to this. Post-Marxism embraces the politics of the new social movements although it gives this an individualist emphasis. Theoretically it criticises Marxism for its philosophical foundation-alism, class reductionism and economic determinism. However, critical realism also criticises such trends in Marxism. But rather than embracing radical contingency, it maintains that the social world is structured in a certain way. Whereas post-Marxism replaces determinism with contingency, critical realism replaces determinism with notions of stratification and emergence so that the structure of society is not top-down or bottom-up, but a complex interaction with some social layers emergent out of lower layers, but not reducible to them. In turn, it has been shown that by maintaining a notion of social structure, critical realism supports a notion of transformative agency.

Laclau and Mouffe criticise and ultimately reject Marxism because they believe that it contains an essentialism that emphasises class and the economic in a foundationalist way. But it has to be said that in criticising Marxism for its economic determinism and class reductionism they portray it in a very one-sided light as monolithic, totalising, mono-linear, reductionist, determinist, essentialist and devoid of any richness or diversity. With Marxism cast in such a light, their version of radical pluralist democracy seems very attractive. But victory over such a weakened opponent only indicates the weakness of their own argument. Critical realists would argue that post-Marxist theory lacks any ontological depth since Laclau and Mouffe's rejection of Marx leads them to reject any notion of structured, stratified, dialectical, intrinsic or necessary relations, connections or mechanisms. Instead Laclau and Mouffe develop a concept of hegemony that sees it as a moment of articulation of contingent elements that have no necessary connection. This is very different to Gramsci's idea of hegemony as a project that brings together different social groups according to their different interests and under particular material conditions. The post-Marxist view of hegemony sees it in relation to discursive articulation, denying any relation to non-discursive or material processes.

The irony is that Laclau and Mouffe's book is called *Hegemony and Socialist Strategy* when their conceptualisation of hegemony denies them any meaningful strategy while there is nothing intrinsically socialist about anything they say. Maybe they are commenting on the socialist strategy of others, nevertheless, their own attempt at theorising hegemony denies any of the necessary conditions for hegemony's meaningful operation, that is, relatively enduring social structures, practices, interests, identities and relations. Without a relation between hegemony and various social structures, there is no possibility of it playing any kind of transformatory role. To properly conceive of hegemony it is necessary to locate it within structural relations which make clear its limitations and its conditions of possibility. That hegemony is possible is due to the fact that social agents play an active and fundamental role in the reproduction of these social structures. Under conditions of structural tension and heightened social awareness, the transformation of these structures becomes a possibility. Such a process requires a hegemonic project that can unite agents around a programme or a set of interests and a group of social agents who are structurally located such that they are in a position to effect a transformation and to counter those forces hostile to their project.

Similar criticisms have been made by a number of writers. For example, Best and Kellner argue that fear of essentialism drives Laclau and Mouffe to reject any social ordering, avoiding the issue of whether some social agents are more central than others or better able to achieve socialist transformation (Best and Kellner 1991: 202). Meanwhile Rosemary Hennessy has argued that since the relation between power and discourse is regarded as contingent, opposition can only be random. She also notes the difficult in seeing how discursively constituted subjects can effect radical social change (Hennessy 1993: 43).

By contrast, critical realism can support a transformational model of social activity because it locates social activity within social structures that are reproduced through such activity and which can therefore be transformed. In contrast to post-Marxism which rejects Marxist attempts to ground social theory, critical realism advocates a depth ontology that can answer such questions without resorting to mechanical materialism. The meaningful nature of transitive discourse pre-supposes the intransitive structures and objects to which it refers. Of course it recognises the discursive turn, supporting the idea that social processes and subjects are *in part* discursively constituted *as well as materially grounded*. But it rejects *all* forms of reductionism including the discursive reductionism of post-Marxism and postmodernism.

Critical realism comes to Marxism 'from outside' in the sense that it is not intrinsically Marxist, but approaches Marxism in a scientific way. By distancing itself from Marxism (by presenting itself as a conceptual analysis) critical realism is better placed to provide a genuinely critical appraisal. It insists on a degree of precision and rigour missing from much of the speculative schemas of Marxist philosophy. It provides a new framework for the conceptualisation of social relations, offering an ontological approach that moves beyond questions of knowledge and action to ask what the world itself must be like for these to be the case. Only if we acknowledge and theorise these relations, can we engage in an emancipatory politics.

Further Reading

Derrida'a *Specters of Marx*, like the rest of his work, is not an easy book. A symposium on this book has been edited by Sprinker (1999). Laclau and Mouffe's *Hegemony and Socialist Strategy* (1985) is not much easier. Norman Geras's reply in *Discourses of* Extremity is very forceful. Roy Bhaskar's earlier works of critical realism are much more readable. The best are *The Possibility of Naturalism* (1989a) and *Reclaiming Reality* (1989b) which contains some essays on Marxism. Bhaskar's later work *Dialectic* (1993) and *Plato, Etc.* (1994) are very complex but also very interesting in outlining a critical realist dialectic that links the struggle for freedom to a process of negation. They are, however, extremely problematic as far as the relationship with Marxism is concerned. Since these works, Bhaskar has taken a further 'spiritual' turn which is decidedly anti-Marxist and anti-social scientific. Andrew Collier's *Critical Realism* (1994) provides a more readable introduction. His earlier *Scientific Realism and Socialist Thought* compares critical realism to structural Marxism. The volume *Critical Realism and Marxism* edited by Brown, Fleetwood and Roberts contains a very good selection of essays on the subject.

9

Conclusion

Introduction

Having examined various Marxist theories and approaches we can conclude by saying that there is no one accepted body of Marxist social theory but a variety of schools with often contradictory standpoints. To say what Marxist social theory might be we therefore have to operate on the basis of a number of shared 'family resemblances' which most basically would include:

A materialist theory of history
The importance of economic production
The concept of ideology
The importance of class
A theory of the state
A commitment to a politics of struggle and an emancipatory theory.

The biggest question to address is that of the materialist theory of history as the other issues flow from this. This conclusion attempts to summarise some of the debates around these issues while broadly endorsing a critical realist approach to Marxist social theory.

The Materialist Theory of History

The Marxist view of history starts with our productive capacities and examines how these have taken various historical forms. These different modes of production are said by Marx to determine the general character of social, political and spiritual life (Marx 1975a: 425). Such a stance is crucial to an account of the fundamental way in which a social system is organised. However, two problems arise. First, to what extent does the determination of social political and spiritual life take place? Second, how do we understand production? Many of the problems in Marxist social theory stem from the fact that social production is defined too narrowly as economic production and that this economic production is given too much determining power.

Marx's 1859 *Preface* clearly gives the economic base pre-eminence. It argues that social relations of production are appropriate to a given stage in the development of the material relations of production and that these form the economic structure of society. This in turn constitutes the foundation on which arises a legal and political superstructure and forms of social consciousness (Marx 1975a: 425). This leads to a schematic view in two senses. First, it is schematic in social terms in that it presents a model of society whereby the economic base determines those layers above it with little or no autonomy given to the legal, political or ideological elements. Second, this picture is schematic in a historical sense for it sees history as driven by this economic structure of society with emphasis given to the development of the material forces of production. This leads to the equally problematic distinction between forces of production and relations of production with primacy often being given to the level of material and technological development of the productive forces. The *Preface* suggests that productive forces shape the development of productive relations which in turn develop the social relations at the level of the superstructure.

Marx's writings on the nature of economic relations, social and political matters and historical development is much more complex than this as Chapter 1 has hopefully indicated. Marx's *Capital* provides a far richer social analysis than the schematic formula presented in the few lines of the *Preface*. Nevertheless, this more schematic view of history had great influence among the heirs of Marx and Engels who were themselves influenced by an array of deterministic and evolutionary ideas drawn from the natural sciences of the time.

It is perhaps at this point that we should mention the coming together of historical materialism and dialectical materialism. Although Marx himself never used these terms, followers like Kautsky and Plekhanov gave the ideas of Marx and Engels views on historical development the most schematic and mechanical interpretation. They took from Hegel a linear model of historical development based on a dialectic of opposing forces which would lead from one stage of history to another, higher one. Dialectical materialism became a theory that could explain all aspects of social development, giving Marxism a total and integrated scientific theory. Historical development is seen as a continuation from the natural world and subject to the same laws. This gave the Marxist historical schema an evolutionary inevitability that guaranteed a transition to socialism.

Rosa Luxemburg at least tried to introduce a subjective factor into historical development. But still there is an argument that capitalism will inevitably collapse and that the working class will be faced with a stark choice of socialism or barbarism. Luxemburg's understanding of barbarism is characteristic of another trend in classical Marxist thinking – that of catastrophism. By barbarism Luxemburg envisages militarism, world wars and the destruction of modern culture and society. To be fair to her, this is pretty much what was happening at the time, leading to her own tragic death. But these are characteristics of a particular historical period and cannot necessarily be generalised into historical laws. Subsequent Marxists – particularly Trotskyists – have attempted to justify the idea that the barbaric collapse of capitalism is an inevitability on the basis of a theory of the stagnation of the productive forces. But this is not an intrinsic feature of capitalism as argued in the next section.

Despite or perhaps because of her catastrophist views, Luxemburg held an unshakable belief in the inherent radicality of the working class. Like the Marx of the *Manifesto*, she believed that the development of capitalism polarises and radicalises the classes and develops within them a spontaneous urge for action. But such a view was strongly opposed by Lenin. It could be argued that in advancing his theories of party organisation and leadership, Lenin better understood the particular conditions of his time and the fact that spontaneous class struggle was not enough to overthrow state power. This was also recognised by Trotsky and his view that in Russia, the conditions of uneven and combined development and the under-development of civil society allowed for the capture of state power, but made the subsequent task of maintaining this power all the more difficult. Thus with Lenin and Trotsky we can see that by stressing the political factor and the need for organisation, direction and leadership, there is an emphasis on actual social conditions and the measures needed to overcome them, rather than on a mechanical historical schema. Indeed Gramsci went so far as to call the Russian Revolution a revolution against Marx's *Capital*.

Gramsci himself is influenced by the idealist wing of philosophy and in particular the philosophy of Hegel. We have categorised Gramsci as a praxis Marxist alongside Lukács and Korsch. They use Hegel to oppose the rigid historical schemas of mechanical Marxism and to shift emphasis to questions of consciousness and the role of the historical subject. For the praxis Marxists, theory and philosophy are inseparable as they reflect the unity of subject and object. This is clearest in Lukács whose understanding of history and class-consciousness is expressed in the Hegelian terms that 'self-knowledge coincides with knowledge of the whole so that the proletariat is at one and the same time the subject and object of its own knowledge' (Lukács 1971: 20). The essence of historical materialism is inseparable from the practical and critical activity of the working class. Social change is now understood in terms of the level of consciousness or self-understanding of the working class subject, rather than in terms of the unfolding of objective social or historical laws.

Bhaskar's critique of the praxis theorists is that they conceive of Marxism as the theoretical expression of a subject – the working class – rather than as theoretical knowledge of an object – capitalist society. The consequence is that Marxism as a social theory is rejected in favour of Marxism as a philosophy and outlook. The praxis Marxists' notion of the inseparability of subject and object means a denial of the intransitive status of social structures and therefore an ultimately idealist philosophy. And this idealist philosophy is driven by notion that consciousness proceeds to ever higher levels of self-understanding (Bhaskar 1989b: 138–39).

If we are to conceive of society in a more objective way, then a focus on social structures is required. One way of doing this is to turn to the work of Althusser. Here emphasis is placed on the different levels of the social totality. In opposition to a crude base-superstructure model, Althusser argues that each level of the social totality is relatively autonomous and has its own particular development. The conjuncture is to be understood as a complex combination of these different levels and Althusser uses the term overdetermination to describe how the social body is 'determined by the various *levels* and *instances* of the social formation it animates' (Althusser 1977: 101). However, it has been argued that although this position gives the different levels some degree of autonomy, Althusser ultimately goes back to the traditional Marxist insistance that the economy is determinate 'in the last instance'. Against such formulations of relative autonomy and determination in the last instance, it is better to accept that the economy determines every instance. The issue now becomes, to what extent? The extent of influence might be very great or it could be miniscule. Likewise, we have to ask to what degree do other factors like the political or cultural determine each instance. Finally, Althusserian structuralism has to be criticised for the way that it undermines the role of agency. The last chapter showed how critical realism attempts to overcome this with its transformational model of social activity where social structures are both the necessary condition for and reproduced outcome of human agency. Structures are given primacy in the sense that they pre-exist human agents and set the conditions for their activity. Consequently most social agency takes the form of reproducing these structures. However, because of their location and because social structures depend on their activity, human agents possess the possibility to occasionally transform these structures although this is always within definite limits.

Like the structuralists and critical realists the critical theorists of the Frankfurt School are also concerned with broadening Marx's analysis by shifting away from the narrow concerns of the economic sphere to other aspects of the social system and in particular culture and communication. While Marx tends to see history and society in terms of the mode of production, Adorno and Horkheimer examine the role of the cultural and political spheres and the dialectic of Enlightenment reason. Their focus on the rationalisation of society has many similarities with Weber's approach and they trace this process as far back as Greek society – hence it is not simply reducible to the development of capitalist society. Adorno and Horkheimer tend to see only the negative side of culture and politics whereas Habermas attempts to rescue the 'project of modernity' by seeking an alternative to the dominance of instrumental rationality in the communicative interaction of members of society.

All the members of the Frankfurt school are interested in how the different social spheres interact with each other. In Habermas this initially takes the form of legitimation and steering crises. The state apparatus has the role of securing legitimacy and mass loyalty and trying to overcome any dysfunctional effects of the economic system. This may help develop social cohesion and consent, however the danger of doing this is that economic crisis may be shifted onto the political system. The increasing intervention of the state into the private realm may also cause a motivation crisis and a loss of meaning in social life. If the state becomes overwhelmed by a crisis in the economic sphere, then it suffers a crisis of legitimacy spread across a range of political, cultural, public and private domains.

In his later work Habermas tries to formulate these relations in a slightly different way. He replaces the notion of base and superstructure with a distinction between system and lifeworld. Instead of economic base and cultural, political and ideological superstructure, his model has systemic functioning and communicative interaction. The system is purposive-rational, instrumental and strategic while the lifeworld is communicative, consensual and normative. This emphasises the fact that societies must reproduce themselves both materially and symbolically. However, because systemic integration must be institutionalised and anchored in the lifeworld, there is always the possibility of the system overextending itself and 'colonising' the lifeworld.

Habermas is optimistic that this colonisation of the lifeworld can be overcome. However, his optimism involves an overemphasis of the possibilities for rationality and agreement. It might be wondered whether such a harmonious balance can ever be achieved under capitalist society. His account of human communicative capacity is universal and transcendental at the expense of being historical. Indeed, by separating the lifeworld from the system in such a way, he dehistoricises it and ushers in a dualism whereby the extra-discursive or extra-communicative material realm invades and distorts an already constituted discursive realm. Habermas's theory of the lifeworld is constituted inter-subjectively and therefore interaction with the material has to be brought in from the outside. There is little account of social structure in this account. Instead, Habermas's critical theory takes on a normative rather than a historically materialist form.

The Economic

To maintain a materialist approach to history it is therefore necessary to focus on the central importance of material production. This can be justified on the basis that society simply would not exist if its material needs were not reproduced. We can argue over the relative weight given to different aspects of the social system. But quite simply, without material production, we would not even be around to have the argument.

We can move from here to say that if the process of production has a fundamental role in society, then the economic has a fundamental role in production. The key issue now becomes how to maintain some kind of focus on economic processes without succumbing to the kind of economic reductionism described above. For a start, we can state that Marx's account of economic development recognises that this in itself is not sufficient to produce social change and that although economic developments produce changes in social classes, for political change to occur, classes must become active 'for themselves' (Marx 1963: 172–73). Marx argues that the bourgeoisie came to power for two reasons. First, economic crisis and social antagonism was already present in the old order, second, the bourgeoisie was willing to act politically in order to overthrow that system. However, this does not necessarily resolve the problem of economic determinism for Marx argues in the *Preface* that although classes need to take action, they can do so only when ordained by certain economic conditions. It is argued that: 'No social order is ever destroyed before all the productive forces for which it is sufficient have been developed' (Marx 1975a: 426). The material conditions for new relations of production must first mature within the framework of the old society. Once this occurs, the old relations of production become fetters on the developing forces of production and an era of social revolution begins.

These statements of course encourage a mechanical form of historical materialism that reduces historical development to stages in economic development. It argues that social change may occur, but only when economic conditions allow. As well as the general schema of relations fettering forces, this is usually expressed in terms of some law of economic crisis. Thus the nature of capitalist competition and the constant drive to accumulate leads to crises of overproduction. The need to revolutionise the forces of production in order to produce cheaper goods reduces the amount of exploitable labour power (variable capital) and causes the rate of profit to fall. Subsequent Marxists including Trotsky made much out of the idea that capitalism had reached its highest point of development and that would no longer develop but only stagnate.

However, even if such claims are true (and not all of them are), this does not portend the impending collapse of the social order. There may well be a tendency of the rate of profit to fall, but it is important to note that Marx calls this a tendency. A critical realist would argue that tendencies are not reducible to their exercise and that it is perfectly possible for this causal power to exist without it being actualised. In fact certain tendencies are usually counteracted by other tendencies. The falling rate of profit may be a real tendency, but it is one that may or may not be realised depending on actual conditions at any particular moment. Tendencies towards crisis may be offset by counteracting tendencies like increased productivity or technological advance, or else by deliberate acts of state intervention. This is one way to understand the economic development of the post-war era which was marked by an interventionist state, Keynesian economic, welfare reforms, nationalisation of some industry and conditions of full employment. As this system of regulation started to break down, it was replaced by neo-liberal free market policies. However, it is worth noting that even neo-liberalism itself can be considered a form of state strategy, a sort of reverse Keynesianism, the conditions for which are enforced through state actions and global institutions like the WTO.

The way out of economic reductionism is to see crises as tendencies rather than inevitabilities and to note that the conditions for economic development are not given but have to be socially (politically, culturally and discursively) secured. The danger with this approach, however, is to go too far the other way and see crises as things that can always be deferred by political intervention. Such is the case with the early Frankfurt School with Adorno concluding that the social world is now so dominated by technology and the economic, cultural and political systems so integrated that social change is now impossible. Little wonder that he retreated into aesthetic theory.

Ideology

Marx's early theory of ideology is discussed in relation to the way the state presents the general interest as the universal interest and how the ruling ideas in society are the ideas of the ruling class. As his theory of human alienation shifts to the effects of the capitalist system of production, so he develops the theory of commodity fetishism to explain how ideology is produced by the normal workings of the capitalist system and how it normalises commodity production and exchange relations. In a sense, this ideology is generated by the system itself rather than by any particular group of people and its effect is to fit our consciousness in with the demands of the market economy. Fetishism as an ideology may therefore be said to play a role in securing a set of beliefs compliant with the needs of the capitalist production and therefore helping to ensure the smooth functioning of the different parts of the social system. It generates misleading or mystified conceptions of social forms like money, capital, the commodity and the wage-relation, concealing the social basis of these forms and hence ensuring compliance with them.

In Althusser, this approach to ideology is given a stronger structural–functional basis. Ideology plays a role in equipping people for their social existence. It acts to simplify social relations so that we can better engage in social processes. Therefore ideology is required in all societies if people are to be equipped to respond to the social demands placed upon them. Althusser rejects the view that ideology is a negative product of class society arguing that it is a necessary feature of all societies. However, under class society the imaginary relation ideology creates between people and their real conditions of existence manages to obscure the real basis of our social relations. One of the ways this is done is through ideological state apparatuses like education, the church, the family, the media and political bodies that help to reproduce the social system.

The concept of ideology is an interesting one since this is something that has recently come under attack from poststructuralists and post-Marxists. First, they argue, that there is a problem with the traditional Marxist view that ideology is false consciousness since this presupposes something like 'true' consciousness. However, this move can be accepted by structuralists and critical realists without having to abandon the concept. As the realist Andrew Sayer has argued, '[t]he danger of ideological beliefs is not that they are completely untrue, for if they were ineffectual they would pose no threat, but that the particular form of their selective practical adequacy has bad consequences' (Sayer 2000: 43). For both critical realism and structuralism, the emphasis is on the practical consequences of ideology and the role that ideas play in the reproduction of social structures. Consequently, these ideas need to be judged in terms of their practical adequacy and their real effects. This approach stands in opposition to the second critique of poststructuralists that ideology presupposes some underlying reality. Quite simply it does, and by focusing on actual social relations and the ideology that is secreted by them, these structural approaches to ideology move away from an emphasis on the truthfulness of consciousness and instead focus on how consciousness is always located in social practices, not in some ideal way of seeing the world.

Nevertheless, the closeness of ideology to these social practices means that there are limits to what ideology can reveal and that it may therefore be misleading in terms of providing a wider understanding of social relations. By tying the notion of ideology to social practices and structures, realists and structuralists are able to locate the production of ideology and account for the reasons for its production. By contrast poststructuralists and post-Marxists criticise the notion of ideology for presupposing such underlying structures. They tend to replace the notion of ideology with that of discourse which is all embracing. Yet once this happens, it becomes difficult to explain the basis of these ideas and therefore we have no means of tying these ideas down and passing judgment on them. Poststructuralists and post-Marxists have difficulty in judging different sets of ideas since they deny that there is any extra-discursive basis to them. By contrast, those Marxists who focus on the relationship between ideology and the material conditions of its production are able to criticise such ideas, criticise the conditions that produce them and thus offer an emancipatory practice that tries to change them.

Class

Marx wrote less on class than might be expected, however, he says enough to make it clear that class should be defined on the basis of place within the system of production. Under capitalism this takes the form of ownership or non-ownership of the means of production. The starting point, then, should be to define class objectively in terms of position within the production process. However, this still leaves much to be decided.

Marx's political writings, and in particular the *Communist Manifesto*, promote the view that the working class is a homogeneous group whose common economic relation provides the basis for a common political expression. In the

Manifesto it is argued that the opposition between working class and bour-geoisie is growing ever clearer which of course leaves Marxist social theory open to the criticisms of sociologists like Weber who argue for a more sophis-ticated form of social stratification based on different social and political interests and status.

Thus it is important to recognise that social classes are not at all homoge-neous but are in fact divided along various lines. This is in keeping with notions of social stratification proposed by recent approaches such as critical realism. If the social world is stratified in different ways, then so too are the social agents who are located within these social relations. One way of under-standing this would be according to Poulantzas's notion of class fractions which are based on different social, economic and political factors. These frac-tions may belong to the same class, but they have competing and often con-flicting interests. These interests can be objectively grounded such as in different forms of capital or different sectors of industry. Identities may also be grounded in such things as the blue-collar white-collar distinction. However, class may also be subjectively determined in the sense of being determined by forms of consciousness or identification. As well as supporting Marxism's traditional focus on class consciousness and 'classes for themselves', this can bring in such Weberian issues as social status, lifestyle and political affiliation. However, the notion of fractions still entails that the fundamental divisions in society are between classes rather than within classes. Thus, despite the different political, sectoral, cultural and ideological divisions, the most funda-mental social division under capitalism is still that between those who own the means of production and those who are forced to work as wage-labourers. A critical realist approach to Marxist social theory can support such an argument on the basis that there is a stratification of social divisions of which some are more significant than others. If the mode of production is considered to be the most important aspect of a society, then the divisions it causes are more fun-damental than other divisions. Yet despite this it should be argued that other forms of social stratification are important and have their own irreducible dynamics.

Following Gramsci, Poulantzas argues that because classes are divided into different fractions, a ruling bloc must be constructed through the building of a complex set of alliances. In fact, the hegemonic class may not even be the eco-nomically dominant one, but the one that can best unify the power bloc. Political rulership is not given, but involves a complex process of construction. This introduces an element of articulation into social relations and guards against the class reductionist view that political power flows directly from eco-nomic interest. However, it does not embrace the post-Marxist version of con-tingency arguing instead that certain social groups are better able to provide hegemonic leadership than others given their favourable relation to dominant social structures. The project of hegemony also relates to these wider social structures in that it requires not only the unity of different social groups and class fractions but also the securing of the cohesion of the social system. This moves us on to the issues surrounding state power.

The Marxist Theory of the State

The chapter on Marx and Engels explained how it is possible to trace three views of the state to Marx and Engels. Of these, it is the crudest version – that of the state as a class instrument – that has carried most influence. In this view, the state is a representative of the ruling class and gives support to the process of economic exploitation by offering political and military coercion. This view should be criticised on two grounds – those of consensus and cohesion. On the first of these, the coercive aspect of the state is overemphasised at the expense of an examination of mechanisms of consent such as might be found in Gramsci's account of hegemony. Although the state has a coercive apparatus, it also has mechanisms for gaining consent and legitimacy such as the parliamentary system, the legal system, welfare and education. These institutions work through civil society and are crucial to the maintenance of social hegemony. State power is not simply something imposed by force, but is a carefully constructed project of legitimation. This leads to the issue of cohesion. Consensus has to be constructed because there are many different social interests that have to be reconciled. The political interests of different groups do not flow automatically from their economic position and, as was argued in relation to class, social groups are stratified in many different ways. Therefore the state becomes a terrain for the power struggles between competing groups and their social, economic and political interests. Given that classes are not homogeneous, the state must act to resolve or contain the conflicts between different groups and interests in order to protect the general needs of the economic system. The state must act as a factor of social cohesion in bringing together the different groups and securing the unity of the power bloc.

It is the view of the state as a factor of social cohesion that offers most for it recognises the stratification of society and social agents. The state must secure cohesion by uniting different social groups, but it must also secure cohesion in relation to the various social structures. Poulantzas argues that the state apparatuses have the role of maintaining the cohesion of the social formation by concentrating and sanctioning class domination, and in this way reproducing social relations (Poulantzas 1978a: 24–25). However, he argues that the state should be seen as capitalist, not because it is the instrument of the capitalist class, but because of its role in the reproduction of the mode of production. Subsequently, Marxists like Bob Jessop and the regulation theorists have argued that the state must be understood in relation to the process of regulation, intervening in order to help secure the conditions for capital accumulation. The state therefore acts as a mediator between the economic and political spheres.

The fact that the state mediates between different spheres of the social formation suggests that the state is something more than just a product of class society. Because the state develops alongside the development of class society, the two are usually understood together. However, this hides the fact that the state may have a more general social function in relation to such things as the distribution of surplus products, the regulation of different interests and the mediation of different conflicts. Of course, under capitalism this involves the extraction of surplus value, defence of private property and support for the interests of the ruling class fractions. But even under a classless society it is possible to envisage the state playing an important role in securing the cohesion and reproduction of the social system. In other words, because of the complexity and stratification of the social world, the state should be seen as playing a necessary social role that is separable from any class form that this might take.

Emancipation

In their early work Marx and Engels see emancipation in Hegelian terms. They focus on conditions of human alienation and apply Hegel's dialectic to see how the proletarian slave might raise its consciousness, become a 'class for itself' and struggle to overthrow the bourgeois master. Controversial though this may sound, such an approach to emancipation is hopelessly wrong and those Marxists who continue to believe in it are deluding themselves. Change does not come from a discovery of our 'true', non-alienated self or by the proletariat becoming the subject–object of history. Marxism is not a world-view that will be confirmed by the proletariat and its revolutionary party. These ideas belong to Hegelian idealism not to Marxist realism.

Lukács, Gramsci, and the praxis Marxists clearly see Marxism as more like a philosophy or world-view than a social science. But whereas Lukács grounds his theory of emancipation in a utopian dialectic of developing class consciousness, Gramsci at least theorises the actual dynamics of class struggle through his concept of hegemony. Rather than imposing a philosophical schema, Gramsci looks at actual struggles and the tactics and strategy necessary for emancipatory projects. Marxist ideas can help to guide such struggles. However, it is important not to conflate the ideas and beliefs guiding these struggles, and the theory of Marxism as a study of society. The two should be combined as theory and practice. But to combine two things they first need to be distinct. Marxism as a theory analyses society and provides the necessary understanding of the conditions under which practice must operate. Marxism as practice involves a more practical set of ideas and beliefs that can mobilise the masses into action, but which is necessarily a simplification of the real situation.

The distinction between Marxism as a social theory and Marxism as a political practice can, however, be a dangerous one. For example, the Frankfurt theorists can be subjected to Bhaskar's criticism that they emphasise the relative autonomy of theory while criticising Marx's concept of labour, resulting in a gradual decentring of the role of the proletariat and eventually the loss of any historically grounded agency of emancipation (Bhaskar 1989b: 140). Althusser also holds a theoreticist understanding of Marxism as reflected in his description of Marxist philosophy as a 'theory of theoretical practice'. His sharp separation of science and ideology is problematic given that he also claims that ideology is secreted by social practices. If this is so, then surely ideology is also produced by Marxist practice. Marxist social theory cannot stand outside or above the social conditions of its production. Thus the sharp distinction between science and ideology must be blurred, especially if Marxism is to have any practical involvement in political activity.

Post-Marxism abandons both the concept of science and the concept of ideology. Knowledge is relativised to whichever discourse is hegemonic. Thus if Laclau and Mouffe are to offer any kind of emancipatory politics it can only be of a liberal nature, reflecting the contingency of its assumptions and their lack of a conception of social structure. Its ultimate expression is that of the autonomous individual.

To offer a more plausible emancipatory theory it is necessary to restore a notion of social structure and to look at how these generate and distribute upon agents certain causal powers, social identities and interests. These powers and interests have to be examined in their structural context and an assessment has to be made as to the enabling and constraining effects these structures have on human action. Critical realism offers a transformational model of social activity to show how the reproduction of social structures is dependent on human activity and how this therefore offers the possibility of social transformation under certain structural conditions and according to definite causal powers.

The political analyst is required to provide an account of these conditions while the political actor must use this to engage in the activities required to enact social change. The role of philosophical critiques such as that provided by critical realism is not to conduct the analysis nor to lead the action, but to provide the philosophical underpinnings to such analysis and action. Working alongside Marxist theory, they can outline an explanatory critique of dominant ideas leading to a negative evaluation of the source of these ideas and, consequently, a positive evaluation of action designed to remedy this. Approaches like critical realism assist Marxist analysis of the social world by emphasising an ontological approach that focuses on the way that the world is objectively structured and how this structure is the source of certain ideas and practices that need to be challenged.

Conclusion

What should Marxist social theory be like? First, it should recognise the mind-independent objectivity of social relations while maintaining that these social relations are nevertheless open to theoretical investigation. This is because these social relations have a structure and are relatively enduring over time. Marxist social theory should not be the expression of a subject, but knowledge of an object. It should see the social world as having ontological depth and attach central importance to the mode of production and the various economic processes associated with this. However, it must also recognise that there are serious problems with the crude base-superstructure and economic determinist models of mainstream Marxist theory. Therefore, an alternative approach must see the social world as structured and stratified, but also contingent and emergent.

Marxist social theory also needs to be clear about how it conceives of the relation between structure and agency. The primacy of structure means agents generally are involved in acts of reproduction. This should be the basis of Marxism's materialism. However, the location of social agents means they have the potential for acts of transformation. Agents are not the mere bearers of structures, nor are structures the mere outcome of agential activity. Social structures enable social agency but they also set definite limits to it.

Marxists should recognise that society has a discursive aspect. But they should resist the notion that society is 'ideas all the way down'. The concept of ideology is important in that it relates discourses to material processes. Nevertheless, discourses are not reducible to these processes. Discourses are as much a part of reality as material things are. This has to be recognised while crude forms of materialism must be opposed. Indeed a critical realist approach moves beyond a simply material-ideational distinction by recognising the reality of the material *and* discursive which may combine in a structural sense. We might consider, therefore, whether it is more appropriate to talk of underlying structural conditions rather than underlying materiality, although a realist would insist on a strong material content to this reality.

Also going against the main trends in Marxist social theory it has been suggested here that rather than being distinct products of class society that are destined to disappear under a future socialist order, ideology and the state are necessary social features which happen to take on a particular social form under class society. Ideology plays a necessary social role in guiding actors through their social conditions of existence. Under capitalism this takes a distorting, mystifying and misleading form, but as Marxist theories of ideology themselves claim, we need to distinguish between the social form of ideology, and some possible underlying necessary basis. The same goes for the state. Indeed, it is difficult to conceive of a society without some kind of body that can assist in regulating social relations and ensuring that society functions in such a way as to benefit everyone. Marxists are not anarchists; they do believe in the need for order in social life, and in a complex social world, some kind of institutional framework is essential.

Marxism itself argues against neutrality in social theory and so an assessment of Marxist theory should also be partisan. The problem with many schools of thought is that they come to understand themselves through endless internal debates between different sub-schools, thus losing sight of that which they are meant to explain. Sometimes it is necessary to approach these debates from the outside by bringing in a philosophical critique of the various assumptions and formulations and questioning the basis of many of the theoretical articulations. I conclude here in partisan spirit by claiming that Marxist social theory is not in terminal decline and can continue to offer the best possible understanding of our changing social world. But it needs to be approached in a critical manner, using philosophical critiques such as the critical realist one. By focusing on Marxism's conceptual basis while looking beyond this to what it implies about the ontology of the social world, we can better understand both social theory and the social reality that it is about and, hopefully, the emancipatory process that allows us to change it.

Bibliography

Adorno, T. (1973 [1966]) *Negative Dialectics*, London: Routledge.

—— (1987) 'Late Capitalism or Industrial Society?', in V. Meja, D. Misgeld and N. Stehr (eds), *Modern German Sociology*, New York: Colombia University Press, pp. 232–47.

—— (1991) *The Culture Industry*, London: Routledge.

Adorno, T. and Horkheimer, M. (1986 [1947]) *Dialectic of Enlightenment*, London: Verso.

Aglietta, M. (1987) *A Theory of Capitalist Regulation: The US Experience*, London and New York: Verso.

Althusser, L. (1977) *For Marx*, London: Verso.

—— (1984) *Essays on Ideology*, London: Verso.

—— and Balibar, E. (1979) *Reading Capital*, London: Verso.

Amin, A. (ed.) (1994) *Post-Fordism: A Reader*, Oxford: Blackwell.

Anderson, B. (1991) *Imagined Communities*, London: Verso.

Anderson, P. (1976) 'The Antimonies of Antonio Gramsci', in *New Left Review* 100: 5–81.

—— (1979) *Considerations on Western Marxism*, London: Verso.

—— (1992) *English Questions*, London: Verso.

Barrett, M. (1988) *Women's Oppression Today: The Marxist / Feminist Encounter*, London: Verso.

Bebel, A. (1971 [1879]) *Woman Under Socialism*, New York: Schocken Books.

Benner, E. (1996) *Really Existing Nationalisms: A Post-Communist View from Marx and Engels*, Oxford: Oxford University Press.

Benton, T. (1984) *The Rise and Fall of Structural Marxism*, London: Macmillan.

Best, S. and Kellner, D. (1991) *Postmodern Theory: Critical Interrogations*, Basingstoke: Macmillan.

Bhaskar, R. (1978) *A Realist Theory of Science*, Sussex: Harvester Press.

—— (1989a) *The Possibility of Naturalism*, Hemel Hempstead: Harvester Wheatsheaf.

—— (1989b) *Reclaiming Reality*, London: Verso.

—— (1991) *Philosophy and the Idea of Freedom*, Oxford: Blackwell.

—— (1993) *Dialectic: The Pulse of Freedom*, London: Verso.

—— (1994) *Plato Etc.*, London: Verso.

Boersner, D. (1981) *The Bolsheviks and the National and Colonial Question (1917–1928)*, Westport, CT: Hyperion Press.

Boggs, C. (1978) *Gramsci's Marxism*, London: Pluto.

Bottomore, T. (1984) *The Frankfurt School*, London: Ellis Horwood and Tavisock.

—— (1991) (ed.) *A Dictionary of Marxist Thought* (2nd edn), Oxford: Blackwell.

Brenner, R. (1985) 'Agrarian Class Structure and Economic Development in Europe', in T.H. Aston and C.H.E. Philipin (eds), *The Brenner Debate*, Cambridge: Cambridge University Press.

Brown, A., Fleetwood, S., and Roberts, J. (eds) (2002) *Critical Realism and Marxism*, London and New York: Routledge.

Butler, J. (1990) *Gender Trouble: Feminism and the Subversion of Identity*, London and New York: Routledge.

Callinicos, A. (1976) *Althusser's Marxism*, London: Pluto.

—— (1983) *Marxism and Philosophy*, Oxford: Oxford University Press.

Cohen, G.A. (1978) *Karl Max's Theory of History: A Defence*, Oxford: Oxford University Press.

Collier, A. (1989) *Scientific Realism and Socialist Thought*, Hemmel Hempstead: Harvester Wheatsheaf.

—— (1994) *Critical Realism*, London: Verso.

Craib, I. (1976) *Existentialism and Sociology: A Study of Jean-Paul Sartre*, Cambridge: Cambridge University Press.

Davis, H. (1967) *Nationalism and Socialism: Marxism and Labor Theories of Nationalism to 1917*, New York and London: Monthly Review Press.

Derrida, J. (1994), *Specters of Marx*, New York: Routledge.

Elliott, G. (1987) *Althusser: The Detour of Theory*, London: Verso.

Engels, F. (1954 [1875–76]) *Dialectics of Nature*, Moscow: Progress Publishers.

—— (1975) *Selected Correspondence*, Moscow: Progress Publishers.

—— (1976 [1876–78]) *Anti-Dühring*, Peking: Foreign Languages Press.

—— (1978 [1884]) *The Origin of the Family, Private Property and the State*, Peking: Foreign Languages Press.

Firestone, S. (1970) *The Dialectic of Sex*, New York: Bantam Books.

Geras, N. (1976) *The Legacy of Rosa Luxemburg*, London: NLB.

—— (1990) *Discourses of Extremity*, London: Verso.

Gramsci, A. (1971 [1929–35]) *Selections from the Prison Notebooks*, eds, Q. Hoare and G. Nowell Smith, London: Lawrence and Wishart.

—— (1977) *Selections from Political Writings 1910–1920*, ed., Q. Hoare, London: Lawrence and Wishart.

—— (1995) *Further Selections from the Prison Notebooks*, ed., D. Bothman, London: Lawrence and Wishart.

Habermas, J. (1978) *Knowledge and Human Interests*, London: Heinemann.

—— (1984) *The Theory of Communicative Action: Volume One*, Cambridge: Polity.

—— (1987a) *The Theory of Communicative Action: Volume Two*, Cambridge: Polity.

—— (1987b) *The Philosophical Discourse of Modernity*, Cambridge: Polity.

—— (1988) *Legitimation Crisis*, Cambridge: Polity.

—— (1989) *The Structural Transformation of the Public Sphere*, Cambridge: Polity.

Hall, S. (1988) *The Hard Road to Renewal: Thatcherism and the Crisis of the Left*, London: Verso.

Hamilton, R. and Barrett, M. (eds) (1986) *The Politics of Diversity*, London: Verso.

Harding, N. (1977) *Lenin's Political Thought*, vol. 1, London: Macmillan.

—— (1987) *Lenin's Political Thought*, vol. 2, London: Macmillan.

Hartmann, H. (1981) 'The Unhappy Marriage of Marxism and Feminism: Towards a More Progressive Union', in Lydia Sargent (ed.), *The Unhappy Marriage of Marxism and Feminism: A Debate on Class and Patriarchy*, London: Pluto, pp. 1–41.

Held, D. (1980) *Introduction to Critical Theory*, Berkeley: University of California Press.

Hennessy, R. (1993) *Materialist Feminism and the Politics of Discourse*, London: Routledge.

Hoffman, J. (1975) *Marxism and the Theory of Praxis*, London: Lawrence and Wishart.

Horkheimer, M. (1972) *Critical Theory: Selected Essays*, New York: Seabury Press.

—— (1987 [1947]) *Eclipse of Reason*, New York: Continuum.

Howard, D. (ed.) (1971) *Selected Political Writings of Rosa Luxemburg*, New York and London: Monthly Review Press.

Jessop, B. (1985) *Nicos Poulantzas: Marxist Theory and Political Strategy*, Basingstoke: Macmillan.

—— (1990) *State Theory: Putting the Capitalist State in its Place*, Cambridge: Polity.

—— (2002a) 'Capitalism, the regulation approach and critical realism', in A. Brown, S. Fleetwood, and J. Roberts (eds), *Critical Realism and Marxism*, London: Routledge, pp. 88–115.

—— (2002b) *The Future of the Capitalist State*, Cambridge: Polity Press.

Jessop, B., Bonnett, K., Bromley, S. and Ling, T. (1988) *Thatcherism: A Tale of Two Nations* Polity, Cambridge: Polity.

Joll, J. (1977) *Gramsci*, Glassgow: Fontana.

Joseph, J. (2002) *Hegemony: A Realist Analysis*, London and New York: Routledge.

—— (2003) *Social Theory: Conflict Cohesion and Consent*, Edinburgh: Edinburgh University Press.

Knei-Paz, B. (1978) *The Social and Political Thought of Leon Trotsky*, Oxford: Clarendon Press.

Kolakowski, L. (1981) *Main Currents of Marxism*, Oxford: Oxford University Press.

Kollontai, A. (1977) *Selected Writings*, trans. and ed. A. Holt, London: Allison & Busby.

Korsch, K. (1970 [1923]) *Marxism and Philosophy*, London: New Left Books.

—— (1971 [1935]) 'Why I am a Marxist', in *Three Essays on Marxism*, London: Pluto.

Laclau, E. and Mouffe, C. (1985) *Hegemony and Socialist Strategy*, London: Verso.

Larrain, J. (1983) *Marxism and Ideology*, London: Macmillan.

Lenin, V.I. (1947 [1902]) *What is to be Done?*, Moscow: Progress Publishers.

—— (1964a) *Collected Works*, vol. 20, Moscow: Progress Publishers.

—— (1964b) *Collected Works*, vol. 21, Moscow: Progress Publishers.

—— (1964c) *Collected Works*, vol. 22, Moscow: Progress Publishers.

—— (1965 [1917]) *The State and Revolution*, Peking: Foreign Languages Press.

—— (1975a [1907]) *The Two Tactics of Social Democracy in the Democratic Revolution*, Peking: Foreign Languages Press.

—— (1975b [1916]) *Imperialism, the Highest Stage of Capitalism*, Peking: Foreign Languages Press.

Linklater, A. (1997) *The Transformation of Political Community*, South Carolina: University of South Carolina Press.

Looker, R. (1974) *Rosa Luxemburg: Selected Political Writings*, New York: Grove Press.

Löwy, M. (1979) *Georg Lukács: From Romanticism to Bolshevism*, London: Verso.

Lukács, G. (1971 [1923]) *History and Class Consciousness*, London: Merlin.

Luxemburg, R. (1976) *The National Question*, ed., H. Davies, New York: Monthly Review Press.

MacLellan, D. (1971) *Thought of Karl Marx*, London: Macmillan.

—— (1998) *Marxism After Marx*, Basingstoke: Macmillan.

Marcuse, H. (1969 [1955]) *Eros and* Civilization, Harmondsworth: Penguin.
—— (2002 [1964]) *One Dimensional Man*, London: Routledge.
Marx, K. (1952) *Wage Labour and Capital*, Progress Publishers: Moscow.
—— (1963 [1847]) *The Poverty of Philosophy*, International Publishers: New York.
—— (1973) *The Revolutions of 1848: Political Writings: Volume 1* (R), Harmondsworth: Penguin.
—— (1973) *Surveys From Exile: Political Writings: Volume 2* (SE), Harmondsworth: Penguin.
—— (1973a [1850]) *The Class Struggles in France* in SE.
—— (1973b [1852]) *The Eighteenth Brumaire of Louis Bonaparte* in SE.
—— (1973c [1857–58]) *Grundrisse*, Harmondsworth: Penguin.
—— (1974) *The First International And After: Political Writings: Volume 3* (FI) Penguin.
—— (1974a [1871]) *The Civil War in France* in FI.
—— (1974b [1875]) *Critique of the Gotha Programme* in FI.
—— (1975) *Early Writings* (EW), Harmondsworth: Penguin.
—— (1975a [1859]) Preface (*to A Contribution to the Critique of Political Economy*) in EW.
—— (1975b [1843]) *Critique of Hegel's Doctrine of the State* in EW.
—— (1975c [1844]) *On The Jewish Question* in EW.
—— (1975d [1944]) *Economic and Philosophical Manuscripts* in EW.
—— (1975e [1843]) *A Contribution to the Critique of Hegel's Philosophy of Right* in EW.
—— (1975f [1845]) *Concerning Feuerbach* in EW.
—— (1976 [1867]) *Capital*, vol. 1, Harmondsworth: Penguin.
—— (1981 [1894]) *Capital*, vol. 3, Harmondsworth: Penguin.
Marx, K. and Engels, F. (1956 [1845]) *The Holy Family*, Moscow: Foreign Language Publishing House.
—— (1965 [1845–46]) *The German Ideology*, London: Lawrence and Wishart.
—— (1971) *Ireland and the Irish Question*, Moscow: Progress Publishers.
—— (1973 [1848]) *The Communist Manifesto* in R.
—— (1975) *Collected Works*, vol. 8, Moscow: Progress Publishers.
Miliband, R. (1970) 'The Capitalist State – Reply to N. Poulantzas', in *New Left Review* 59: 53–60.
—— (1973a) *The State in Capitalist Society*, London: Quartet Books.
—— (1973b) 'Poulantzas and the Capitalist State', in *New Left Review* 82: 83–92.
—— (1977) *Marxism and Politics*, Oxford: Oxford University Press.
—— (1983) 'State Power and Class Interests', in *New Left Review* 138: 57–68.
Mitchell, J. (1971) *Woman's Estate*, Harmondsworth: Penguin.
Munck, R. (1986) *The Difficult Dialogue: Marxism and Nationalism*, London: Zed Books.
Nairn, T. (1981) *The Break-up of Britain*, London: Verso.
Outhwaite, W. (1994) *Habermas: A Critical Introduction*, Oxford: Polity Press.
Plekhanov, G. (1920 [1908]) *Fundamental Problems of Marxism*, Moscow: Foreign Languages Press.
Poster, M. (1979) *Sartre's Marxism*, London: Pluto.
Poulantzas, N. (1967) 'Marxist Political Theory in Great Britain', in *New Left Review* 43: 57–74.

—— (1969) 'The Problem of the Capitalist State', in *New Left Review* 58: 67–78.

—— (1973) *Political Power and Social Classes*, London: NLB and Sheed and Ward.

—— (1976) 'The Capitalist State: A Reply to Miliband and Laclau', in *New Left Review* 95: 63–83.

—— (1978a) *Classes in Contemporary Capitalism*, London: Verso.

—— (1978b) *State, Power, Socialism*, London: New Left Books.

Ransome, P. (1992) *Antonio Gramsci: A New Introduction*, Hemel Hempstead: Harvester Wheatsheaf.

Rigby, S.H. (1998) *Marxism and History: A Critical Introduction*, Manchester: Manchester University Press.

Roderick, R. (1986) *Habermas and the Foundations of Critical Theory*, London: Macmillan.

Salvadori, M. (1990) *Karl Kautsky and the Socialist Revolution 1880–1938*, London: Verso.

Sargent, L. (ed.) (1981) *The Unhappy Marriage of Marxism and Feminism: A Debate on Class and Patriarchy*, London: Pluto.

Sartre, J.-P. (1963) *Search for a Method*, New York: Vintage.

—— (1991a [1960]) *Critique of Dialectical Reason*, vol. 1, London: Verso.

—— (1991b [1960]) *Critique of Dialectical Reason*, vol. 2, London: Verso.

Sayer, A. (2000) *Realism and Social Science*, London: Sage.

Sprinker, M. (ed.) (1999) *Ghostly Demarcations*, London: Verso.

Stalin, J. (1954) *Works*, vol. 11, Moscow: Foreign Languages Publishing House.

Swingewood, A. (1975) *Marx and Modern Social Theory*, London: Macmillan.

Thompson, E.P. (1968) *The Making of the English Working Class*, Harmondsworth: Penguin.

—— (1978) *The Poverty of Theory*, London: Merlin.

Trotsky, L. (1969) *The Permanent Revolution and Results and Prospects*, New York: Pathfinder.

—— (1971) *The Struggle Against Fascism in Germany*, New York: Pathfinder.

—— (1972 [1937]) *The Revolution Betrayed: What is the Soviet Union and Where is it Going?*, New York: Pathfinder.

—— (1974) *The First Five Years of the Communist International, volume 2*, London: New Park.

—— (1977) *The Transitional Programme for Socialist Revolution*, New York: Pathfinder.

—— (1991) *Literature and Revolution*, London: Redwords.

Vogel, L. (1983) *Marxism and the Oppression of Women: Toward a Unitary Theory*, London: Pluto.

Wheen, F. (1999) *Karl Marx*, London: Fourth Estate.

Young, I. (1981) 'Beyond the Unhappy Marriage: A Critique of the Dual Systems Theory', in *Women and Revolution: A Discussion of the Unhappy Marriage of Marxism and Feminism*, ed. Lydia Sargent Boston, MA: South End Press, pp. 43–70.

Zetkin, C. (1984) 'Speech at the Party Congress of the Social Democratic Party of Germany, Gotha, October 16th, 1896', in *Clara Zetkin: Selected Writings*, ed. Philip Foner, trans. Kai Schoenhals, International Publishers. Retrieved November 16, 2003, from http://www.marxists.org/archive/zetkin/works/women.htm

Index